Puccini

Unlocking the Masters Series, No. 16

Puccini

A Listener's Guide

John Bell Young

AMADEUS
PRESS

An Imprint of Hal Leonard Corporation
New York

Published in 2008 by Amadeus Press
An Imprint of Hal Leonard Corporation
7777 West Bluemound Road
Milwaukee, WI 53213

Trade Book Division Editorial Offices
19 West 21st Street, New York, NY 10010

Printed in the United States of America

Book design by Snow Creative Services

Library of Congress Cataloging-in-Publication Data

Young, John Bell.
    Puccini : a listener's guide / John Bell Young. -- 1st pbk. ed.
       p. cm. -- (Unlocking the masters series ; no. 16)
    ISBN 978-1-57467-172-8 (alk. paper)
    1. Puccini, Giacomo, 1858-1924. Operas. 2. Opera--18th century--History and criticism. 3. Opera--19th century--History and criticism. I. Title.

ML410.P89Y68 2008
782.1092--dc22
                                            2008045419

www.amadeuspress.com

For

Joanna Porackova

a magnificent soprano and a great Puccini interpreter

Contents

Acknowledgments

Writing about music, or any work of art governed by abstraction, is no easy task. One is easily persuaded by force of habit and by long-held beliefs in the veracity of a point of view, as if objectivity were the only thing that mattered.

But as any musicians worth their salt know only too well, there are no ivory towers: music is so complex and abundant as to invite any number of perspectives. And where those perspectives are informed and imaginative, they are worthy of contemplation.

Much the same can be said of any artistic endeavor, and writing is no exception. I am indebted for their assistance and advice to a number of friends and colleagues, several of whom did not live to see the completion of this project nor were even aware that what I learned from them would contribute to it so substantially.

Above all there is my late mother, Dorothy Burgess Young, without whose support and unflinching belief in my abilities I could never have written this volume or even so much as played a single note. Whether eerie coincidence or something born of a grander scheme, Amadeus Press offered me the formidable challenge of writing a dozen books for its distinguished roster only thirty minutes after my mother's passing in July 2007 at age eighty-eight. And so it is in honor of her that I commit to this enormous and challenging project.

There are in addition a number of individuals to whom I am indebted for their support and advice, literary and otherwise, while writing this book. First and foremost, I thank my best friend and partner, Michael Vincent Connelly, for his uncompromising friendship, patience, solidarity, tireless assistance, and unwavering faith in my abilities; Joseph Early and Sandra Rush, whose infinite patience, innumerable kindnesses, critical overview, and thoughtful consideration were not only proof of the deepest friendship, but equal to the best editorial advice; Reni Santoni and Tracy Newman, without whose assistance and counsel at a time when I most needed it I would surely never have been able to complete these works; Joseph and Veronique Fabio for their continued encouragement; Roberto Poli, a superb pianist whose encyclopedic knowledge of all things Italian and musical was an invaluable resource in this study of Puccini; Joanna Porackova, a phenomenal dramatic soprano and an extraordinary Puccini interpreter who taught me a great deal about opera; Alan Schneider, a splendid tenor; Michael York and Hugh Downs, both experienced authors, whose support has been unwavering and who have also shown tremendous patience in reading and critiquing my manuscripts; Mark and Camilla Tarmy, whose understanding and generosity of spirit know no bounds and who have patiently put up with my sometimes impossible demands for convenience and quietude; Tatyana Dudochkin and Mark Churchill of the New England Conservatory; Margarita Fyodorova, who taught me all about intonation and much more; Rick Bechard, whose eye and ear as a documentary filmmaker were invaluable, as he helped me to reconsider both style and narrative, which I can only hope find in these volumes a writer who does them justice; my friend of thirty years, Lord Montagu of Beaulieu, for his gracious assistance; Gordon and Emily Jones, Joseph Fichter, Julie Marden, and others in the extended Putney School family, for their encouragement, kindness, and help; and John Cerullo, the publisher of Amadeus Press. Thanks also to my editor at Amadeus Press, Jessica Burr, and my meticulous copy editor, Angela Buckley.

Finally, to those who are no longer with us, I extend my gratitude in ways that I can only hope will be borne aloft on the wings of angels. From these individuals I learned much of what I know of music. Among them are Constance Keene, a great pianist who was also my teacher and mentor for nearly thirty years; Michel Block, likewise among the great pianists of the twentieth century, whose extraordinary musical savoir faire and personal gentility were a continual source of knowledge and enrichment; James Landrum Fessenden, a brilliant philosopher and musician whose premature death was a blow to all who knew him and whose willingness to share his phenomenally authoritative knowledge of any number of disciplines, from the aesthetics of opera to epistemology and psychoanalysis, has proven invaluable; and to both Claudio Arrau and Ernst Levy, the celebrated pianists who, in my few brief encounters with them, taught me more about music making than most could have done in a lifetime.

—John Bell Young
Putney, Vermont
February 2008

Introduction

In this volume for Amadeus Press, it is my objective to survey great music from a personal perspective, just as anyone would. Whatever I can convey of my ideas about listening, though informed by analytical scrutiny and historical data, will not be enslaved by technical analysis. While academia continues to do its job in the classroom, pointing out idiosyncratic formalities as it teaches students to more effectively recognize compositional strategies, I prefer to do what I can to bring music to life in a kind of dialectical dance. This volume, then, is part musical analysis and part interpretation, but above all a personal appreciation. It is not intended to be nor should it be construed as a work of scholarship.

Nowhere will I presume that the reader will be following my musical observations, or the accompanying CD, with a score in hand. So often when we listen to music, things seem to fly off the page of the score or from the hands of the performer in ways that strike us as inexplicably new and exciting, as if we had just heard the piece for the first time. Perhaps that's simply how it should be. In any case, in attempting to put myself in the shoes of listeners, both those who are familiar with this music and those who may not be, I will do my best to bring them into the dynamic fold of the music as it reveals itself. And while there are certainly advantages to examining the score, there is also much to be said for letting your ears do what they do best when you trust your instincts: listening!

Though I presume that readers will have a minimal knowledge of the vocabulary of music, or access to information that would explain such things as meter, rhythm, note values, bar lines, and the array of Italian-language tempo and dynamic markings, I will nevertheless attempt, where appropriate, to demystify some of the larger issues pertaining to musical experience. To this end, I will evaluate and describe the more salient points of the compositional process, at least where such are relevant to opera. However, to move into strictly musical dimensions at the expense of drama, story, and stagecraft would defeat the purpose of evaluating opera in the first place, much less conveying its substance. Even so, as we begin this survey of Puccini's operas, it might benefit us all to look at a few basic technical concepts, albeit nothing too intimidating.

Let's start with the notion of *tonality*. What does that really mean? If you think of a work of tonal music—that is, music that depends for its very existence on the organization of its parts into tonal regions, or keys, and their relationships—as a kind of solar system, with planets, asteroids, meteors, light, and space, you will also have to conclude that somewhere or other there lurks a sun, too. And just about everything in this musically configured solar system orbits around that sun.

What I am getting at here is that the home key is akin to the sun, and its purpose similar. The home (tonic) key is a kind of sonorous landscape that gives sanctuary to all the parts of a composition and welcomes them home after they drift away or go off on their own into other keys. This tonal center exerts its own kind of gravitational pull, too. Everything in its sphere of influence moves inexorably toward it, and we experience this movement as fulfilling. The moment we return to the home key, we sense a certain satisfaction, as if things were meant to return there all along. In turn, the parts of the composition—its rhythmically organized notes and motives—are irradiated by the heat of this musical sun, which not only envelops its progeny in its ever-present rays, but assures them of its power and permanence.

If I may digress for a moment, I propose changing the paradigm for the discussion and analysis of music. For those who may not be so comfortable with technical terminology, no matter how fundamental or arcane, have no fear: While I could certainly refer to the home key of any tonal composition as the "tonic," or to its closest relations as the "dominant, subdominant, and mediant" (the common terminology of harmonic analysis), I prefer, for the purposes of this book, to deal less with technical matters and instead raise more experiential questions: How is it possible for our ears to recognize a musical event as it happens in real time, and once we do, how do we determine its significance? Are some events more significant than others? And while it's all well and good to identify the various elements of a musical composition by name, what use is that kind of exercise for listeners who are unable to do so?

To appreciate and recognize significant compositional events as they occur, it may prove more productive to focus our attention on both the rhythmic and melodic progression of the work at hand. In other words, what we ought to ask ourselves as listeners is not to which key this or that chord belongs, or how the imposition of a Schenker graph would illuminate both form and harmonic structure, but something even more essential: Where are things—by which I mean melodies and rhythms—going, where did they come from in the first place, and how did they get there? By what visceral or aural means can listeners untrained in the vocabulary and complexes of music find their way "home" and back?

Think of it this way: all of us know very well our own homes. We know how they are laid out, where the furniture is, where we've made open space or indifferently created clutter. If we are particularly well organized, we may even know what lurks in the darkest recesses of every closet and behind the rakes and shovels in the garage. Even during a power failure, when everything is thrown into total darkness, we can find our way around, though the gentle illumination of a small candle would be welcome and might prevent us from stumbling over the unforeseen.

If this sounds like the stuff of an Alfred Hitchcock thriller, it is indeed possible to make an analogy to the genre of the mystery novel. Just as Agatha Christie keeps us on our toes in anticipation of whodunit, providing clues alluded to by the heroes and villains of her texts, so does a composer proffer information, albeit in musical categories. These musical clues are called *motives*, which are the musical equivalent to literary characters.

We can easily recognize a motive, no matter how brief, by its rhythm, pitch organization, melody, or mood. The eminently familiar first four notes of Beethoven's Fifth Symphony, for example, form the driving motive of that work. In opera, a composer often uses an array of motivic fragments in association with, or in an effort to paint, a character or even a situation. For instance, in *La bohème*, we instantly recognize Mimì, or even the thought of Mimì, whenever we hear a strain of her famous introductory aria, "Mi chiamano Mimì." Likewise, whenever we hear a reference to "O suave fanciulla," we know it relates to the passion that binds Mimì to Rodolpho.

Any composers worth their salt are resourceful, never failing to organize the elements of their music clearly and intelligibly so we can follow their train of thought. They will provide signposts and goals, and as the work progresses, they develop, vary, and elaborate their materials. Eventually the home key—our "sun"—will reappear on the compositional horizon and beckon us back to the familiar place where the journey began.

Savvy listeners will strive to cultivate their listening habits and inscribe themselves within the musical activity, as if they themselves were composing the music as it unfolds in time. To a certain extent the listener, as a real-time participant who processes the stream of sound, is doing just that. Complexity in art music—that is, the myriad parts, rhythms, harmonies, and, not least, their interrelationships—is not something to be feared, but to be embraced. Listeners who are untrained in the context of analysis and find themselves unable to name this or that compositional form, harmony, or technical particle should not be intimidated. Not everyone is a professional musician, or can be, and woe be unto a society replete with professionals but wanting for amateurs.

In the final analysis, having an encyclopedic knowledge of music in all its details is unnecessary and unimportant for the nonprofessional music lover, because when it gets right down to it, what really matters is listening with an open mind and an open heart. In opera, the dramatic dimensions and visual stimuli are in many ways every bit as important as the music that drives them; opera is not merely about music, but offers a broader range of aesthetic experiences that bring the plastic and performing arts together as one. Opera, which is nearly always the result of a collaborative effort between a composer and a writer (librettist), relies for its very life on the understanding and response of its audiences.

To say, as some do, that in opera only the music matters is naive. For no matter how sophisticated its organization in compositional terms, the musical dimensions of opera, while perfectly capable of surviving autonomously as abstract musical compositions, cannot *be* opera in the absence of theater. To this end, I have resolved to bring the stories of Puccini's operas to life as best I can, providing a scaffold for listening that will point the reader to whatever salient musical points circumscribe and inform the drama. There are innumerable places where we can hang our hats as we take in an opera, and we do this by discerning the manner in which dramatic action—and thus articulated human behavior conveyed by singer/actors—relates to musical data and its presentation.

To this end we are charged, if we are to come away from a work of art fulfilled and with a greater understanding, to decipher its form, whether in its smallest incarnation (the motive), which is a fragment of a larger picture, or in its largest expression, be it a fugue, a sonata, or a symphony. In opera, where episodic development is de rigueur, even conventional forms exist in miniature: an aria, for example, can thrive in the space of a few minutes as its form, be it binary or tertiary, unfolds. But devotees of opera, save for music scholars whose life and living depend on it, need not fear that the only way they can get the most out of an opera is by means of musical analysis. On the contrary, opera is one art form that demands we watch as well as listen, and that we do so attentively *and* intuitively. Opera is complex precisely because it links word and tone, image and action, and it is up to conscientious observers to imaginatively evaluate, in their own way, these idiosyncratic connections. My objective here is to fill in a few of the gaps in order to illuminate the myriad references, links, aesthetic and historical influences, and stimuli, both dramatic and musical, that make of opera something more than merely a play with music.

In drama and in music, form—or, more accurately put, formal organization—matters. Repetition, that is, the manner in which certain melodies and gestures are repeated within a work (be it a play or a piece of music), is vital to our understanding of how ideas flow and work in tandem. Certainly, it is not without purpose, either structural or pragmatic, that the laws of composition have traditionally demanded the repetition of whole sections; composers and dramatists continually recycle, develop, and vary ideas in order that we might consider them from multiple perspectives and contemplate them in continually evolving contexts. Contemplation of this variety strikes me as the essence of civilization.

As we listen to music, doing our best to follow its melodies, fascinating rhythms, and changing harmonies, patterns emerge, then embed themselves in our perception and memory. It is to these patterns that our ears become accustomed. With this, and the composer's help, the destiny of each motive evolves before our eyes (or should I say, our ears) and "catches fire on form," to cite the German philosopher and critic Theodor W. Adorno. Finally, a motive takes its place within the larger formal context it informs, influences, and ultimately helps to create.

Music is an adventure. Opera is an event. Together they form a rich tapestry that can provide a particularly intense, even opulent experience. In opera we have everything: great music and theater, human behavior, drama, historical perspective, philosophical contemplation, and emotional catharsis. It is my hope that my comments here will succeed in cultivating in readers a renewed or even a new curiosity about opera.

Certainly I make no claims to be right or wrong; the most rigorous harmonic and formal analyses are probably better served by theorists and scholars whose work is more useful to each other than it is to nonexpert music lovers. The latter, after all, are those who simply strive to become as intimate with musical experience—and theatrical experience, too—as they can without becoming scientists. It is to these *amateurs de la musique* that I dedicate this volume, and I hope they will find within its pages something of value.

Giacomo Puccini:
An Overview

Whatever it is about Puccini's music that stirs the passions to the extent it does may never be known. If, as Heraclitus so ably put it, the truth is nowhere—it has no location—then it may be a very long time indeed until anyone can come up with a satisfactory explanation. While Puccini's music, which expressed itself almost exclusively in opera, is celebrated by an overwhelming majority of listeners for its opulent melodies, dramatic efficacy, and harmonic originality, it is often maligned by others who see in it little more than cheap entertainment, a potpourri of popular tunes masquerading as through-composition and geared for the masses.

To come to grips with Puccini, and the possible reasons for the disparity of taste that would either extol him as a great composer or marginalize him as merely an early progenitor of pop music—which, as we shall see, he most certainly was not—it might be a good idea to reconsider some very common assumptions about music itself, and particularly in relation to the average, if nonexpert, music lover. So let us digress for a moment and see where that takes us.

Certainly, it is true that in the 115 years or so since the publication and premiere of his first major success, *Manon Lescaut*, Puccini's operas have rarely if ever failed to enthrall audiences; they have always been, and remain, popular. In the world of classical music culture, *popular* is a dirty word, one that has long been pejorative, though perhaps less so nowadays than it once was. The idea, long since reified as common wisdom, that the technical and aesthetic complexities that inform classical music can be fully appreciated and understood only by those who study it, still has currency and is not entirely without merit. Great music, or any music for that matter, rewards those who reward themselves through getting to know it better. And while that can be accomplished by means of diligent study, practice, and experience, objective study ought not exclude the equally important discipline of listening.

But for now, in order to disavow ourselves of any prejudice in relation to Puccini's music, we would do well to consider the entire notion of popularity, especially as it relates to classical music. Some people find the fact that his operas appeal to such a broad spectrum of people, across so many cultures and nationalities, to be troubling, as if Puccini's success in communicating with audiences were merely formulaic. Great art, in the minds of some, is great only by virtue of its immanent complexity. If everyone can understand and is moved by a musical composition—so this mindset would have it—then it can't possibly be worthwhile, and certainly not "serious," which is to say, intellectually viable, genuine, and aesthetically substantial. This conclusion may arise because the notion of "popular" presumes, for one thing, a lack of complexity within the artwork itself, as if the bundle of ideas, structures, technical strategies and procedures, traditions, and, for lack of a better word, laws that govern a "serious" musical composition are all that matter.

Granted, in a civilized society, art is and always has been the measure of socialized values, a reflection of a culture's standards, beliefs, and aspirations. Without moving into a discussion that would go far afield of this work, suffice it to say that art, at its best, codifies that which cannot be expressed any other way. Indeed, in a language that is not exactly a language (which is to say that music is capable of expressing only itself—it cannot, like words, convey specific information about anything outside itself)—music codifies ideas, states of mind, and feelings. This it does by means of an exceptionally rich and sophisticated compositional vocabulary. What's more, it does so on its own terms, without having to rely on anyone's wholly subjective impressions or reactions to its unique message or inner workings. Music simply is what it is: ineffable, ungraspable. Our response to and perceptions of music, while contributing to our individual experience, are not equal to it.

Music has the power to inspire anyone who cares to listen, and if it does so through association with extramusical phenomena, so be it. Certainly, trained musicians may experience music on a number of levels that the average person may not; a musician can hear *across* a composition, no matter its genre, be it a Chopin prelude or Wagner's *Ring*, and detect within a compositional edifice many, if not all, of its parts and the relationships of these parts to each other. If musicians have any advantage, it lies in their ability to grasp what is substantial or novel about a work's harmony, rhythm, architecture, and counterpoint, how these are organized, and what they engender. In other words, the expert listener is both capable of and satisfied with the act of interpretation.

That's just fine, but is it fair or even smart to suggest that because a musical composition, no matter its genre or complexity (and Puccini's music, by the way, is nothing if not complex in compositional as well as dramatic categories), has the ability to speak to its audience and to move them, the work is somehow inadequate or unintelligible? Is our principal obligation as listeners, and even as professional musicians, to evaluate, analyze, and think about music in a manner that segregates our listening apparatus from our gut feeling?

It seems to me that if we favor the division of labor in art to such an extent where we abstract the artwork itself—which is already an abstraction—from our enjoyment and experience of it emotionally, we do ourselves a disservice. That is *not* by any means to suggest that we should abandon our pursuit of knowledge, or fail to move into the interior workings of a composition as a means of enlightenment, intellectual stimulation, and thoughtful interaction. But the moment we shrink away from music precisely because it moves in on us, exploiting our emotional responses for reasons and in ways that remain mysterious, we begin to miss the point altogether. After all, Beethoven's Ninth or Mahler's Third excites our imaginations, stimulates our gray matter, and compels us to think about what we are listening to and how we are listening to it. But these works also move us, sometimes to laughter or tears; their power is precisely such that they can toss and buffet us, like so many leaves in a brisk wind or gentle breeze, exposing us to the elements of art that we cannot always, and need not always, explain.

The operas of Puccini elicit precisely these kinds of emotional responses, and those who find it reasonable or even pleasurable to demean these works because they reach deep into the hearts of those who hear them, no matter their station in life or experience, have little if anything to gain from those opinions. Perhaps it has something to do with immediacy; music that takes hold of anyone, on first hearing, with such inexorable power is viewed as suspect in some quarters, and nowhere more often than in academia. That's hardly surprising, of course, among those who devote their attention to talking, writing, and thinking about music—sometimes rather than making it. That's not a critique so much as it is an observation, because the fact remains that, without intelligible, probative analysis, and immanent critique, music would not have gotten much farther along than blowing into bones.

My point is precisely this: let's not miss the point. As Stella Adler, the actress and celebrated drama coach, once told me over lunch at her home as I pressed her for ideas about the dramatic arts, "Let the given circumstances of the situation you find yourself in onstage *move in* on you." A more apt expression of intent and reason for making art in the first place I cannot imagine.

The man and his music

Few if any composers have a name quite as long as Puccini's. Giacomo Antonio Domenico Michele Secondo Maria Puccini was a born musician, almost literally. His father, Michele Puccini (1813–1864), was a composer, an organist, and the choirmaster of the Cathedral of San Martino in the Tuscan city of Lucca, where the Puccini family had roots going back to the early eighteenth century. Michele was also the director of a music school, the Istituto Pacini, in Lucca. Giacomo's great-great-grandfather and eponym, Giacomo (1712–1781), was likewise an organist, while his grandfather Domenico Puccini (1772–1815) was a reasonably successful composer of operas.

Puccini was not quite six years old when his father died in 1864. His mother, Albina, intuited the boy's musical gifts early on and sent him to his uncle Fortunato Magi for piano and voice lessons. At sixteen, Puccini enrolled full-time in the Istituto Pacini, where he studied composition with Carlo Angeloni. Puccini had already established himself as a proficient organist and kept himself employed in local churches.

Even then, he had a sense of humor. Already enamored of one of Italy's favorite pastimes, the opera, he was known for improvising medleys on famous operatic tunes and throwing these, like so much extra pork, into his hymns, a feat that, while remarkable, did not exactly win him friends among the clergy. Indeed, Puccini was so enthralled with opera that, in order to see a production of Verdi's *Aida*, he actually walked to Pisa, some nineteen miles from Lucca, which in those days would have been quite an exercise.

He graduated the Istituto in 1880, an occasion marked by the composition and debut of his *Messa di Gloria* (its original title was *Messa a Quattro Voci*), for mixed chorus, tenor and baritone soloists, and orchestra. It was a smart choice, given his pedigree and the fact that Lucca had long had a reputation as a center for the composition and production of sacred music. His *Messa* was a critical and public success, and though it hardly made him famous, it got him noticed.

Upon being graduated from the Istituto, Puccini had a dream come true: with a stipend from Queen Margherita, he moved to Milan, where he studied composition with Amilcare Ponchielli and Antonio Bazzini. He submitted his first opera, *Le villi*, for a competition but failed to win, as his work was deemed ineligible, for reasons, it seems, of legibility! Fortunately, the work attracted the attention of a few prominent individuals, including the composers Boito and Catalani, and an important journalist, Marco Sala. With their support, *Le villi* had its premiere at the Teatro Dal Verme in Milan in May 1884.

The success of *Le villi*, while not overwhelming, brought Puccini a certain local acclaim and also the interest of Giulio Ricordi, the influential music publisher, who found in Puccini the rightful musical heir to Verdi. With this, Puccini, who would form an impenetrable personal and professional bond with Ricordi until the day he died, and with the Ricordi firm until the day Puccini himself died, was on his way. Ricordi provided him with a reasonable stipend, enough to keep him going while he composed his next opera, *Edgar*, which was not a success. Ricordi, who had a nose for the crème de la crème in music, did not abandon him on that account; on the contrary, he drew closer and supported Puccini all the more.

But with the premiere of his third opera, *Manon Lescaut*, at the Teatro Regio in Turin in February 1893, Puccini's bright future became a fait accompli. With the royalties and revenues he earned from its publication and many productions throughout Europe, he became a wealthy man, but he also remained a frugal one; in his student days in Milan, as he occasionally reminisced, he sometimes had to make do in a way not unlike one of the characters in *La bohème*, burning manuscript paper to keep warm. He never wanted to find himself in that situation again, and he never did. In 1891 he rented rooms at Torre del Lago and in 1900 built the magnificent villa that would become his permanent residence.

Success upon success followed. *La bohème*, likewise produced at the Teatro Regio, was given its premiere on February 1, 1896, attaining to even greater international acclaim than *Manon Lescaut* and thus increasing his fortunes all the more. *Tosca*, based on a play of the same name by Victorien Sardou, was next in line and had its notable premiere on January 14, 1901, at the Teatro Costanzi in Rome. *Madama Butterfly* followed, but its opening night at La Scala on February 17, 1904, was a dismal failure; the Milanese crowd, or at least the part of it that took its seats in the rafters, booed and hissed. This rejection was likely due to a long-simmering feud between Ricordi and rival publisher Edoardo Sonzogno, who battled each other for dominance. Sonzogno, it seems, used the occasion of *Madama Butterfly* to fuel the antagonisms of some sectors of the public, particularly young composers who had been marginalized by Ricordi in favor of his star client, Puccini. The music-publishing world in those days pretty much controlled which composers became successful, and it influenced to a perhaps unhealthy degree the revenues that an opera house could take in. A few months later in May 1904, Puccini's revised version of *Madama Butterfly* was given a second chance in Brescia, where it became an immediate hit.

The Metropolitan Opera in New York played host to the premiere of *La fanciulla del West* on December 10, 1910, to largely favorable but not unanimously stellar notices. Certainly, the public loved it. Musically, it was one of Puccini's most original creations, but the critical reaction was not exactly what he had hoped it would be. In 1916 he completed his comic opera *La rondine*, the composition and production of which were delayed by the onset of World War I. Its debut in Monte Carlo on March 27, 1917, was something of a personal triumph, given the work's genesis; it was commissioned by an Austrian publishing house that sold the rights back to an Italian—Edoardo's son, Lorenzo Sonzogno—as the political situation in Europe, particularly between Germany and Italy, made its production something of a burden.

The year 1918 saw the Metropolitan Opera production of his triple bill *Il trittico*, which included three one-act operas, *Il tabarrro*, *Gianni Schicchi*, and *Suor Angelica*. Only two years later, Puccini set to work on his last opera, *Turandot*, which he would not complete; he finished only the first two and a half acts, up to Liù's funeral cortege. Puccini developed cancer of the throat and died in Brussels in November 25, 1924. *Turandot* was completed by his student Franco Alfano and had its premiere at La Scala in Milan on April 25, 1926, under the direction of Arturo Toscanini, a conductor with whom Puccini had a long and stormy relationship.

Puccini's personal life could sometimes be as dramatic and entangled as any of his operas. In 1886 he met Elvira Gemignani, who at that time was married to a Luccan businessman. Puccini, who throughout his life remained a womanizer unable to keep himself from getting embroiled in affairs, became enamored of Elvira, a tall, dark-eyed beauty, and they entered into a serious relationship. As her husband would not grant her a divorce, she was compelled to live with Puccini without the legal and, perhaps more significant at that time, social benefits of matrimony. She had two children, one of whom, her daughter Fosca, was entrusted to her care upon her separation from her husband. In 1886 she bore Puccini a son, Tonio, who would some years later make a failed attempt at suicide over a soured love affair of his own. When Elvira's husband Gemignani died in 1904, she and Puccini were finally able to wed.

The union would survive many rough roads and last until Puccini's final breath. It was not an easy affair, though. Like Tosca, Elvira had a jealous streak a mile long, and probably with good reason, given the number of affairs her husband saw fit to have. But she was in part responsible for their problems, as she was unable to control her temper. She never cared for Puccini's passions, which included hunting, boating, cars, and card games. She could be difficult when with his friends or family, and her wildly suspicious nature inspired her worst, and perhaps psychotic, behavior.

A particularly gruesome episode in 1909 involved their maid, Doria Manfredi. Elvira, convinced that Doria was having an affair with her husband, stalked the poor girl mercilessly after dismissing her. Worse still, she denounced Doria to the village priest and other prominent citizens, cursed her in public, and even threatened to kill her by drowning her in Lake Massaciuccoli. Given her social status as the wife of an internationally celebrated composer, people took her seriously, even those who didn't particularly like her. Her community roundly ostracized Doria, and the scandal Elvira created depressed and devastated the woman. Doria poisoned herself and, after a few days in utter agony, died. To make matters worse, morally if not legally, Doria's autopsy revealed that she died a virgin. Her family brought suit against the Puccinis and Elvira was indicted and subsequently found guilty; she was fined, as well as sentenced to more than five months in prison. Thanks to their status, the Puccinis appealed successfully, and the matter was settled out of court. Puccini came close to leaving Elvira, as the entire episode was extraordinarily stressful and compromised his ability to work, specifically on *La fanciulla del West*. Puccini and Elvira reconciled soon enough but agreed never to bring up the matter again.

If anything, the nasty business surrounding that incident tells us something of Puccini's overall relationship to women, which was sufficiently complex to merit a study all its own. (It is said that, during visits to Doria's gravesite, he would refer to her as his little "Butterfly.") It is no secret now, any more than it was in his lifetime, that he was a ladies' man and had a devil of a time keeping his affairs under control. Even his sister, Iginia, later known as Suor Giulia Enrichetta, who was the mother superior at a convent near Lucca, chided him for it. Nonetheless, and with few exceptions (Minnie in *La fanciulla del West* being one of them), the women of Puccini's operas tend to be facile, weak-willed, and dependent creatures, at once manipulative and demanding, who invariably bring down the men in their lives, whether by an act of fate (Manon, Butterfly, Mimì, Magda) or pure desperation (Tosca, Turandot). Whether this was an expression of the composer's private disposition toward the fair sex or just the stuff of good drama may never be known, but it is fair to presume that some bit of Puccini's disposition informed his decision to choose, for operatic treatment, literary works that featured women of this type.

Puccini used his enormous wealth wisely but also enjoyed treating himself to some of the more expensive "toys" of his day, not the least of which were high-end automobiles, including a De Dion-Bouton. A New York financier, whom he met in the United States during the production of *La fanciulla del West*, offered him any sum he named so long as he agreed to pen a private autograph of themes from *La bohème*. He did, and he used the three thousand dollars he made that day to buy a speedboat, which soon became all the rage at Torre del Lago.

Puccini's operas have always enjoyed popularity. That warm reception was not due, at least entirely, to any special lobbying; and certainly, given the absence of mass media as we know it today, no one can accuse Puccini of exploiting any such thing. Nor can it be said that he pandered to the public, choosing to write music only to please a crowd. Puccini's music, like it or not, was enormously sophisticated and imaginative. What's more, the depth of his understanding of theatrical conventions cannot be underestimated. He admired and learned a great deal from his contemporaries and was not afraid to say so. He was impressed, if not moved, by Debussy's *Pelléas et Mélisande*, was likewise intrigued by Schoenberg's half-spoken, half-sung *Pierrot lunaire*, and had the greatest respect for Richard Strauss. Stravinsky's music, especially *Petrushka*, fascinated him, and he was invariably courteous, at least in public, to his Italian colleagues. We can only surmise what Puccini might have thought of Scriabin, who like Stravinsky fashioned a world of bizarre harmonies. Certainly, Puccini had unusually keen instincts about what good theater involved, and he knew well what would appeal to the public. Thus his savoir faire extended beyond the purely musical and into the marketplace. He was nothing if not a shrewd surveyor of public taste, nor was he in the least embarrassed to turn it to his advantage.

Indeed, what he knew about theater would fill the Library of Congress and then some, while his profound understanding of the relationship of music to drama put the *Gesamtkunstwerk* crowd to shame. His unparalleled success brought him fame and fortune that he put to use in ways that can only be called modern; his glamorous homes, expensive cars, sleek speedboats, and international travel set him apart in a unique way from other artists of the day, including Liszt, Wagner, and Brahms, who only a short time earlier also enjoyed substantial success. In a very real sense, Puccini invented the modern jet-setting concert artist, but he also adumbrated the lifestyle and public personas that movie stars would assume decades later, long after his death. That element of the theatrical was in his blood, and it stayed there whether he was onstage, so to speak, or off.

Whether it was the abundance of melody so uniquely wrought on the wings of his imaginative and often bizarre orchestrations, or the gritty, if not always so naturalistic, dramas that he took such pains to realize musically, his music never failed to take on a life of its own. Though some would deny it, Puccini's aesthetic ideals owed themselves to the innovations and philosophy of the Giovane Scuola, which was roughly the Italian equivalent, in western Europe, of the kuchkists in Russia, though their aesthetic concepts and goals were entirely different. Here was a group, whose "members" included Mascagni, Leoncavallo, and Giordano, that embraced verismo as its artistic capital, but on its own terms. In verismo—a philosophy as much as it was a style of writing, singing, and composition that valued the everyday, the true to life, and even the vulgar—they found a legitimate agenda worthy of artistic pursuit and development. However, the term *Giovane Scuola* was not contemporary; it was coined only years later, in the 1960s, as a means of categorizing what appeared to be a camaraderie of approach and style in late nineteenth- and early twentieth-century Italy. Were Puccini alive today, and were he to be asked about it, he'd only scratch his head and confess he had no idea what his interviewer was talking about.

What were Puccini's innovations? There were many. So many, in fact, that they merit a book of their own if the subject is to be adequately examined. Suffice it to say that, beyond his ample melodic gifts, he had an ear for orchestral color second to none. His imagination blossomed, you might say, in tutti. Like an artist with many brushes and an unusually colorful palette, he was a painter in sound, coloring vast expanses of migrating sonorities where exotic instrumental combinations and audacious contrasts, simultaneously affected or in juxtaposition, could create an entirely different mood or character within the blink of an eye.

Here was a composer who took risks, imposing a quartet of cellos, for example, in the middle of grand opera to give emphasis to elegy, or throwing a wash of church bells against a sheen of muted strings and English horns. Nor was he immune to the magical effects, which he never engineered for their own sake, that the percussion family could engender. Nowhere else will you find (save for Mahler, perhaps, whose genius was of a different order) triangles, piccolos, cymbals, snare drums, and sheep bells astride bass clarinets, horns, and trumpets. That Puccini's mastery of orchestration allowed him to dissolve one instrumental combination into another in a split second is astonishing enough in its own right.

But it is Puccini's intimate understanding of the human voice that bears the most fruit. Certainly, he demanded as much from singers as he did from librettists. His long, melisma-like melodic lines that seem to stretch out at times to infinity require a great deal of a singer, so much so that young singers are often (and wisely) advised to be very careful about which of his roles to take on. To be sure, and without exception, every one of his tenor roles, be it Rodolfo or Pinkerton, though suitable for a lyric voice, brings with it heldentenor demands. Whatever its tessitura or type, the voice that takes on a Puccini role faces an enormous challenge that requires unusual stamina, as well as an ability to sustain a long line and even longer breaths. The Puccini singer is one who is capable of soaring above the rich orchestration so as to be heard, and heard clearly, but also one capable of singing a velvety *pianissimo* in a high register, which, as every singer knows, is not so easy.

As for acting, Puccini's music is rarely static, and its brand of verismo demands a kind of naturalistic acting that is rarely seen on an operatic stage. There is good physical reason for this rarity, beyond the acting talent (or lack of it) of a given singer. To preserve the breath and maximize the use of the lungs and vocal cords, a singer has to remain reasonably still, though not moribund. Too much physical motion—bending down, running onstage while singing, and so forth—can compromise the voice, sometimes for good. Puccini's operas require an artist who can reconcile the specific demands of the role to the demands of the voice and yet make it all look and sound natural. The days of the singing cardboard cutout, whose entire dramatic vocabulary is defined by large and general gestures without the benefit of the underlying intent that drives them, are over.

Puccini's harmonic vocabulary was at once fluid and exotic. He had a fondness for a number of compositional strategies that in less gifted hands would have come off as merely cheesy. His mastery extended to a particularly rich use of double thirds, piled up atop each other and often proceeding in whole tones; he enjoyed juxtaposing such exotic writing with sudden dips into Wagnerian chromaticism, thus migrating from wide open sonorities that boast rootlessness and independence, to those that are closed and labyrinthine. In Puccini, dual tonalities, or opposing modalities, lurk side by side without sounding in the least dissonant; this is often the consequence of part writing that favors pitting offstage players or voices against those who have a more vigorous presence onstage. He had a liking, too, for augmented fourths, lowered leading tones, falling fifths, and dominant-quality harmonies, all appropriated in the service of expressive specificity.

As for his appropriation of the leitmotif (or motive), his vision was entirely individual. Unlike Wagner, who drew out, endlessly elaborated, and extolled the virtue of the motive as a compositional device capable in its own right of defining and even expanding the psychological dimensions of a character, Puccini's use of it was more fundamental. For him, the motive was a contextual device, which, as we shall see in this exploration of his operas, served a mnemonic function. Though a Puccini motive can indeed be construed to represent a character or a situation, it rarely if ever makes a meal out of either. Instead, motives are put to work as a means of recollection, reminiscence, and premonition. They are pieces of a larger design or musical mosaic that lend the whole its integrity without becoming merely a crutch or a substitute.

Finally there is the idea of *mestizia toscana*, or "Tuscan mournfulness," a deep-rooted melancholy that sings the Tuscan soul. It permeates Puccini's music, under which runs a perpetual current of profound sadness. The concept can be a bit glib, as it refers to nothing specific. According to the Venetian-born pianist Roberto Poli, *mestizia toscana* was pretty much encapsulated by late nineteenth-century Tuscan poetry, which drew a kind of perverse inspiration from the desolate Tuscan countryside known as the Maremma. In winter, it is an especially barren, vast, and open landscape of swamps, valleys, beaches, and pine trees, which in Puccini's day was populated largely by shepherds.

It may be helpful to bring in, as a kind of quasi metaphor, and because I am more familiar with it, the Slavic equivalent of *mestizia toscana*, which is *zhal'*. *Zhal'* is not easily translated, having deep roots in several Slavic languages. In addition to sorrow, pity, and grief, *zhal'* conveys the grittier emotional environment of complaint, resentment, and even loyalty. It is the site of what Charles Rosen has so aptly coined *morbid intensity*, where even musical humor (which Puccini only rarely exploits), in contrast to the music of say, Beethoven, Haydn, or Schumann, is wistfully forsaken.

Though Puccini is known primarily for his operas, he was not immune to other genres. Alas, neither these nor his two earliest operas, *Le villi* or *Edgar*, is examined in this volume, which is necessarily limited, by space and other considerations, to his major and best-known operas. Nor have I surveyed *La fanciulla del West*, one of his most innovative and compositionally complex works; to do this great if infrequently performed opera the justice it deserves would require a book in its own right. His piano music, what little there is of it, is unremarkable; "Scossa elettrica" (Electric shock), for example, was a second thought, a rather nondescript but scintillating march commissioned in 1899 by the Como Exposition and the World Conference of Telegraphers on the occasion of the centennial of the invention of the electric battery.

He wrote five works for string quartet, but none more successful than *Crisantemi* (CD Track 1), which he composed in 1890. This brief one-movement work, which Puccini claimed to have written in a single night, is no less an example of his *mestizia toscana* than his operatic output. It is an elegy composed in memory of Duke Amadeo di Savoia, an Italian nobleman. Certainly, it clearly shows his debt to Wagner: Puccini's infatuation with the composer of the *Ring* was hardly unusual at a time when every young composer was condemned to stand in Wagner's rather overwhelming shadow. Nevertheless, *Crisantemi* (Chrysanthemums—which are funeral flowers) is densely chromatic, given to long pauses and drooping motivic sighs. Perhaps its greatest significance is not what it stands for in its own right, but what Puccini was able to harvest from it: two themes, which he extracted and used in the concluding act of *Manon Lescaut*.

From all accounts, Puccini was a kind and gentle man, generous to others, and rarely if ever confrontational. He had strong opinions, of course, as any artist worth his salt does, and wasn't afraid to articulate these in private. Artistically he was a demanding and difficult collaborator, one very much set in his ways, who tolerated no dissent once his artistic vision was formulated. That said, the ideas that his librettists set forth inform every one of his operas and are no less remarkable than the music itself. The contributions of Luigi Illica (*Manon Lescaut*, *La bohème*, *Madama Butterfly*, *Tosca*), Giuseppe Giacosa (*La bohème*, *Madama Butterfly*, *Tosca*), Giuseppe Adami (*La rondine*, *Il tabarro*, *Turandot*), Guelfo Civinini (*La fanciulla del West*), Carl Zangarini (*La fanciulla del West*), Giovacchino Forzano (*Il tabarro*, *Suor Angelica*, *Gianni Schicchi*), Renato Simoni (*Turandot*), and even Ferdinando Fontana (*Le villi* and *Edgar*) cannot be underestimated. Were that I had another volume to evaluate the work of these librettists exclusively, I would; but as rewarding as that task would be, it falls outside the scope of this volume.

The characters that populate Puccini's operas are rich, voluptuous, and complex, and they demand extraordinary discipline from singers with exceptional vocal authority. But they also demand no-less-comprehensive dramatic skills. Mouthing in the shadows, twirling a mustache, or protesting another's villainy with wrenched hands, like an old silent-film actor, simply won't do. In these works, the behavior of any given character must be conveyed, if it is to be credible, with earnest compassion and, to whatever extent may be possible onstage, with naturalistic demeanor.

No less difficult are the vocal demands. As the great tenor Nicolai Gedda observed, "Indeed, young singers are often cautioned against assuming these roles too early in their careers; the voice is a very delicate instrument and must be treated with the greatest care." He is right. Singers who push too hard too soon expose their instruments to danger of irreparable ruin. For example, the Puccinian tenor is more often than not an equivalent of the Wagnerian heldentenor, that is, one who is capable of tremendous stamina, dynamic range, power, and refined vocal declamation. Nor does Puccini let his female singers off the hook: more often than not his heroines require the nearly superhuman skills of a dramatic soprano. As the tenor Marcello Giordani observed recently during an offstage interview at the Metropolitan Opera, even bel canto singing in Puccini demands something of the *lirico spinto*, which refers to the dramatic intent and authority normally associated with a heldentenor.

Even so, there are certain roles, such as Mimì in *La bohème*, that can be carried off beautifully by a young singer. Unlike the often brazen, extraverted Tosca, for example, Mimì is characterized by introversion and quiescence. That is not to say the role is a breeze; on the contrary, it requires musical cultivation that pays homage to subtle inflection. Manon Lescaut, on the other hand, is a dramatic soprano's meat and potatoes; in the New Orleans death scene, for example, where she intones her big aria, "Sola, perduta, abbandonata," the soprano must summon every available vocal resource. The singing here must be crystal clear, often *forte*, and yet flexible, all the while suspending any disbelief in the character's desperate situation. To sing out with the power of an ox while making the audience believe she is dying of fever, thirst, and starvation is no easy task.

Throughout this book, I have made every effort to draw out the titles of the arias and other relevant material. The customary practice is to name an aria by its first few words. More often than not, that information is simply inadequate, as it's nearly impossible to grasp from it at a glance what the aria is all about, absent any familiarity with the libretto. Thus, by translating at least the first line or two, or more, I hope those readers who may not be so familiar with these beautiful works will find the thrust and literal meaning of the arias a little easier to grasp.

For all the popularity Puccini's operas have enjoyed, they continue to stand on their own merits as musico-dramatic compositions of substance, integrity, and imagination. They have moved audiences the world over for more than a century, and, given the depth of their humanity and the innumerable beauties of the music, I expect they will continue to move and inspire listeners for centuries to come.

Manon Lescaut

Characters	Voice Type
Manon Lescaut, a young beauty	Soprano
Lescaut, a soldier; Manon's brother	Baritone
Chevalier des Grieux, a student	Tenor
Géronte de Revoir, a treasury official	Bass
Edmondo, a student	Tenor
Innkeeper	Bass
Singer	Mezzo-soprano

In four acts. Libretto by Luigi Illica and Domenico Oliva. Based on the novel *L'histoire du Chevalier des Grieux et de Manon Lescaut* by Antoine François Prévost. Premiere at the Teatro Regio, Turin. February 1, 1893.

When the Abbé Prévost penned the seventh volume of his *Memoirs and Adventures of a Man of Quality* in 1731, who could have predicted the effect it would have on a public hungry for stories of tragic love and sordid passion? But it was just such an episode, "The Story of the Chevalier des Grieux and Manon Lescaut," that Prévost set in literary stone within the pages of that imaginary memoir. Something about his tale of a femme fatale whose effect on the men she loves, and even those she does not, brings them to ruin appealed to the sensibilities of baroque-era men of letters as much as it did to the barely literate.

Indeed, the dramatic thrust, if not the specific substance, of the story continued to resonate for centuries. Not even fifty years later, the twenty-five-year-old Goethe penned *The Sorrows of Young Werther* (1774), which, like its predecessor, became something of a cause célèbre. But literature was the cinema of the eighteenth century; impressionable readers were often sent into raptures over a gesture or an idea, and hundreds of young men throughout Europe traded reason for romantic idealism, emulating Werther by doing themselves in with pistol or daggers, or allowing themselves to be railroaded by courtesans whose exploits were better left to the imaginations of writers.

But unlike *Werther*, the Abbé Prévost's slim volume detailing the infamy of two young lovers was forbidden fruit in France; pirated copies surfaced among those no less thirsty for romance than Manon herself is for water in act 4 of Puccini's opera.

The story, as retold by Puccini and his coterie of librettists, is straightforward enough; though not exactly a rough adaptation, it is hardly a precise re-creation of Prévost's woeful tale. But no matter, as it is the opera that concerns us here. A cynical young student, the Chevalier des Grieux, encounters a soldier, Lescaut, and his sister, an eighteen-year-old beauty named Manon. As their love blossoms on first sight, they resolve to elope, much to the embarrassment of a Parisian functionary, the elderly and exceptionally wealthy Géronte, who had likewise set his sights on Manon. As des Grieux has no means of supporting himself, much less a ravishingly beautiful woman with expensive tastes, the union doesn't last. Soon enough, Manon breaks away and installs herself in Géronte's elegant Parisian flat. And the devilish Lescaut, who has seen fit to befriend the heartbroken des Grieux, has converted the young man into a corrupt and dishonest gambler like himself.

Sensing Manon's sadness over having left des Grieux, whom she still loves, Lescaut calls for him. In the throes of passion they are discovered by Géronte, who denounces her publicly and then has her arrested on charges of sedition and prostitution. Off she goes to jail, where she awaits deportation to America, at that time quite the worst penalty anyone could possibly endure. Des Grieux and Lescaut plot her escape but are foiled by the guards. Along with other disreputable women, Manon is herded onto a dingy prison ship, but not before des Grieux throws himself at the mercy of the ship's captain, begging for and receiving a place aboard as a cabin boy.

When they arrive in New Orleans, they are destitute and unable to find either food or shelter. (Here, Puccini parts company with Prévost, who in his novel had generously given the pair a brief but respectable life together in the French Quarter, only to be undermined by political machinery that took a dim view of their unmarried status; this situation in turn led to their exile following des Grieux's murder of a political figure's son.) Manon, now sick and weakened by her experience, begs des Grieux's forgiveness and dies a broken woman.

Manon Lescaut first became the subject of an opera in 1856, when a French composer, Daniel-François-Esprit Auber, took it on. In 1884, Jules Massanet, another Frenchman, offered it with certain success to the European public. Puccini's effort, which made him a star in the operatic firmament, was only his third opera and was given its premiere on February 1, 1893, in Teatro Regio in Turin. It became an immediate commercial and critical success.

The always hard-to-please Puccini could go through librettists as often as some people go through shirts. Although the libretto of *Manon Lescaut* has no attribution, it is in fact a composite of the work of Luigi Illica and Domenico Oliva. Following his decision to make *Manon* his own, and largely indifferent to the fact that only ten years earlier, Massanet's *Manon* had been widely celebrated, Puccini began his search in earnest for a librettist. That search turned into a literary pastiche of sorts that began with the playwright Marco Praga, who, inexperienced with opera, demanded that Oliva join the team and be made responsible for the libretto's versification.

Dissatisfied with what Praga and Oliva produced, and unwilling to withstand Puccini's frequent and often pungent criticism, Praga withdrew from the project, On the advice of his publisher Ricordi, Puccini turned briefly to Ruggero Leoncavallo, whose star as both a composer and librettist was rising fast. But what Leoncavallo had to offer was not suitable to Puccini's vision, and the two parted ways cordially. Even so, Puccini preserved two of the four lines Leoncavallo penned, and both can be found to this day in act 2, just before Manon is arrested. Enter Illica, whose long association with Puccini would prove historic in operatic circles. Illica, at least as dissatisfied as Puccini with what he had read so far, made the commitment to complete it.

Though Puccini was never entirely satisfied with any of his works, he was sufficiently happy with *Manon Lescaut* to leave it alone, at first. Even so, as time went on, he found reason to make slight alterations, even removing from the 1909 edition one of the most famous arias,

"Sola, perduta, abbandonata," Manon's searing elegy. Were it not for Arturo Toscanini, who conducted a revival of the opera at La Scala in 1922 and persuaded the composer to reconsider, it might have remained on the cutting-room floor.

Act I

A square in eighteenth-century Amiens

In the exceptionally bright, even blinding opening fanfare that inaugurates this otherwise dark tragedy, there is virtually no hint of what is to develop. Indeed, whatever it was about crowd scenes and cafés that appealed to Puccini, as they do here and in *La bohème*, a certain joie de vivre permeates the stage and its characters, at least for a while. Even the key, A major, is well chosen, in that it provides an edgy tonal ambience suited to the festive disposition.

Manon Lescaut opens with a brief prelude, an Allegro brilliante in 3/4 time. It's a festive tune, a kind of frenetic minuet brightened all the more by the inclusion of violins playing in a high register amid a spattering of metallic triangles. The motivic cell that inaugurates and, indeed, informs the initial two-bar phrase is a Scottish snap, that is, a vigorously accentuated dotted motive wherein the first of its two notes is the shorter value. Its motivic importance is inestimable, as it returns to color the ensuing music, and thus dramatic action, throughout the act. An accompanying sequence of jaunty syncopes punctuates the theme with certain discretion in advance of a considerably warmer, more lyrical theme that surfaces in contrast.

The setting is a public square in eighteenth-century Amiens, on the outskirts of Paris, where an amiable crowd of students, passersby, soldiers, and young girls enjoy the balmy springtime weather with its efflorescent aromas and the birdsong of swallows. Edmondo, a young student, has joined his comrades at a table at the tavern, drinking wine and singing the praises of youth, poetry, and love. Though he is chided by his comrades for such romantic flights of fancy, Edmondo's cheerfulness is infectious, and he remains unperturbed. A few of the girls catch his eye, and together they engage in a frivolous "madrigal" of Edmondo's invention. The ensuing dialogue between Edmondo and the chorus of girls is conversational, but not consistently blithe; Puccini occasionally dots the musical landscape with brief though attenuated undercurrents of gravitas.

The Chevalier des Grieux, an aristocratic but poor young student, is as cynical as his friend Edmondo is optimistic and will hear nothing of love. He neither believes in nor has any use for it, or so he says. His entrance is barely announced through the distant strain of cellos and winds, outlining a descending scale, that accompany his appearance. Even so, just as he comes into view, the orchestral texture lightens and the strings blossom into an ethereal, open progression that complements the first word on his lips: *amore* (love).

Even in the midst of all the pretty faces, the impetuous des Grieux can hardly resist a challenge; like an early version of Calaf in *Turandot*, he dares the girls with a temptation he knows they cannot, or will not, accede to. He is at once impertinent and boastful as he addresses, in his first aria, the beautiful young ladies surrounding him. ("Tra voi, belle, brune e bionde, si nasconde giovinetta vaga e vezzosa dal labbro rosa che m'aspetta?"—Among you, dark and fair beauties, is there hiding a pretty, charming girl with rosy lips who waits for me?) Here, the busy thematic gestuary of the opening fanfare is transformed, but also slowed; indeed, the melodic design of des Grieux's aria is a variant of the introductory material. The optimistic, even ardent scent of the music belies what des Grieux says about love and makes the girls' rejection of his diatribe that much easier to believe. The closing period of his aria proffers a tense motivic fragment in the minor, highlighting des Grieux's pretentious dare that the girls show him, within their number, his destiny. It is a motive that Puccini will return to as he enshrouds his young hero in the fate that awaits him.

Fate doesn't wait to intervene. As the spirited crowd congratulates itself, reveling in its passions, and the opening fanfare again raises its thematic head, a postillion horn flourish adumbrates the appearance of the remaining principal characters. A resplendent coach, coming from Arras and carrying the soldier Lescaut, his sister Manon, and Géronte de Ravoir, a government functionary attached to the Department of the Treasury, makes its way through the crowd and to the front of the inn.

Here, the musical choruses and broad arias that have thus far informed the musical texture are suspended in favor of parlando and recitative. The orchestral texture has thinned, too, while the rhythmic spine is broadened within the context of a deliberate 9/8. Lescaut, brandishing his machismo like an ax, is the first out of the coach, making way for the elderly, elegantly attired Géronte. A radiant Manon alights gracefully, led to the inn by Géronte, the man who, before the act is over, will become her mortal enemy.

As the crowd, and especially des Grieux, remarks on Manon's exceptional beauty, the innkeeper send his charges to collect the bags of these distinguished visitors. Amid all the vocal babble there emerges a vague hint of Manon's principal motive, a somewhat pious figure that essentially surveys a G-major triad, colored by the second and fourth degrees of the scale, in third position. The crowd, at first fascinated by the strangers and their finery, loses interest soon enough and resumes its activities in front of the inn. As a short interlude recycles the introduction's piquant themes, des Grieux remains onstage, transfixed by Manon; he is lost to and thoroughly ensorcelled by her beauty.

Working up his courage, he approaches Manon and, giving voice to a simple, broadly ascending melody, flatters her for her loveliness: "Cortese damigella, il priego mio accettate" (Gentle lady, please accept my plea). His tone is subdued, and the wash of flutes and muted violins accentuates his sincerity; the contrast with his earlier, rather stentorian protestations is thus made all the more remarkable in both musical and dramatic categories. Impressed, and perhaps touched, Manon introduces herself, now in the full flower of her very own motive, its descending line (in G major) forming a reasonable complement to des Grieux's ascending one. Here Puccini avails himself of what will become a familiar theatrical and compositional device, one he will use again in *La bohème* only three years after *Manon*'s composition. In allowing his heroine to simply state her name, he lays the mnemonic groundwork that imprints her character, as both gesture and motive, in the imagination of his listeners.

Manon speaks sadly of her own fate, as her family has seen fit to send her to a convent. As she does, the music tightens and the violins angle upward in a sinewy chromatic strain, evoking, too, a hint of Wagner's *Siegfried Idyll*. Her brother, Lescaut, though unhappy with that decision, has nevertheless assumed responsibility as her chaperone. But Lescaut is still out of sight, allowing the pair to engage each other in a hovering recitative, rather than a full-fledged duet; evidently it's too early for such a blatant display of affection, a nod toward dramatic restraint that Puccini and his librettists would abandon altogether in the first act of *La bohème*. With each response, Puccini draws the key upward as a harp lends the music, and thus the characters, a pious air, as if to envelop them in a halo of sanctity. Fleeting allusions to the thematic material of the introduction infect their exchange, thus exploiting another mnemonic commitment, namely, the implicit presence of Edmondo and the other students.

Lescaut interrupts the lovers' acquaintance, calling out from the inn for Manon. She excuses herself with a reluctant promise to meet des Grieux secretly after dark. Her beauty, as well as her assurances, sends des Grieux into ecstatic spasms that will remain, for obvious reasons of theatrical discretion, merely an abstraction. Nevertheless, he makes his feelings plain in a passionate aria, "Donna non vidi mai simile a questa!" (Never have I seen such a woman!). Here he holds on to Manon by intoning her name, and the very words—and motivic fragment—that she used to introduce herself. Des Grieux's impassioned tenor gains both tension and perspective within the bucolic, but also higher, key of B-flat major.

Edmondo and the students have not been far behind and have held des Grieux under friendly surveillance. Having seen him migrate within minutes from haughty insolence to a schoolboy crush, his comrades take pleasure in teasing him. Des Grieux, regaining his composure and perhaps no little impertinence, is not amused, and he flees the busy square for more comfortable climes. Their enthusiastic revelry, expressed with equal boisterousness by the orchestra, proves in vain, as the object of their gentle chiding has already flown.

That des Grieux has temporarily vanished does nothing to compromise the students' mood, which remains thoroughly upbeat. Indeed, here Puccini introduces an audacious new theme in 3/8 time that bull-dogs its way upward in disorienting hemiolas. As if on cue, Lescaut and Géronte, oblivious to either the concerns or the frivolity of the crowd, emerge, though hardly arm in arm. Unknown to either, Edmondo, who has nothing better to do, has tucked himself discreetly behind a nearby tree, so that he might eavesdrop on the pair. In eighteenth-century France, after all, what could be better than spying on strangers? Yet, in another of those mysterious moments left unexplained by the libretto, Géronte, who has presumably just shared a coach with Manon and Lescaut for days if not weeks, inquires, as if for the first time, as to Manon's situation. He is dismayed, as is Lescaut, that Manon has been compelled to don the veil and become a nun.

After accepting Géronte's invitation to dinner, which he will oblige along with Manon, Lescaut finds himself drawn to the students he has ignored. A shrewd gambler, he joins them in a game of cards and will stop at nothing to win. Géronte is no less shrewd; he has returned to the inn to have a word with its proprietor, whom he promptly bribes to have a coach on the ready in one hour, so that he may kidnap Manon. Here Puccini proffers a rather Lisztian motive, its sentiment at once quiescent and diabolical. It creeps and lumbers along staccato in 3/8 time, like a hoof-footed goblin stumbling clumsily onto every down-beat. This uncomfortable motivic association with Géronte, who won't appear again after act 2, is deliberate and forecasts his behavior.

Appalled by what he has just overheard, his agitation made all the more anxious by the continual repetition of the tense hemiola motive, Edmondo curses Géronte under his breath. As the orchestral accompaniment dwindles to the thinnest whisper, Edmondo discloses to des Grieux what he has learned and assures him that he will do what he can to thwart Manon's abduction. A brief orchestral interlude, which tosses about the hemiola motive alongside fragments of Manon's theme, unfolds in anticipation of Manon's entrance. She protests that it would be best if they did not see each other again, but her words fall on deaf ears. Des Grieux will have none of it, and with this what had been a dialogue between them blossoms into an impassioned love duet.

The austerity of the occasion is distinguished by the emergence of a new theme, marked "Andante amoroso," which proceeds in 6/8 time but conveys itself in duple meter, swinging to and fro gracefully on the wings of the supportive pedal points and seventh chords that underlie it. To this opulent melody, Manon sings of happiness that was once hers, while des Grieux, at once moved and determined, appropriates the theme as he looks into and speaks of Manon's eyes: "Nelle pupille fulgide profonde" (In the brilliant depths of your eyes). The orchestra swells underneath, the strings awash in doublings.

Here, the lovers definitively declare their passions, their voices rising in bold thematic unison on the words "Mio sospiro infinito" (My infinite desire). Lescaut, unaware of either des Grieux's designs or his sister's acquiescence in them, demands another glass of wine. Des Grieux takes advantage of Lescaut's negligence, restraining Manon from entering the inn at the sound of her brother's voice. The hemiola motive, now infused with even greater energy, and briefly given over to inversion, succumbs to greater urgency. Des Grieux reveals Géronte's plot to steal her away and convinces her to elope with him instead. As the orchestral textures increase in density and the tempo quickens, a rush of syncopes destabilizes the musical ambience, creating a sense of unease and impatience. Urged on by Edmondo, who has made suitable arrangements, the pair flee the inn and install themselves in the carriage Géronte had intended to use to nefarious purpose.

Accompanied now by the jocular, hoof-footed motive that defines and demonizes him, Géronte joins Lescaut, who is still preoccupied with the card game. But the distant sound of the postillion horn alarms him, as it's too early. Edmondo breaks the news: Manon and des Grieux, imposing their will in a kind of familial coup d'état, have fled together. To Géronte's consternation, Edmondo, his fellow students, the young girls, and the townspeople gather to snub their noses at Lescaut and the old man, in effect celebrating the young lovers' elopement. Though hardly amused by the crowd's behavior, Lescaut remains unconcerned; he persuades an annoyed Géronte that the union can't possibly last, as des Grieux has no means to support Manon. Indeed, he assures the aging bureaucrat, she'll be back in Géronte's corner the moment the money runs out. As act 1 draws to a close, the orchestral accompaniment harvests Géronte's unctuous motive in breathless repartee with Lescaut. Lescaut's cynical, even sinister, reference to Manon as Géronte's potential daughter seems to assuage the old goat. As the students laugh and make merry, the act concludes in the dominant key of E major, thus raising harmonic tension as this turn of events insinuates itself within the drama.

Act 2

A lavishly decorated suite in Géronte's home in Paris

Just as Lescaut predicted, Manon abandoned des Grieux shortly after their elopement. Puccini and his librettists saw no good reason to spend time creating a history of their time together, preferring instead to jump into the consequences of their affair. We learn that Manon, unaccustomed to either struggle or poverty, and unwilling to tolerate either, willingly retreated into the far more secure haute-bourgeois environment that Géronte sought to provide her in the first place. Géronte, unlike des Grieux, is sufficiently well-heeled to look after whomever he pleases. For the charming but impatient Manon, the temptation to indulge herself in such lavish material comforts proves too great to resist.

Act 2 opens with a sumptuously attired Manon preening herself in Géronte's luxurious flat. Though she is no Straussian Marschallin, neither aristocrat nor peasant, she complains to her hairdresser and two assistants, ordering them about in a shrill fit of vanity. Des Grieux is never far from her thoughts: as the act opens, a fragment of his first aria informs the music, which Puccini delicately embroiders with a flute and harp. Indeed, with this nod to the favored instrumentarium of eighteenth-century chamber music, he pays homage to the French baroque.

Manon's tone here is staccato, even brittle, and thus proffers a contrast to the often dulcet, if rich, compassion of her act 1 arioso. She has gained the world but has lost her soul, or so it seems. But as Lescaut, who has likewise planted himself in the flat, compliments his sister on her cosmetic savoir faire, her facade begins to crumble. She weakens further when Lescaut boasts of his part in saving her from herself, or

so he believes, when she fled des Grieux: "È mia la gloria se sei salva
dall'amor d'uno studente" (Mine is the glory for saving you from the
love of a student).

Even so, Manon cannot resist asking, at fist timorously, what has
become of des Grieux. Without so much as breathing his name, Lescaut
intuits the information she covets. Suddenly, her tone and timbre
change, and she launches into a dark and earnest aria—"In quelle trine
morbide" (In those soft lace hangings)—that codifies her regret as
well as her longing. The intensity of her feeling is expressed poignantly
enough by the thematic design, which moves her thoughts forward, in
its first period, in a vacillating array of eighth-notes and half-notes in
mostly stepwise motion astride barely perceptible syncopated thrusts in
the accompanying woodwinds. The strings are no less expansive, supporting Manon with fervor as the theme exfoliates in a higher register.
Migrating from E-flat major to G-flat major, Puccini wraps up the aria
with a plaintive oboe giving shape to an expansive theme in 2/4 time
(a retreat from the broader 4/4 with which the aria began). Intoning
a single pitch above it, Manon sings of the modest circumstances—
"O mia dimora umile, tu mi ritorni innanzi" (Oh, my humble dwell-
ing, you again appear before me)—that she quit in favor of Géronte's
apartment. It is a song replete with regret, as if she will never see des
Grieux again.

But Lescaut has news. In spite of Manon's absence, des Grieux has
become not only Lescaut's friend, but a protégé: Lescaut has transformed the once-responsible young student into a compulsive gambler.
With this development, Lescaut is convinced des Grieux can position
himself competitively and command Manon's favor once again. Lescaut
and Manon hurl themselves into an intense duet, which, for those who
do not speak Italian or know the story, might be mistaken for another
kind of love affair altogether, and one a good deal more sordid. But
incest has no place here; the passions articulated are an expression
of a kind of twisted familial sincerity, wherein each character speaks
at cross-purposes. Indeed, as Manon speaks of rapture, caresses, and
burning kisses, Lescaut holds forth with the pride of a confidence man,
attesting to the skill des Grieux has acquired, under his tutelage, to
fleece less savvy gamblers.

The mood is broken as vanity returns. A coterie of soprano instruments, to wit, the flute, piccolo, and harp, accompanied by the bass in pizzicato, restores act 2's opening motive, which no longer seems to remind anyone of des Grieux, least of all Manon. She returns to her mirror in an effort to forget the man she loves. Géronte, who like other fops of the day imagines himself an artist, has composed a set of madrigals and hired a band of castrati to entertain his paramour, all to persuade her to remain a kept woman. No one needs worry: real castrati have not graced opera stages, so far as anyone knows, for nearly two hundred years. The singing here is assigned to a solo mezzo-soprano, accompanied by a small group of sopranos and contraltos. The madrigal on this occasion (which Puccini appropriated from one of his earlier works, a Mass) is a kind of musical frieze, à la Poussin or Fragonard; in "Sulla vetta tu del monte erri, O Clori" (On the mountaintop you roam, O Clori), Géronte has cast himself and Manon as merely decorative figures of antiquity, namely, the shepherd and shepherdess Philenus and Chloris. If there were any question about the relationship posed by the duet between Manon and Lescaut, no one should think the worse of her now, or Géronte, either, for their relationship to sheep. It's just an opera, after all.

Manon insists that Lescaut pay the singers, but even the thought of handing over an honorarium is too much for the avaricious gambler Lescaut to bear; he can use the money, and so takes the gold pieces for himself. But the entertainment has only begun; in advance of Géronte's entrance with a dancing instructor, a string quartet takes its collective seat, and, as is wont for ensembles, its members tune their instruments in a series of open fifths. (As played by the orchestra's string section, which enlarges the sonority, the pomposity of the situation is accorded even greater emphasis.) Lescaut, eager to throw a wrench into paradise, takes his leave en route to find des Grieux, with whom he will return, to the surprise, then horror of his sister.

Bored with it all, Manon tries taking cues from the dancing master in a stately minuet, played by a thin complement of strings. Géronte is pleased, and so are his tiresome guests, their finery shimmering and powdered wigs all a-twitter as they lavish praise on Manon and, by proxy, on their host, Géronte. Manon offers a lyrical pastoral of her

own, and the ensuing concertato dissolves into a polite, sparsely orchestrated dialogue between her and Géronte. Attending to his guests, he
leads them on an evening promenade, unctuously but not impatiently
imploring Manon to join them, Cleopatra-like, in a gilded sedan chair.
She begs his pardon, asking for a few moments to prepare; she will join
Géronte and his friends in a short while.

An upward chromatic whoosh, like a cold wind, is given over to
lower strings on the heels of a distant rumble of timpani that presciently
anticipate a significant change of circumstances. Manon hears someone
at the door and presumes it to be a servant ready, though sooner than
she had hoped, with her sedan chair. "Tu, tu, amore?" she cries in astonishment as she eyes des Grieux in the doorway. She doesn't have much
time to express her regrets or to confess her sins, much less profess her
love, as Géronte is waiting. As she bears witness to the still-inflamed
feelings that bind them, in breathless melisma, the string-heavy orchestration surges in chromatically inflected sequences that pull the lovers,
like a gravitational field, into a sweeping sonic vortex. A climax on
"Ah, voglio io tuo perdono" (I want your forgiveness) is followed by
sudden silence. With this, the pair merges into a rhapsodic duet, born
of the motivic material from des Grieux's "Donna non vidi mai," their
song of kisses, love, and death a persistent reminder that Wagner's
Tristan und Isolde was still much on everyone's musical minds, including Puccini's. Here, Manon and her lover reconcile, not only with each
other, but to their fate, their respective statements of "Io t'amo" (I love
you) expressed *forte* and in unison astride lush orchestration. Indeed,
when des Grieux swears his destiny is to be found in his lover's eyes—
"Nell'occhio tuo profondo io leggo il mio destin"—the musical mood
transforms itself completely.

With these words, des Grieux momentarily rejects the serpentine
chromaticism that has so effectively infested the lovers' duet up to this
point, in favor of a new, if motivically derivative (it echoes two earlier
arias, "Donna non vidi mai" and "In quelle trine morbide"), diatonic
theme. This startling new fragment vaguely recollects, like a shaft of
early morning sunlight, a moment or two from Wagner's *Meistersinger*;
it also anticipates, unfortunately, a far more banal tune that would make
its way into a popular science-fiction fantasy, a cinematic confection,

some eighty years later. Lest the association, whether a case of plagiarism or not, should ruin either work for anyone, that wholly vapid, if oddly endearing, work will remain unnamed here.

The lovers sink into each other's arms as the strings shimmer *pianissimo* behind them, giving way to the ethereal "Dolcissimo soffrir" (Such sweet suffering), but not before a rather exquisite, if not so unsubtle, allusion, in the household of harmonic progression, to Isolde's "Liebestod."

Géronte's interruption of the lovers is perhaps not unexpected. Certainly, as in any melodrama, behind every silver lining is a cloud. A jarring, even furious fugato presages Géronte's appearance. He feigns indifference upon discovering the lovers on his own turf, savoring his malevolent ambitions with the courtly manners of a gentleman unperturbed, his fury seething within. In displacing Géronte's diabolical motive into a high registration entrusted to the woodwinds, the violins, and a particularly metallic triangle—like a dancing skeleton—Puccini makes of the old man's resolve something even more sinister.

Manon wastes no time in mocking Géronte, who continues to keep his anger in check. But he does not leave without an implied threat: "Arrivederci—e presto!" (Till we meet again—and soon!). Manon, convinced that she is at last free of her keeper, relishes the moment as she protests having to flee her master's house without the luxuries to which she has become accustomed. Here the dancing instructor's minuet again raises its airy and charming head, as if to say that her material possessions are already a memory. But des Grieux intuits something dangerous, and in a bitter aria, "Ah! Manon, mi tradisce il tuo folle pensier" (Ah, Manon, your foolish thoughts betray me), reveals his despair that he has fallen under her spell yet again and, to that end, allowed himself to become a less than honorable man.

His worries are realized when Lescaut, genuinely fearful and in a state of extreme anxiety, runs into the room and throws himself on a chair. The fugato returns, the strings tumbling over each other in ascending and then descending spirals. The dialogue becomes feverish as Lescaut discloses that the police are on their way; Géronte has denounced Manon as an immoral woman, a crime punishable by exile in those days. A rush of derivative motivic fragments gasps for air as the music moves forward in a spirited 6/8, but all the bluster hardly separates the hysterical Manon from her greed. In spite of the pleas of des Grieux and Lescaut, she refuses to leave without a few valuable souvenirs. She wants the jewelry that just an hour or so earlier had ornamented her sadness. "Vuota i cassetti!" (Open the drawers!), she screams, her panic having overtaken whatever good sense she once might have possessed. With that, she fills her overcoat to the brim with rare stones.

Her sudden, unanticipated bustle proves to be a move that will cost her dearly and compromise her escape. The trio's singing becomes as frenzied as the orchestral accompaniment, tossed about like detritus in a volcano, as Puccini highlights the tension with violent syncopes, rapid passagework, abrupt crescendos, and vocal roulades that have the words and vocal lines bouncing off each other. Manon is too late; the police arrive with Géronte in full vendetta mode, and now it is his turn to mock Manon. The attempt to escape proves futile—there is no place to hide. Manon, her fear having thoroughly overwhelmed her, runs right into the arms of the gendarmes, where she lets go of her coat, only to have the stolen jewelry fall out of it onto the floor. The gendarmes detain her, holding her roughly against her will. Des Grieux reaches for his sword, but Lescaut grabs it from him, protesting that he will do Manon no good, nor be able to free her, if he, too, is arrested. His desperate cries of "Oh, my Manon" yield neither sympathy nor results, and he watches helplessly as his lover is engaged by her fate.

Act 3

Intermezzo: The imprisonment, the journey to Le Havre

It is no accident that, in the score, Puccini cites a passage from the Abbé Prévost's novel, as if to remind the listener that some things are best left unsaid, at least onstage. The passage is testimony to des Grieux's struggle to free Manon, and it codifies his anguish and despair:

> How I love her! My passion is so strong that I feel I am the unhappiest creature alive. The attempts I made in Paris to obtain her release! I have implored the powerful, I have knocked and

petitioned at every door! I have even resorted to violence. All
was in vain. Only one way remains for me—to follow her! And
I will follow her! Wherever she may go! ... Even to the ends of
the earth!

Like the cited passage, act 3 emerges in a halo of grief, a solo cello
wailing its woes and joined by the dark ruminations of a viola. The
theme itself is a chromatically inflected variant of Manon's suave introductory motive in act 1, where she introduces herself to des Grieux
("Manon Lescaut mi chiamo"). While traces of thematic material only
sparsely distributed in the lovers' duet in act 2 also inform it, its character remains its own. Its Wagnerian overtones are discernable and
unapologetic; the ambiguous, vacillating tonality in tandem with its
dense chromaticism again recalls Isolde's "Liebestod," as well as that
most operatic of nonoperatic chamber works, *Siegfried Idyll*.

The excruciating pain conveyed by this all-too-brief introduction
empties into another, but considerably longer and more elaborate,
thematic tributary. Here, Puccini takes us back again to the soaring
love duet of act 2, appropriating and harvesting its thematic content,
particularly that voiced by Manon in her climactic paean of regret
and impassioned appeal for des Grieux's forgiveness ("Un' altra volta
... deh, mi perdona!" and "Ah, voglio il tuo perdono"). The string-
rich orchestration is lush, and the participation of a harp throughout
serves to communicate the sincerity of the message. A reference to des
Grieux's noble atonement from act 2, paying tribute to his lover's eyes
and the destiny he sees within them, bleeds into the orchestral fabric.
An expansive elaboration, Brahmsian in its demeanor, washes over the
music in a slowly descending chordal progression. Suddenly, for only
a moment, despair dissipates, at least in compositional categories, and
amid a thin shudder of violins and a harp, something akin to hope surfaces, like the sun breaking through a thick wood. But just as quickly,
a cavalry of trumpets postures itself with voluminous menace, only to
fade just as swiftly, via a B-major triad, into another pious restatement
of the same thematic material.

The scene set, des Grieux and Lescaut have pressed ahead with their
ill-conceived plan to free the unjustly imprisoned Manon, who now
awaits exile to America, and to New Orleans specifically. Dawn breaks

as they enter the harbor (Le Havre), where Manon, awaiting deportation, is imprisoned in a barracks along with other scarlet-letter women. Lescaut has bribed a sentry, thus providing des Grieux an opportunity to see her one last time. The music darkens as muted strings punctuate the anguished recitative in a sequence of surging, if truncated, chromatic fragments.

With a prearranged signal, the corrupt guard makes himself scarce, and Manon, like an apparition of the undead, comes into view behind a barred window. In the ensuing love duet, the orchestra appropriates several motivic ideas as a means to manipulate our emotional response to the story thus far. First, Puccini reintroduces, in a high register of the strings, the melodic substance of des Grieux's first encounter with Manon in act 1 ("Cortese damigella"). Motivic material from the Intermezzo combines with a restatement of Manon's introductory motive, as if to say that, in parting, the lovers are only just getting to know each other.

No sooner do Manon and des Grieux rekindle their affection than a lamplighter strolls by, forcing them to separate and giving voice to a disturbing song, in imitation of folk music, as he extinguishes the candles. "Why tempt a poor maid's heart? The Lord made me beautiful for a husband," he intones, thus relating an old tale of woe about a king and a maiden, a story that Puccini would reinvent years later, for comedic purposes, in *La rondine*. It is an eerie presentiment, and not one lost on either protagonist. Indeed, des Grieux persuades Manon to meet Lescaut at the courtyard, where, with the help of the bribed sentry, she will be liberated. Here Puccini borrows a persuasive melody from an earlier, unrelated work, his elegy for strings, *Crisantemi* (Chrysanthemums). This melody defines itself as an exceptionally expressive dotted motive, at once introverted and gracefully drawn within a sequence of close-quartered intervals of a third, a fourth, and a fifth.

Desperate and confused, des Grieux threatens suicide in the event the rescue fails. As if she were not terrified enough, Manon consents, only to be ripped away again from des Grieux when the sound of a gunshot pierces the hush. With their game now afoot, distant voices, presumably those of the guards, can be heard offstage in a chorus of "All'armi!" (To arms!).

Lescaut devastates des Grieux with the news that their plot has failed; Manon cannot be saved. The music brightens as a crowd assembles to observe the procession of women from the barracks onto the prison ship. A drumroll precipitates a roll call, one by one, of the condemned. Amid the ribald disparagement of the crowd, which sees in these women nothing more than poor excuses for human beings, a sergeant gives solemn utterance to the name of each offender. He sets forth each name in static recitative on the identical pitch, thus rendering equal and essentially reifying each of the women as they pass. While the other women, prostitutes all, mock their captors and their fate, Manon seems oddly out of place to the crowd, which responds sympathetically. The ambience is all the more severe for the sparse orchestration, the muffled interjections of the crowd, and the extended space that separates the roll call. Manon's own dejected recitative suffocates on a single pitch until it broadens into an anguished wail and blossoms into a full concertato with Lescaut, des Grieux, and the crowd, all the while punctuated by the shrill and impervious roll call.

A dark variant of Manon's act 2 aria, "In quelle trine morbide," lingers ominously in the lower strings as the sergeant pushes Manon forward onto the ship. Frantic and alarmed, des Grieux imposes himself in an effort to protect her, a gesture so desperate and unexpected that it draws the attention of the ship's captain. Des Grieux prostrates himself before the commander, begging to be allowed to join Manon, even if that means becoming a miserable cabin boy en route to the American jungle. His arioso "No! Pazzo son! Guardate!" (No! I am crazy! Look at me!) avails itself of the same motivic variant of "In quelle trine morbide" that accompanied Manon onto the ship, but now set within the impassioned context of *forte* set astride a pulsating sequence carried forth first by the strings and then the brass. A stroke of the timpani augurs the authority of the captain, who, amused if not impressed, takes pity on des Grieux and consents: "Ah! Popolar le Americhe, giovinotto, desiate? Ebben—sia pur!" (Ah, so you want to populate America do you, young man? Well, then—so be it!). As act 2 draws to a close, a *fortissimo* announcement of des Grieux's hopeful "Nell'occhio" theme blasts forth courageously in the full orchestra, its brass ablaze.

Act 4

In America

New Orleans in 1730 may well have been host to a primitive, ravaged landscape even worse than the devastation left behind nearly three centuries later by Hurricane Katrina. Like Australia, New Orleans in those days served as a penal colony for criminals and ne'er-do-wells; the story exploits that fact in order to implicitly demean America. Puccini was evidently complicit with that view. Yet there is no justification for making of the composer a rabid anti-American; he was not. He admired America and enjoyed one of his greatest successes in New York City with the premiere of *La fanciulla del West* at the Metropolitan Opera. Even so, the indifference with which Puccini seems to indict America, both here and through the character of Pinkerton in *Madama Butterfly*, as a kind of vast wasteland of cruelty, while hardly the stuff of political invective, suggests either indifference or a touch of snobbism.

History has a way of putting things in perspective. Where banishment to New Orleans might have been a fate worse than death for the fictional Manon and des Grieux, we can now only gloat, with bemused contentment, at the fervor with which either character, real or not (and a matter of authorial intent), would have gladly paid for the privilege of living there today.

But as no one wants to take the blossom off a tragic love story, perhaps it's best not to politicize it any more than it deserves. It is just an adult fairy tale, after all. In any case, as the curtain opens, Manon and des Grieux, gaunt, hungry, and distraught, are seen wandering aimlessly in the wasteland that was once rural New Orleans. The horizon is broad, the perspective endless, as they seek food and shelter. They are both thirsty and starving, and Manon has not weathered the voyage well; she is dying. So that she may recapture her strength, what little is left of it, she pleads with des Grieux to rest, if only for a moment. Music from the Intermezzo imposes itself here, as their dialogue, littered with reminiscences of earlier motives—not the least of which, again, is Manon's theme of introduction from act 1, now severely attenuated—sputters. In "Vedi, son io che piango" (Look, it is I who weep), des Grieux bemoans their misfortune, alternately addressing Manon and himself with an intensified variant of the Brahmsian tag of the Intermezzo, as if to dissuade her from thinking about the grave illness that will destroy her soon enough. Des Grieux takes off in search of water, leaving Manon to fend for herself.

With her lover absent, Manon belts out an aria of self-condemnation, "Sola, perduta, abbandonata" (Alone, lost, abandoned) (CD Track 2). Here, she blames her beauty for her demise. The melodic material, a vigorous lament in F minor that has the soprano using every bit of her chest voice as she exploits both high and low registers, emerges to the accompaniment of a lone and haunting oboe. The descending vocal line, set against a sparse orchestral accompaniment, articulates the desolation of Manon's soul with penetrating ardor. Only midway through the aria, at "Terra di pace mi sembrava questa!" (This seemed a peaceful land to me), is there some sense of relief, with its subtle drift toward a major key and the affective rhythmic lilt that Puccini so elegantly embroiders within it.

Des Grieux returns to find Manon in a delirium, barely able to speak (a problem, of course, that opera so niftily accommodates, allowing the crippled to walk and the fatally ill to sing with the greatest virtuosic finesse). Motivic fragments from all four acts invade the thin orchestral texture, as well as the lovers' increasingly dispirited pronouncements of love. Even a brief hint of the dancing instructor's minuet finds a moment in the Louisiana sun, but now as only a slow and ghostly recollection that slows the music, and its onstage protagonists, to a crawl. As Manon expires, des Grieux, overcome with grief, throws himself on her lifeless body. And there he will remain until the curtain closes, and opens again, when all will be well, and the singers, no doubt exhausted from one of the most trying operas in the repertoire, will do it all over again the next evening.

La bohème

Characters	Voice Type
Rodolfo, a poet	Tenor
Mimì, a seamstress	Soprano
Marcello, a painter	Baritone
Schaunard, a musician	Baritone
Colline, a philosopher	Bass
Benoît, their landlord	Bass
Musetta, a singer	Soprano
Alcindoro, a state councilor	Bass
Parpignol, a toy vendor	Tenor
A customs sergeant	Bass

Students, working girls, townsfolk, shopkeepers, street vendors, soldiers, waiters, children

In four acts. Libretto by Giuseppe Giacosa and Luigi Illica. Based on *Scènes de la vie de bohème* by Henry Mürger. Premiere: Teatro Regio, Turin, February 1, 1896.

Few operas in the history of the genre in have commanded as much affection—indeed, public ardor—as this one. Given its vivacity, and the stellar place it has taken in the operatic repertoire, it's hard to believe that at its premiere in Turin it failed to grab much attention. That reception was in part the fault of the critics, who disparaged *La bohème* on musical grounds as being somehow inferior to the composer's weightier *Manon Lescaut*. Some even predicted that *La bohème* would never survive to see the light of day in the operatic diaspora.

La bohème was inspired by a real story—sort of. Like so much else in the world of theater, it is nothing if not a confection born of innumerable influences and the collaboration of many. In Puccini's case, the period of gestation for *La bohème* was nearly as dramatic as the opera itself. He set to work on it in 1893. Plagued by delays and disagreements among its creators, its birth was an artistic cesarean section. Even so, in order to understand why a composer of Puccini's stature and taste was intrigued by a popular story whose currency made headway some fifty years earlier, we need to take a closer look at the modest volume of short stories that inspired it.

By the 1840s, the French Revolution was long over, though its legacy of fraternity and independence, to speak nothing of the supremacy of art, had left its mark. At that time, Paris was the center of the artistic universe, and the relationship of the City of Light to the world of music was certainly no exception; Chopin and Liszt, neither of whom wrote operas, prevailed in Parisian musical culture, though any number of less gifted though equally popular luminaries, such as the pianists Henri Herz and S. Thalberg, and the devilish fiddler Nicolò Paganini, wowed audiences with their instrumental virtuosity. Greater talents, such as Hector Berlioz (1803–1869) and Giacomo Meyerbeer (1791–1864), likewise held court and turned heads, while Wagner was only just beginning to make a name for himself in neighboring Germany. Gioachino Rossini (1792–1868) had been a celebrity in the operatic firmament for years and served as the director of the Théâtre-Italien in Paris until his retirement in 1829. In literature, Prosper Merimée, a linguist and literary scholar, whose novella *Carmen* eventually became Bizet's popular opera of the same name, was likewise at work. George Sand, a female novelist with a man's name and manners, spent every possible moment in the company of her paramour Chopin, while the world of painting saw the emergence of great talents such as Delacroix and Courbet.

It was in this environment that an aspiring young novelist, Henri Mürger, penned *Scènes de la vie de bohème* (Scenes from Bohemian Life), a sprint of short stories first published by an avant-garde magazine, *Le Corsair-Satan*. Bohemians were the mid-nineteenth century's version of hippies, though with a *zigeuner* (gypsy) twist. Happy-go-lucky and with high expectations, these young men and women valued art above commerce; no matter what, they were determined to prove themselves worthy of the moniker "artist."

The characters of Mürger's imagination, and the short stories that represented it, were for the most part starving artists with whom the very word *bohemian* became synonymous. Each aspired to greatness in an urban climate that was unforgiving to those whose talents failed to gain recognition; they simply could not live up to what the public demanded. Perhaps it was much the same then as it is today, but those who labored to make dreams come true were exposed to cruel reality, dismissal, poverty, and, at worst, pestilence.

Mürger's work is autobiographical, in that he was himself a young bohemian who bravely, or stupidly, set forth to make his mark as an artist in a world that would most certainly ignore him. It is perhaps no little irony that the one, admittedly modest, work he produced in consequence of his experience not only became his only major success, but outlived him to become one of the most important stories of the human condition of all time. Not only would his tale of four young men and the women they loved serve as the basis for Puccini's and Leoncavallo's operas, both titled *La bohème*, but it would inform the story of American musical theater in the late twentieth century: Jonathan Larson's *Rent* is the same story, and, in an eerie twist, that young songwriter, like Mürger himself, as well as *La bohème*'s Mimì, died while still a young man.

The students who inhabited digs with Mürger in Paris were poor but from good families; their poverty was largely of their own making, giving way to a kind of camaraderie of want that was as fashionable at the time as making a statement of independence was a badge of honor. The principal characters of *Scènes de la vie de bohème*, while inspired by those Mürger knew, are also composites that include elements of his own personality as well as those of his friends.

The four principal male characters in Mürger's original confection share a garret apartment overlooking the mansard roofs of Paris. First among them is bald, thick-bearded poet and journalist, and sometimes playwright, Rodolphe; next is Marcel, a painter whose one great work, *The Passage of the Red Sea*, was so often rejected by the French art establishment that the embarrassment served only to fuel his ambitions. Schaunard is a cosmopolitan by nature but a musician and poet by day, distinguished by his enormous nose and a fondness for an old overcoat; and Gustave Colline is a philosopher. Among the women, who though likewise artistic are largely marginalized by their roles as mistress, there is Phémie, Schaunard's unlikely paramour; Musette, a popular singer who lives out her life in the Latin Quarter when she isn't flirting with anyone that moves en route to Marcel, who loves her; and finally, Mimì, a vivacious ne'er-do-well of whom Rodolphe is enamored.

Yet another character, Francine, whose attributes become Mimì's in the opera, is the subject of a different Mürger story, titled "Francine's Muff"; she, too, was based on a real person, one of Mürger's lovers who died in hospital before the young writer had a chance to bid her good-bye. In *Scènes* she is an impoverished seamstress with a heart of gold who, loved by the sculptor, Jacques, returns to the bohemian's flat in abject poverty on Christmas Eve. Seeing her deathly ill with consumption, the artists chip in what they can, selling their simple possessions to get her admittance to hospital, where, like Mürger's real love, she dies.

With the first performance in 1849 of *La vie de bohème*, a play based on his popular stories, Mürger's fortunes improved. He wrote it with the cooperation of Theodore Barriere, in the manner of a singspiel— that is, something along the lines of musical theater wherein folk tunes and other musical numbers, penned by a mediocre composer of questionable talent, were introduced throughout the play.

More than twenty years after Mürger's death, another "member" of this lively bohemian collective of artistic wannabes, Alexandre Schanne, came out with the memoir *Souvenirs de Schaunard*. While this may have been nothing more than a belated effort to cash in on his colleague's success, it sheds light on just who each of these characters was and what informed their desires. Schanne, who was affectionately called Schannard by his friends, was the inspiration for Mürger's Schaunard; it was only because of a typographical error in the first publication of *Scènes*, in which the second "n" was replaced by "u," that his name was modified. Schaunard, a minor composer, eventually abandoned his artistic ambitions to pursue a career as a toy manufacturer, thus betraying the youthful naiveté of his fellow bohemians.

Had it not been for Puccini's steely fortitude and the rigorous support of his publisher, Ricordi, this *La bohème* might never have seen the light of day. Over coffee at a café in Milan one day in March 1893, Puccini was amused to hear from his colleague Leoncavallo that he, too, had contracted to set Mürger's touching story to music. But when Leoncavallo learned that Puccini had likewise committed to turn it into an opera, he was not amused. On the contrary, an infuriated Leoncavallo went to the press, where he let it be known in *Il corriere della sera* that he was proprietor of the *Bohème* idea, if not the work itself. Of course, Puccini could not have cared less; he was fully aware, and said so publicly, that where art is concerned, ideas are owned by no one. Even so, the publisher Ricordi made an attempt to secure the copyright to the original *Scènes*, only to discover that, since Mürger's death, the work had reverted to the public domain and was therefore up for grabs. The subsequent play was still under copyright (to the extent that copyrights existed in those days), but it held no interest for either Puccini or Leoncavallo, who found its loosely arranged, episodic treatment of the original to be wanting in more than one category.

In spite of Leoncavallo's impertinence, Puccini pressed on with the project, though after the unprecedented success of *Manon Lescaut*, his self-assurance—some would say arrogance—had grown significantly. Few composers were as tough on their librettists as Puccini, whose demands for perfection were rarely satisfied. Once again and on the heels of *Manon Lescaut*, his diligent librettist was the hotheaded Luigi Illica, who by now was barely able to maintain an uneasy peace with the composer and sometimes found that the best way to communicate with Puccini was through the mediation of Guilio Ricordi, or his son, Tito Ricordi.

Enter Giuseppe Giacosa, whom the elder Ricordi determined would make an ideal third partner for this venture, in which much had been invested. Giacosa, a pudgy and obsequious presence on the Italian arts scene, was a poet, playwright, and prominent literary figure. His task now was to versify Illica's prosaic prose, polishing whatever dialogue he came up with and adding finishing touches to the overall narrative. But even Giacosa nearly came to wit's end with Puccini's continued dissatisfaction, complaining to Ricordi, "I must confess to you that I'm exhausted by this continuous redoing, retouching, adding, correcting, cutting, sticking back together, expanding here in order to shrink there . . . I swear to you that I'll never again be caught writing librettos."

Puccini was hard to pin down. Traveling constantly within Europe to supervise, attend, or otherwise consult on production of *Manon Lescaut*, he declined, or at least delayed, to commit himself to *La bohème* with his customary fervor. Indeed, Ricordi had even approached him to compose music for a new opera, *La lupa*, based on a novel by Giovanni Verga, with the author as librettist. But after careful consideration and giving Verga every hope that he would follow through, Puccini rejected it as an inadequate vehicle for his talents and came back to *Bohème*.

All four members of the *Bohème* "team"—Puccini, Illica, Giacosa, and even Ricordi (whose negotiating abilities were as important to the project as his intuitive dramatic judgment)—were well aware that if the ostensibly busy crosscurrents of *La bohème* were to be successful, and move the public, the original story would have to be consolidated and cut back. While this kind of reductionism was hardly anything new to opera, it was also crucial to communicating the essence of a story in such a way as to move its audiences.

Thus certain characters had to be eliminated in the interest of dramatic economy, while others became composites of those who populated Mürger's original *Scènes*. Mürger himself had already done a share of the work; indeed, through Rodolphe (who becomes Rodolfo in the opera), Mürger speaks of his own experience in the bohemian collective, while Marcel is based on a writer, Champfleury, as well as two painters who were also members, Lazare and Tabar. Likewise, Colline combines Jean Wallon, a philosophy student whose weighted pockets buckled with books, and another artist, Trapadoux, an exceptionally large man who likewise treasured an old and ragged overcoat. And as we have seen, Mimi was herself a complex creation, in whom Mürger focused the attributes of Marie Vimal, a beauty who made her living perpetuating fraud; his own, tubercular girlfriend, Lucille Louvet; and the aforementioned seamstress Francine.

Puccini originally conceived of *La bohème* as a three-act opera, beginning with what is now the second act. Puccini was adamant about the Latin Quarter act, where the action takes place. In his view, the cultivation of a festive atmosphere in the midst of all the illness and poverty was every bit as important as the development of a human character. Unfortunately, all the hustle and bustle in the Latin Quarter contributes little if anything to the development of the opera's principal characters, while introducing a few minor ones and offering crowd scenes. Aside from Musetta's one memorable aria, the real value of act 2 is the remarkable opulence of its orchestration, which, in combination with the myriad choruses and the soloists' fragmented ariosos, blossoms into a breathtaking but remarkably coherent tumble of polyphony. In a perhaps unconscious nod to Gesamtkunstwerk, the writing renders the characters, the scenery, and even the props equal to the music itself, as if each of these was a melodic line in its own right and thus part of the counterpoint.

A final meeting of the La bohème team in July 1894 at last saw the cooperation of all involved and agreement on the text. Even Illica, who attended only begrudgingly, was able to turn in a complete revision of his libretto that satisfied both the composer and the publisher.

It was not until January 1895 that Puccini began to score La bohème in earnest. Thrown out was the notion of beginning the opera with the Latin Quarter; instead, the Bohème team delivered "The Garret" as act 1, in which all the principal characters save Musetta are introduced with cheerful dispatch. This approach contributed, too, to a certain symmetry. The first and last acts, which take place in the confines of a room among friends, frame the two middle ones, which are at once ambulatory, ribald, and festive.

Puccini entrusted conductor Arturo Toscanini with the first performance of La bohème at the Teatro Regio in Turin on February 1, 1896. It was well received, but not as well as had been anticipated. The composer was accorded only fifteen curtain calls, suggesting the public did not care for the work as much as it had Manon Lescaut a few years earlier. The opera gained capital and critical acclaim soon enough, and a performance in Palermo the following April was a triumph. Here and in Florence the number of curtain calls rose into the dozens, certifying La bohème as a bona fide triumph.

Act I

The garret

A brief orchestral introduction in 3/8 time provides a spirited opening salvo in an ascent of thirds, fifths, and sixths over an F pedal. While this figure, which will be reiterated throughout the act, embodies optimism, it also represents the carefree character of the bohemians. As the curtain opens onto a bright but desolate flat overlooking the mansard roofs of Paris in 1830, Rodolfo and Marcello, shivering and frockcoated, tease each other with playful banter. Marcello bemoans his fate with Musetta, whom he portrays as an ice queen as he attempts to convince himself she is unworthy of his attentions; Rodolfo can barely contain his frustration with the smoke that rises so blissfully from the other buildings in his view, while the failing stove in their own apartment is barely capable of keeping the bohemians warm. The somewhat static though oddly philosophical melody that Rodolfo gives voice to in "Nei cieli bigi guardo fumar dai mille comignoli Parigi" (As I look at Paris, seeing how the skies gray from the smoke of a thousand chimneys) is reflective at first, but it also adumbrates tragedy to come. This melody, which Puccini inaugurates with a simple B-flat-major triad, drifts calmly in 6/8 time over an ascending montage of quiet major chords below. This is very much Rodolfo's melody and will serve as his leitmotiv throughout the opera.

Chilled to the bone, the two men enter into a competition of sorts. Marcello offers to burn his painting, *The Passage of the Red Sea*, the rejection of which has caused him no little anxiety. Rodolfo, not to be outdone, grabs a pile of papers on the table, a manuscript for a five-act tragedy whose destiny he now envisions as more appropriate as fiery detritus than as art. Puccini himself would look at this scene fondly, as it reminded him of his student days when, living on beans and herring, he, too, burned his manuscripts to keep warm.

The collegial atmosphere is made all the more chummy when we learn that it is Christmas Eve. With the arrival of Colline, the philosopher, the banter borders on comedic. With a bumptious, heavily accented tune to accompany him, Colline complains bitterly that not a single pawnshop is open, and thus he is unable to satisfy his own wants. Nevertheless, he is delighted that at least his friends have managed to get a fire going. Alongside two young porters who carry in the prerequisite batch of cigars, along with food and wine, Schaunard, the itinerant musician, makes his entrance to the strains of a cheerful ascending melody, a quasi-Siciliana in 6/8 time that will likewise represent his presence as the story continues. The somewhat sarcastic Schaunard regales his friends with his own story of sacrifice: simply in order to make a few francs, he allowed himself to be indulged by a decadent Englishman who paid him to kill his parrot by singing to it for three days. The plan didn't work, but as Schaunard insists, it succumbed to a sprig of parsley that he fed it with a little help from the servant girl he had been making love to.

Schaunard, hungry and impatient, insists the lot of them go out for dinner, money be damned, even though he's strewn about a batch of coins with the image of King Louis-Philippe affixed. But his comrades could not care less and pay Schaunard no attention. A knock on the door introduces the gruff and elderly landlord Benoît, whom the crew welcomes with bad intent. His tenants embarrass this married man with accounts of having seen him at the Bal Mabille with a pretty young girl, using the indiscretion to indict him. An easygoing melody, docilely harmonized, endows the boastful Benoît, who speaks shamelessly of his taste for younger women as his phrase endings drift interrogatively off in duplets. Marcello, who has had enough and sees in all this an opportunity to dismiss the man to whom he and his cronies owe money, denounces Benoît and unceremoniously throws him out.

Here Puccini, like an errant Wotan toying with unsuspecting humans, anticipates act 2 with a reference to the jaunty, descending chordal "Café Momus" theme that will eventually introduce the lively goings-on in the Latin Quarter and become a musical emblem of joie de vivre. Distributed quietly among the lower strings, woodwinds, and trumpets, against a harp halo, it emphasizes Schaunard's entreaty to spend the evening out. Echoes of the introductory motive in thirds combine with Rodolfo's theme.

As the three jocular bohemians take their leave to the accompaniment of a lone clarinet as it pipes out Schaunard's bumptious motive, Rodolfo begs off in a flurry of artistic conscientiousness, claiming he has work left to do. What occupies his attention is an article (perhaps an allusion on Mürger's part to *Scènes de la vie de bohème* itself) for a journal of dubious value, *The Beaver*. Puccini brings the first half of act 1 to a close with reference to the introductory theme.

Another knock at the door fails to produce anyone asking for money or heat. In a characteristic dramatic flourish that Puccini favored in

virtually every one of his operas, his heroine here, Mimì, is first introduced musically, and in advance of her physical manifestation onstage.
This tenuous, slow-moving (lento), and endearing melody, which will
blossom into her leitmotif, emerges here almost imperceptibly, given
voice by strings and a clarinet in 4/4 time, thus providing a more
grounded, deliberate musical context than the dancelike 6/8 that
informed so much of the motivic material of the first half. But then, just
as inconspicuously as it had begun, its sincerity affirmed, it hemorrhages
into an expressive descending figure that hovers uneasily above a root-
less seventh chord in tremolo. The effect is startling, in that it corrupts
Mimì's theme, enshrouding it with a certain faiblesse and uncertainty,
as if the motive itself had suddenly become ill.

Sickly, drawn, coughing, and delicate, Mimì needs a flame for her
extinguished candle, itself a prescient metaphor for the frail life that
will itself be extinguished by disease. Rodolfo, smitten at sight, helps
her to a chair and offers a glass of wine. As she is about to leave, she
turns back, having forgotten her key, only to encounter a draft that
blows out both their candles. Scrambling in the dark, Rodolfo finds
the key and, looking for a pretext for continued proximity to Mimì,
surreptitiously squirrels it away in his pocket. His hand finds its way
onto hers. (Not coincidentally, in "Francine's Muff" it is Francine who
initiates the flirtation by brushing the key under a table as Rodolphe
deliberately hides the matches.)

What follows is one of opera's most famous moments. Taking her
chilly hand in his, Rodolfo opens his aria "Che gelida manina, se la
lasci riscaldar" (How cold your little hand is! Let me warm it for you).
Pulsating warmly in D-flat major against a delicate spray of flutes, it
is a theme that will reappear to great effect in the final act, where it
becomes all sad reminiscence and faded hope. Rodolfo, now warmed
in spite of the lack of heat, confides in Mimì, telling her of his artistic
aspirations and his labors as a poet, and saying that what he lacks in
wealth he makes up in abundance of spirit. In one of those operatic
moments the purpose of which is to totally suspend disbelief—and
in this opera, it somehow does—he professes what amounts to his
love for her, though he has known her for only a few minutes. Here
Puccini elaborates the design of Rodolfo's aria, in a particularly ardent

expression of love that will inform the remainder of the opera. But here, for some eighteen measures, he sings of the enchantments of Mimì's gaze: "Talor dal mio forziere ruban tutti i gioielli due ladri: gli occhi belli" (But sometimes my strongbox is robbed of all its jewels by two thieves: a pair of pretty eyes).

Mimì's response—her celebrated aria "Sì, mi chiamano Mimì" (Yes, they call me Mimì) (CD Track 3)—codifies her passion, present and future. In a nod to Mürger's own lost love, she tells Rodolfo that, although her real name is Lucia, she is known as Mimì. Here the delicate chromatically inflected theme, which tapers off into an augmented fourth, and which was introduced in advance of her appearance, gently exfoliates. She describes her simple existence, alone and uncared-for; how she longs for springtime; and she finally offers a touched Rodolfo an apology for being a bothersome neighbor. As her aria moves into its second half, its serpentine melody enriched by the doubling in the bass and embodying just a trace of Rodolfo's theme, she speaks of life's small pleasures and her love of embroidering flowers on exotic silks. She explains, "Mi piaccion quelle cose che han sì dolce malìa, che parlano d'amor" (I love all things that have gentle magic, that talk of love). That confession suggests an artistic dimension all her own, and by this means Puccini and his team have endowed her as a symbol of vulnerability and art itself. The dramatic advantages of this posturing will become evident soon enough.

Mimì is an antiheroine; she demands our attention neither with virtuosic flourishes and impressive vocal roulades, nor with overt theatrical gestures meant to impose a character on the listener's consciousness to the possible detriment of all else. Rather, Mimì blends into the modest, even drab scenery, her pathetic weakness and compromising illness individualized as if in a continual state of the last breath. Her aria doesn't expand so much as it winds down, relieving itself in so much chatter, or recitative.

From offstage the sounds of voices interrupt (CD Track 4) as the music dwindles, only to swell up again in a string- and woodwind-drenched duet that soars above the rafters. In this ecstatic, wholly ardent expression of their love for each other, Rodolfo and Mimì embrace in tone to the strains of Rodolfo's endearing leitmotif. Oddly

fulfilled, and alone no more, Rodolfo, his poetic sensibility truly awak-
ened, calls out to his comrades below to save a table for them both at the
Café Momus. Seeing Mimì engulfed by moonlight (which in Paris, as I
can tell you from experience, bounces light off the neighboring roofs in
the most enchanting, even ghostly, way), Rodolfo is ensorcelled, his love
in full bloom. As the lovers embrace and move into musical unison with
each other, they are engulfed in *forte* amid horns and a distant, perhaps
ominous rumble of timpani. A now coquettish Mimì disengages herself
from his embrace and assures Rodolfo she will always be near him, and
arm in arm, the two swiftly depart for the festivities below.

Act 2

The Latin Quarter

Trumpets announce act 2, where we find a bustling Parisian square
replete with revelers, dancers, soldiers, students, singers, children, and
passersby. Indeed, here the *La bohème* team has taken pains to ensure
that the character of the populace is not only represented, but becomes
just that—a character in its own right equal to any one of those performed by the singers. The Café Momus theme, which was introduced
at a distance in act 1, here becomes a thrilling fanfare in 2/8 time.

As to be expected, the bohemians pursue their material needs, and
what better time to do so than on Christmas Eve? Schaunard has found
an old horn, while Colline, his academic curiosity a-flutter, searches
for more books with which to fill the already bulging pockets of his
beloved overcoat, which he has just had sewn up. Marcello proves
himself a cad, reveling in machismo as he flirts with local girls in a bid
to bed them. Elsewhere, Mimì, disclosing a material side of her own,
entreats Rodolfo to buy her a new embroidered bonnet, though she is
not so successful in persuading him to grab her a coral necklace. Even
so, Rodolfo promises to find her something even better one day. The
music is no less a-bustle, drifting first into A-flat major with a curva-
ceous motivic fragment in eighths that ends in a tail of four sixteenths;
and then a vague variant of Rodolfo's "Talor del mio forziere" theme

flutters in the background as the Bohemian soloists and crowd give singing voice to their good cheer.

The quartet, eager to sit together but finding no available tables outside—a curious desire, given the blustery winter chill that they took such pains to eliminate in their flat—move indoors. Mimì and Rodolfo, already beyond the throes of passion but in love (in the wholly irrational world of opera, minutes become the equivalent of years, after all), join Colline, Schaunard, and Marcello, who express their satisfaction with meeting Rodolfo's new love. The accompanying music is as conversational in tone as the fast-paced dialogue that it accompanies. A strain of the second half of Mimì's motif infests Rodolfo's introduction of her to his colleagues: "Perché son io il poeta, essa la poesia" (For I am a poet, and she is poetry itself). An image of his own love motif likewise rears its head. Thus it is that Puccini telegraphs, whenever these themes are heard, the burgeoning intimacy that connects the two lovers.

Their merrymaking is punctuated by the arrival of a group of small children, accompanied by their mothers and the popular toymaker Parpignol. A playful, deftly articulated tune in 2/4 time gallops in, its toy-soldier ambience making it a perfect representative of the children it accompanies. Puccini's scoring is no less suggestive: in juxtaposing this theme with the Café Momus motive, he colors it with dulcet trumpets and a child's favorite instrument, the xylophone. As the children compete with each other in to give voice to their Christmas wishes, entreating Parpignol, like an errant Santa Claus, to fulfill them, a single, small boy pipes in with a wish of his own: "Vo' la tromba, la cavallin!" (I want the horn and toy horse!). As the bohemians, now expanded by Mimì's presence to five, order their much-awaited meal, the children retreat to the accompaniment of the strings playing *col legno* (on the wood of the bow).

Like Brahms, Puccini was rarely satisfied with his own work; he was never above making improvements even years after its publication or official premiere. Certainly, *La bohème* was no different. In an earlier version, the children have barely taken off when Marcello is heard announcing the arrival of Musetta and Alcindoro, her doddering and presumably septuagenarian escort. But Puccini had a change of mind, pulling that sequence and replacing it with a scene that focused on

Mimì's character and needs. In response to the rather cynical Marcello's query, Mimì delights in her new bonnet, but even more so in the kindness and thoughtfulness of the man who bought it for her.

Marcello, perhaps in a burst of self-pity, orders a glass of poison as he spots in the distance his onetime paramour Musetta in the distance, accompanied by the aforementioned Alcindoro, a foppish, submissive old man whose prevailing interest, like that of the landlord Benoît, is focused on one thing only. Musetta's motif sums up her brazen coquetry with ideal panache; it is a stepwise staccato theme that fluctuates and constantly changes, both in character and in meter, migrating from 9/8 to 3/4 time. As if to tease the tormented Marcello, Musetta orders her antique admirer, whom she calls Lulu, to find them a table just next to the bohemians', so as to be able to tease her ex-lover Marcello all the more. Marcello feigns disinterest, while Mimì innocently asks Rodolfo just who this lively, well-dressed woman is. But it is Marcello who responds, with his usual sarcasm, opining that her last name is Temptation and casting her as bird of prey: "Cognome . . . Tentazione! . . . E come la civetta è uccello sanguinario."

Musetta, infuriated by Marcello's apparent indifference, hurls a plate to ground, smashing it to bits while her embarrassed companion Alcindoro looks on and implores her to mind her manners. But by now, her gaze firmly affixed on Marcello, she has forgotten all about her aged escort, who, for her, is no more important than a dog. In a bid to gain Marcello's attention, Musetta breaks out into her sultry siren song—"Quando m'en vo soletta per la via" (As I walk alone through the streets, people stop to look at my beauty)—which has long since become one of *La bohème*'s most endearing arias and is nothing if not a waltz of persuasion. Here, to a nearly diaphanous string accompaniment, Musetta boasts of her coquetry, her seductive prowess, and the lovers she has made, through her irresistible charms, her own. It is perhaps all the more ironic that Puccini appropriated this lovely melody, now in the brighter, contrasting key of E major, from an earlier, incidental work he had written in honor of a vehicle of war, not love; it was originally a paean of sorts that accompanied the inauguration of a battleship at Genoa.

Musetta, seeing that Marcello is coming around, feigns severe discomfort and complains that she has hurt her foot. Sending the boorish Alcindoro away on the pretense of finding her a new pair of shoes, she falls into Marcello's arms. Taking up her song, Marcello is now completely bewitched by his ex-and-now-on-again lover's charms, and they declare their love for each other. The orchestra, now emboldened, enriches the vocal texture in tutti, while Mimì and Rodolfo reflect on the power of love.

Suddenly, the distant strains of a military marching band emerge. Just as he did Schaunard's coins from act 1, Puccini characterizes this *ritirata*, or "tattoo," in the score as a "Fanfare from the Age of Louis-Philippe." As it hears the approaching sounds of fifes, drums, and trumpets, alongside echoes of the jubilant Café Momus theme, the crowd, including the children, expresses its delight. The tattoo having entered the square, and its trumpets now clarion clear with their anthemlike march, the crowd erupts in patriotic fervor as it cheers on the bold tattoo.

Cleverly combining their dinner bills, which none of the bohemians can afford to pay, Musetta sets them down on Alcindoro's table, claiming he will pay when he returns with her new shoes. Carried aloft on the shoulders of her Bohemian comrades, including Marcello and Schaunard blowing his horn, Musetta takes off along with the rest of the crowd, following the tattoo in parade. An exasperated Alcindoro, finding no one to greet him upon his return, says nothing (in the original version he never reappeared) and, at last resigned to his fate, falls listlessly into a chair.

Act 3

The barrier

As the curtain opens, the scene has changed from one of boisterous mirth and colorful festivity to barren enterprise. The *Bohème* team would have been hard-pressed to dream up, alongside Mürger, anything drearier than the customs gate and abutting tavern that fleshes out this act. In stunning contrast to the previous act, and even to the first, the atmosphere is murky, unsettling, and even dangerous. Cold is hardly shunned or relieved, but embraced for what it adds to the overall ambience. A stage direction—not uniformly obeyed in every production—notes that just off to the side is an entrance to one of the streets leading back to the Latin Quarter. This image holds out in some small way the hope of better things to come, as in Stendhal's dictum that "la beauté est une promesse du bonheur" (beauty is a promise of happiness). But given the pervasive sense of foreboding conveyed by the set and circumstances of act 3, no one should forget that happiness is not obliged to keep its promise.

The sinister, uneasy string tremolo pedal point that accompanies a sequence of falling fifths in the flutes—an echo of the Café Momus fanfare—is prescient. The introduction of a harp brightens things just a bit as a chorus of milkmaids and peasant women welcomes the day. The *Bohème* team takes some things for granted, as it expects operagoers to know that, in between the acts, things have not gone so swimmingly for either pair of lovers. Mimì and Rodolfo, testing each other, have not been getting on particularly well and have quarreled incessantly. Rodolfo has hinted at separation, while Mimì, a frail but needy creature, has remained timorous, if not altogether submissive. Elsewhere, the extravagant Musetta has steadfastly declined to give up her opulent lifestyle, which does not sit well with the frugal Marcello, who questions her faithfulness yet again.

Marcello has found a certain satisfaction, however; his painting *The Passage of the Red Sea* has at last found acceptance and now hangs over the entrance of the dingy tavern, where it has been renamed *The Port of Marseilles*. As dawn breaks, the sound of distant laughter mingles with the clinking of glasses; somewhere the revelry is not quite over. Customs officers scurry about in an effort to warm themselves, while one of their number, wine glass in hand, emerges quietly from the tavern. The open fifths of the orchestral introduction serve to emphasize both the cold and the desolation, while the extramusical sound effects—in addition to glassware, there are horse bells and an assortment of noises associated with steeds—provide a somewhat disembodied accompaniment. A trace of Musetta's famous waltz lingers in her familiar voice in the distance, too, like a memory manqué.

A growing crowd of passersby clamors for the gatekeepers to open the barrier, but their entreaties fall on deaf ears. Finally, as if by routine, one of the guards gives in and opens the gate, so that the matinal hangers-on can get back to work. It's a new day, after all. The produce vendors and marketers, compelled to submit their wares for inspection of the customs officers, only want to get on with their day.

With her plaintive cough, Mimì emerges from the shadows, giving voice to her ardent "Mi chiamano" theme as she queries the sergeant in attendance. But this time her theme bears the stamp of neither innocence nor tenderness, but of desperation. Even the rhythm of her speech here is uncertain and tenuous, an homage of sorts to the verismo style Puccini has taken pains to engage. Where is the tavern, a soldier asks, that houses the young painter Marcello? A servant woman passes her by, but not before Mimì grabs hold of her and asks her to deliver an urgent message to Marcello. It isn't long before Marcello responds; he invites her inside, urging her to get out of the damp cold. But, embarrassed, she declines. Taking her aside, he explains that he has been living and working at the tavern for some weeks, decorating it with his pictures— one a portrait of a Turk, which in those days was the equivalent, in French culture, of a fashion statement—and spending his time with Musetta, who supports the household, too, by giving voice lessons.

Mimì, distraught and in tears, begs Marcello to help her with Rodolfo, whose irrational jealousy has become an insurmountable obstacle to their happiness. She confides her grievances with a passion she has usually reserved for her lover: "Mi grida ad ogni istante: non fai per me, prenditi un altro amante" (All the time he yells at me: "You're not for me, find another"). Marcello concurs it would be best if she and Rodolfo go their separate ways, as a life without laughter, such as he and Musetta enjoy, is not a life at all. Their ensuing duo, a naturalistic dialogue that endears them one to the other, makes its musical capital on an oscillating, though largely descending, motivic fragment in 3/4 time that moves back and forth woefully in intervals of a third and is capped off by an expressive triplet. Mimì can barely carry this tune, however, as the naturalism of Puccini's antiheroine demands a periodic return to parlante (speaking) style in order to emphasize her state of mind and the overall emotional environment. Naturally, it is only a matter of operatic convenience that Rodolfo just happens to be asleep in the tavern. As he awakes, Marcello, touched by Mimì's situation and concerned for her health, urges her to hide herself behind a tree so that he can have a word with her on-again, off-again lover. A suggestion of Marcello's Paris roof motive, the first that identified him in advance of his meeting Mimì, anticipates his appearance.

Marcello proves less than a sympathetic listener as Rodolfo expresses his dissatisfaction with Mimì, giving voice to his vapid conviction that she has been flirting with an aristocrat, thus providing reason enough to separate. Marcello objects, convincing his friend that, given his propensity for biased jealousy and naming a litany of his masculine faults that are no better or worse than Mimì's, he should reconsider. Rodolfo confesses that his love for Mimì is every bit as real and deep as it has always been and that it is her health, not her flirtations, that is the real source of his consternation; he has one overriding fear, and that is that Mimì is dying. For this he blames himself. The very mention of death brings with it six measures of dark, brooding chords, a funeral dirge of sorts in 2/4 time that moves ominously forward over a plaintive exchange of open fifths in the bass. To this grim music Rodolfo intones, "Mimì è tanto malata, ogni dì più declina. La povera piccina è condannata" (Mimì is terribly ill, she grows weaker every day. The poor little thing is doomed!). Worse still, Rodolfo bemoans his inability to do anything substantive to help her. "Love is not enough," he sings, resigned to his lot.

Mimì, still hidden, overhears the entire dialogue, and, as if her naiveté weren't already hard enough to believe, declaims in secret asides her astonishment that she is fatally ill and that her life may be over. Perhaps all this time she's just thought she's had a cold; whatever the case, her denial is about to become her oblivion. Crying through her hacking, Mimì can hide no longer. As a surprised Rodolfo acknowledges her presence and sheepishly eats his cruel words, Marcello rushes to her aid, but not for long; on the heels of a tense vocal trio, Musetta's derisive laughter, in the form of her original flirtation motive from act 2, pierces the repartee. Marcello, now every bit as jealous as his old friend Rodolfo, is convinced that the incorrigible Musetta is once again flirting with a person or persons unknown, and he nervously returns to the inn.

As Rodolfo welcomes and tries to comfort Mimì, a bouquet of earlier motives combines, not the least of which are the first two motives, from act 1, that define her character. Given the fragile state of her health, and now convinced, after Rodolfo's conviction, that she is already at death's door, she resolves to let Rodolfo go. Her arioso "Donde lieta uscì al tuo grido d'amore torna sola Mimì" (Back to the place I left at the call of your love) is rife with motivic and thematic throwbacks, each an eerie and heartbreaking reminder of happier times. She implores Rodolfo to gather the few things she owns, including her prayer book, and keep them for her until she sends for them. But then, in a moment of supreme self-pity, she also asks him to hold on to her embroidered bonnet, as a memento of their passion.

But it is all a ruse; she doesn't really want to, nor plan to, leave him, any more than he wants the same. As Mimì bids him farewell, and as Rodolfo finds reasons to reject her departure, Mimì pipes in with the delicate thematic material that informs the ensuing vocal quartet: "Addio dolce svegliare alla mattina" (Good-bye to our sweet wakening). Here the supportive orchestration is sparse, as the strings play in pizzicato to the wispy punctuations of clarinets. For this, Puccini harvested a tune from one of his early songs for soprano and piano, "Sole e amore." As the pair come to their senses, knowing full well that their love is far too strong to abandon, they agree to see what another season, the spring, brings them, when they expect their love to blossom again as fully as the flora. Thus the litany of their "good-byes" becomes merely perfunctory; they may not be able to live together, but their affection for each other is safe. Indeed, the harmonic color of this "Addio" theme breeds conciliation and quiescence as it proceeds largely in whole tones—the structure of a pentatonic scale—and engenders a nearly Oriental calm. As they sing to each other with sentimental affection bordering on cheap poetry, Marcello and Musetta engage in hostile epithets, insulting each other in the heat of argument. While they call each other toad and witch, Mimì and Rodolfo profess their ultimate devotion to each other. It is certainly an unusual quartet, at least for grand opera, in that all the participants are not physically in each other's presence; thus it is not so much a quartet as two independent duos exploiting dramatic and even thematic contrasts as they weave themselves, with exquisite finesse, into a larger musical fabric. With that, Musetta flees the tavern, while Marcello remains. As the curtain falls, Mimì and Rodolfo embrace and move graciously offstage.

Act 4

The garret

As it is in the beginning, so it is in the end. Here the *Bohème* team brings us back to the garret where it all began. But now the atmosphere is not so much joyful as it is a bundle of reminiscences about past joys and woes. The boisterous bohemian motive that inaugurated the opera returns to open this act, as Rodolfo and Marcello again find themselves at their respective implements, a desk and an easel. The dramatists evidently saw this as a perfect opportunity for the two protagonists to tease each other, rather than their respective love interests. Rodolfo reveals an encounter with Musetta, whom he saw riding in a carriage, yet another emblem of her material aspirations. In its evocation of her life as a plaything for wealthy older men, that image serves only to infuriate Marcello, who is told that Musetta has had no change of heart but has lost it altogether under her expensive velvet finery.

Not to be outdone, Marcello informs Rodolfo of an encounter of his own, but with Mimì. Likewise, he says in obvious jest the purpose of which is to sting, he saw the tubercular creature in a carriage, beautifully coiffed. Echoes of Musetta's waltz combine with Rodolfo's impassioned "Che gelida manina" (How cold is your hand) motive as the two old friends pine for their lovers in this unusually affectionate duet. As their duet draws to a close, a solo violin and solo cello, given over to the most sinuous vibrato, sweetly echo the "hand" melody. In so doing, they give Mimì a kind of abstract, albeit entirely instrumental, existence. As Rodolfo lingers over Mimì's pink bonnet, Marcel pours his heart out over a crumpled old ribbon that brings Musetta very much to mind.

Puccini and his librettists, Illica and Giacosa, valued dramatic symmetry. That much is obvious when, in a replay of act 1, Schaunard and

Colline make a brusque entrance, carrying bread and herring. The foursome fawn over their dinner of mushrooms and salmon, though the champagne, Schaunard discloses, has gone flat. Colline dominates the action for a few minutes, his boisterous 6/8 Siciliana motive from act 1 generously distributed in his favor. Colline attempts to excuse himself for a "meeting" with the king, only to be rebuffed by his jovial, and perhaps slightly tipsy, comrades. Schaunard, always the joker, suggests a simulation of a ballroom dance. Marcello demands a minuet, while Rodolfo recommends a slow and sad pavane to reflect his own feelings. Schaunard, unattached and determined to preserve at least some sense of merriment, pipes in with a call for a spirited Spanish fandango, where roses and thorns are drawn between the teeth. Colline, with his customary sobriety, is in favor of a quadrille, which finally appeals to them all. As they move furniture to make way for their faux ball, the music migrates into a potpourri of dance tunes. Playing their parts well, Schaunard and Colline pick a pretend fight as an excuse to enter into a mock duel with fireplace tongs and a poker. But the merriment, which is accompanied by music that is at once lively and largely in major key, comes to an abrupt halt with the sudden introduction of an E-minor chord played by the full orchestra.

An unusually subdued Musetta, her voice barely a whisper upon her finding herself confronted with real crisis, bursts into the garret. Unable to support her en route to the flat, she has left Mimì behind on the stairs below. Rodolfo finds her there and, cad no more, carries her inside. Mimì is delirious, in the throes of a delusion that would have her believe she is on the road to recovery. Meanwhile, Musetta recounts how she had heard that Mimì had left the viscount, the very aristocrat whom Rodolfo had accused her of flirting with—correctly, it now seems. Finding her alone in the streets of Paris, deathly sick and wandering aimlessly about, Musetta resolved to bring her to a place where she is loved.

Showing her true colors, Musetta casts off her earrings and asks Marcello to sell them so that Mimì might have a sip of spirits and a doctor brought to her without delay. As Mimì asks for her muff, which Musetta promises to bring, she compliments everyone, leaving no one untouched by her kind words. She singles out Musetta, especially, for her kindness. In a mournful arioso, Colline's ominous basso swells up in tearful regret as he offers his treasured overcoat to Marcello and Schaunard, entreating them to sell it, as well. As he concludes his arioso, Schaunard's once-amusing theme in 6/8 reappears and attains to a new gravitas, enriched still in a dark orchestral harmonization.

Everyone leaves for a while, allowing the lovers Rodolfo and Mimì alone to share their last moments together in private. Mimì here intones a grim new theme in C minor that avails itself of a persistent dotted figure—an allusion to a funeral march—to accompany her confession that she was pretending to sleep; under the circumstances she could find no more delicate way to ask them to leave. Her action, though born out of an understandable selfishness, is hardly one of guile but of thoughtfulness. Here, with tender affection accompanied by the endearing melodies that shaped her character long ago, Mimì and Rodolfo revisit their memories of their first meeting: of their time together, of the candle that went out, of the key that she lost and he surreptitiously found, of his very first declaration of love. She asks him if he still thinks she's pretty, but when he replies that she is as "fair as the dawn" (bella come un'aurora), she reprimands him gently, saying, "No, as fair as the sunset!" (bella come un tramonto). Here Puccini introduces with subtle solemnity a trace of the funereal dirge that accompanied Rodolfo's words of concern in act 3 when he predicted her days were numbered. Like a weakened heart winding down, gentle syncopes pulsate below, making all the more poignant Mimì's confession that she knew all along that Rodolfo had deliberately pocketed the key. "Aiutavo il destino," he muses (I was helping fate).

Schaunard returns, to be followed moments later by Musetta, Marcello, and Colline. Musetta's frolicking eighth-note motive from act 2, now reborn, proffers itself in a somewhat less lively manner; only briefly assigned to a lone oboe, it is now possessed of a Wagnerian climate that infuses it, Isolde-like, with a sense of isolation. As she sets a candle on the table next to the ailing Mimì, the flicker of light assumes an entirely new meaning, one at once suggestive of something profoundly Catholic (just as it is when Tosca arranges the candles around the mortally wounded Scarpia) and deeply melancholy. Here, the purpose of the candle is not to shed light as much as it is to diminish it—a theatrical metaphor, perhaps, for a life about to be extinguished.

Fading rapidly, Mimì asks why her friends are crying. The orchestration diminishes to almost nothing, save for a few pulsating arpeggios, pungently assuaged by two violins in tandem. Musetta hands her the muff, which Mimì clutches and holds next to her heart. The pace slows to a crawl as a distant strain of Rodolfo's "Che gelida manina" emerges, as if from the silence of a womb; we know now who consumes Mimì so completely, to an extent far greater than her disease, as she lies dying. As she sputters and drifts into silence, and the bass plucks below in homage to her withering heartbeat, the last words on her pale lips are in deference to the man she loves: "Qui, amor . . . sempre con te! Le mani . . . al caldo . . . e dormire" (Here, beloved . . . with you always! My hands . . . the warmth . . . to sleep).

A hush of horns, like a clarion call from the gods, interrupts the silence as Musetta offers a prayer. Rodolfo, either unaware or unaccepting of the gripping reality of that moment, when the magic has flown and the one person he loves has vanished forever, inquires about the doctor still en route. Even Musetta, not quite aware of what has happened, holds out hope until Schaunard, in utter desolation, mutters under his breath to an anguished Marcello, "È spirata" (She is dead).

Colline's reappearance with the money needed to help proves in vain; his final words and avuncular basso hemorrhage soulfully into a subdominant cadence as they yield to a moment of thoughtful reverence. As Colline inquires as to her condition, a thin and diaphanous cloud of thematic recollections shimmers in a high register of the violins, as if her soul, now released from the body, were hovering before departing to some other reality. The room grows quiet; the only voice in the din of silence is that of Rodolfo, who shudders when he sees, on the no less ashen faces of his comrades, the evidence of death. In an existential moment so searing and powerful as to rip the coldest heart asunder, Rodolfo moves away from song, with a cry so shrill and desolate as to defy the blaring brass that accompanies his grief.

Nothing in life prepares us for the death of a loved one. Indeed, its re-creation onstage, when treated artfully and realistically as it is in *La bohème*, devastates us with no less poignancy. Without exception, and with every performance, no matter its efficacy, Puccini's *La bohème* not only codifies, but also conveys, heartbreak with shattering power and compelling force.

Tosca

Characters	Voice Type
Floria Tosca, a celebrated singer	Soprano
Mario Cavaradossi, a painter	Tenor
Baron Scarpia, chief of police	Baritone
Cesare Angelotti, former consul of the Roman Republic	Bass
A sacristan	Bass
Spoletta, a police agent	Tenor
Sciarrone, a gendarme	Bass
A jailer	Bass
A shepherd boy	Alto

Soldiers, police agents, noblemen and -women, townsfolk, artisans

In three acts. Libretto by Giuseppe Giacosa and Luigi Illica, Based on *Tosca*, a play by Victorien Sardou. Premiere at the Teatro Costanzi, Rome, January 14, 1900.

*T*osca is an opera of action. Of Puccini's works, it is perhaps the most intense in its portrayal of its characters and in what it reveals of their individual psychology. Nothing is what it appears to be in this story; every one of the characters, including Tosca herself, is in some way duplicitous, dishonest, or just plain evil. Everyone has something to hide.

The historical dimensions of Victorien Sardou's play, and Puccini's opera, are significant and require some explanation. From 1798 to September 1799, French occupying forces had established a Republican regime in Rome under the command of Napoleon. The pope, under siege, fled to Tuscany. But in the spring of 1799, Napoleon suffered a setback, when General Suvorov defeated his troops in northern Italy, paving the way for the Bourbons, under the command of Ferdinand IV, who was the king of Naples and Sicily. Ferdinand, a descendant of the Bourbons and a distant cousin of Louis XVI (who was sent to the guillotine), was married to Queen Maria Carolina, the sister of Marie Antoinette and a reactionary anti-Republican. Maria and Ferdinand had long had offices and a residence in Rome at the Farnese Palace, the site of Scarpia's lair in *Tosca* and where the entire second act of the opera takes place. The restoration of the monarchy in Rome brought with it tragic consequences, not the least of which was a brutal campaign against Republican sympathizers, many of whom were intellectuals, scientists, and artists. As Pope Pius IV had died in exile, Queen Maria assumed regency and, with it, the right to purge the state of anyone she considered unsympathetic to its agenda. Rome turned into a police state. Public executions, numbering in the thousands, took place at the ancient Castel Sant'Angelo in Rome, the site of *Tosca*'s act 3. Dissent was not tolerated.

In the spring of 1800, Napoleon tried again, crossing the Alps to Marengo to do battle with the Austrians, who were led by General Mélas, the only historical figure actually mentioned in *Tosca* besides Napoleon. Mélas's troops boasted supremacy, outnumbering the French by a substantial margin. On the heels of a virulent skirmish with the French on July 14, 1800, the Austrians took control, but only briefly. A short time later Napoleon's troops revived and, in a strategy of surprise, roundly clobbered the Austrians. The Austrian victory at dawn had been co-opted by the French at dusk.

It is in this environment, a hotbed of political intrigue, that *Tosca* takes place. The time period for the play's action is specific: from June 17, 1800, to the crack of dawn on June 18, 1800. It was during this time that news of the battle at Marengo was reaching Rome; at first the news was good, at least for the status quo, and an occasion to celebrate the Austrian victory. But by nightfall, the reversal of fortunes cast a long shadow over the city and the vicious, murderous aristocrats who ran it.

Tosca is an ingenue, a celebrated concert singer with a jealous streak. She is in love with the painter, and Republican sympathizer, Mario Cavaradossi. Cavaradossi has been commissioned, by the church of

Sant'Andrea della Valle, to paint a portrait of Mary Magdalene. Tosca, finding him there, insists he is in the throes of an affair, though he is not. Angelotti, an escaped political prisoner, has sought refuge in the church, where his family has a chapel. Seeing Cavaradossi, an old friend, he bemoans his situation. Cavaradossi makes a solemn promise to help Angelotti flee, and that they do. Soon enough, Scarpia, the chief of police and the opera's villain, arrives in search of Angelotti. Tosca returns, and, seeing her, Scarpia interrogates her, then uses her to lead him to the fugitives.

In act 2, Cavaradossi has been apprehended and brought to Scarpia's headquarters at the Farnese Palace for questioning. Tosca, who is singing at a celebratory function nearby, is brought to Scarpia's flat, where she sees Cavaradossi, who has been tortured ruthlessly. She pleads with Scarpia to let him go, and the police chief says he will—but only if she agrees to sleep with him. She refuses but is persuaded to comply when the torture resumes. She makes only one condition: safe conduct out of the country for Cavaradossi and herself. Scarpia agrees and tells her that Cavaradossi's pending execution will be faked. As Scarpia prepares the documents, Tosca seizes a knife and stabs him to death. She runs to the Castel Sant'Angelo, where Cavaradossi awaits execution. After she advises him of the sham, he confidently faces the firing squad, which shoots him, not with blanks as Scarpia had promised, but with real bullets. Discovering the deception, and devastated by his death, Tosca throws herself off the parapet of the castle to her death.

In *Tosca*, several important dramatic themes complement the music. Politics, history, lust, amorous passion, and idealism fuse in a drama of intrigue second to none. Puccini's skill in bringing all these elements together is persuasive and coalesces in the opera with unusual power. He appropriates and puts motivic material to work in a most impressive manner, investing each character and situation with thematic fragments that they carry with them like medals throughout. The opera is in itself a kind of military campaign, fraught as it is with battles, skirmishes, political authority, and military bravado. Two arias, Tosca's sad if eloquent "Vissi d'arte" and Cavaradossi's elegiac "E lucevan le stelle," are among Puccini's most well-known works and stand out in an opera of many memorable moments.

Thus does Puccini ask us to imagine Tosca, an innocent ingenue who, exploited for selfish interests by political authority, is turned into an unwilling participant in a nightmare that should never have happened in the first place.

Act I

Inside the church of Sant'Andrea della Valle

Puccini was not especially fond of opening an opera with an overture, though that had been for centuries a rather common compositional procedure. Once again, he dives right into the action, framing the drama to come with harmonies and motivic fragments that encapsulate the "spine" of the play, that is, the fundamental spirit that drives it.

Three chords, played *fortississimo* (triple *forte*) and entrusted to the entire orchestra, inaugurate *Tosca*. Their significance lies in what and whom they will soon come to represent: Scarpia, the opera's villain. It is no accident that, in an interrupted progression from a B-flat-major triad to an E-major triad, Puccini wraps the music in the menacing ambience of an augmented fourth, also known as the *diabolus in musica* (the devil in music). The path from the first chord to the last is in no way compromised by the remote A-flat triad that stands between them; indeed, the essential qualities of the *diabolus* implicitly prevail in both foreground and background, and thus grip the listener.

Though ostensibly only a minor detail, this small motivic cell, the augmented fourth, is significant. In the household of musical composition, an augmented fourth (in this case, B-flat to E-natural) boasts rather peculiar properties. Among them is its ability to divide a scale precisely in half, so that even in inversion it maintains exactly the same intervallic proportions. Whereas a major third, for example, becomes a minor sixth when inverted, the augmented fourth remains the same. What's more, its harmonic tendencies are ambiguous, in that it simultaneously yearns to resolve inward to a major third or outward to a minor sixth. Thus, in the context of a large phrase period, the augmented fourth can convey mystery and uncertainty, ambiguity, and even danger; it is a kind of compositional lost soul in search of resolution that it can never fully achieve.

It is into this harmonic atmosphere that *Tosca* is born, on the heels of these growling chords. As the curtain opens, the baroque interior of the splendid church of Sant'Andrea della Valle in Rome discloses itself. Here, in this majestic basilica, with its sweep of white marble, flying buttresses, and seraphic frescoes by Domenichino, is an artist's scaffold, covered in a cloth and surrounded by accoutrements: brushes, palettes, and paint. Long shards of sunlight penetrate the stained-glass windows, and the air smells of oil paint and burning wax. A basket of fresh food lies undisturbed, suggesting that someone had just been there, while on the right is the Attavanti Chapel (a fictional name, as no such chapel exists in the real Sant'Andrea della Valle; what Puccini in fact describes is the Barberini Chapel).

A descending and uneasy rush of four syncopated chords, which we can henceforth refer to as the "fugitive" motive, serve to introduce Cesare Angelotti, an escaped political prisoner and former Republican consul in the employ of the French occupying forces. The first character to be seen onstage, he steals into the church, careful not to make much noise. He is a wanted man, and the careers of certain powerful individuals, including the chief of police, Scarpia, depend on his capture. Exhausted and unkempt, he grasps in one hand a letter from his sister, the Marchesa Attavanti, who has provided him precise instructions on where to find a wardrobe of woman's clothes, including a fan. With these he will be able to effectively disguise himself and avoid capture. His sister has left a key to their family chapel, and it is here that he will find what he needs. As he darts about in a frantic search for it, a distant strain of the aforementioned *diabolus* motive swells from below. As if under the protection of some higher power, he finds the key carefully hidden next to a statue of the Madonna and makes his way to the sanctuary the chapel will provide him.

Suddenly, the bumptious sacristan appears out of nowhere, as if he had been there the whole time. Accompanied by a jaunty, even banal theme in 6/8 time that reflects his awkward, if not uncouth, behavior, the sacristan cuts a nervous but not quite comical character with an unfortunate tic in his neck. That he is often portrayed as a buffoon does not necessarily, or at least easily, make him so; the sacristan is an ironical creature who is self-absorbed to the point of distraction, and while that trait can certainly be conveyed as merely comical, his character runs deeper than that. After all, good intentions, as the saying goes, pave the road to hell. A savvy basso will know just how to color the sacristan so as to make him human, not a caricature.

Under the impression that the painter Mario Cavaradossi, whom the church has commissioned to paint a portrait of Mary Magdalene, is somewhere nearby, the sacristan busies himself with his petty obligations. The impressive opulence of the basilica, with its skylit cupola, blankets of gold leaf, and Mattia Preti's exquisite paintings of St. Andrew's martyrdom, has become, for the sacristan, merely a routine impression. A few paintbrushes have found their way into the sacristan's fidgety hand, giving him good reason to level tepid complaints about the extra work Cavaradossi creates for him. Even so, he apologizes to the absent Cavaradossi for neglecting to clean his brushes. Amid the bustle emerges the barest trace of a lyrical new motive that will later gain capital as an emblem of the painting of the Magdalene. This "unveiling" motive is a string of descending whole tones delicately colored by a raised fourth degree of the scale.

As the Angelus bell is heard tolling in the rafters, the sacristan kneels and prays. The drone of the Angelus bell is compelling, and with good reason: It extends over an exceptionally long pedal point on F. It isn't long before Cavaradossi enters and, hoisting himself onto the scaffold, removes the cloth cover that obscures the painting of the Magdalene. The motivic whole-tone descent that peeked through the orchestral din earlier blossoms here without shame. A bit of motivic dovetailing enriches the orchestral music and its dramatic meaning, as Puccini forecasts a florid melodic fragment of the first love duet between Cavaradossi and Tosca ("Si, lo sento, ti tormento").

The sacristan expresses astonishment, as the face in the painting bears a striking resemblance to the Marchesa Attavanti, a parishioner who has of late been praying a great deal. He is not amused that Cavaradossi would have exploited such a pious woman, with or without her knowledge and consent, in the house that Pope Pius built.

In Cavaradossi's right pocket is a small medallion that frames a portrait of Floria Tosca, a well-known singer from peasant stock with whom he is in love. Eager to get back to work, he asks the sacristan to bring him his paints. The now taciturn, now querulous sacristan complies, all the while cleaning Cavaradossi's brushes in a handheld bucket. The painter compares Tosca's sultry dark eyes with the bright blue gaze of the blond Magdalene and wonders aloud, in an expansive aria, about the "hidden harmony of contrasting beauties" (Recondita armonia di bellezze diverse!). Introduced by a gentle hover of parallel fourths played by the flutes, his aria blossoms into an impassioned expanse that gives voice to two opposing themes. The first, a soaring if close-quartered profusion that lingers around only three pitches in a high tessitura ("Recondita armonia"), precedes a lyrical melodic pendulum ("E te, beltade ignota"), distinguished by a lilting dotted triplet and significant for its reference to the painting (and thus to the Marchesa Attavanti herself). But Cavaradossi's feelings for Tosca prevail in the impassioned cadential prolongation of her name as the aria comes to its emotional conclusion. ("Ma nel ritrar costei il mio solo pensiero, Tosca, sei tu!"—Yet as I paint her portrait, Tosca, my sole thought is of you!)

For the grumpy sacristan, to even speak of such a thing in a house of worship is an act of sacrilege. The sacristan is curious about only one thing: why hasn't Cavaradossi eaten the lunch that he, the sacristan, has taken so much trouble to prepare? "Fame non ho" (I'm not hungry) is the only response he gets. With that, the sacristan mockingly accuses Cavaradossi of irreverence, crosses himself, and takes his leave to the accompaniment of his own bumbling motive.

Meanwhile, Angelotti, whose paranoia has already become fetish, remains squirreled away in his private chapel. Hearing the sacristan leave, he presumes he is now alone and safe to roam about. His gait is rugged as he leaves the Attavanti Chapel, putting the key back in the lock as he does so, his fugitive motive in pursuit. The sight of Cavaradossi startles him, until he recognizes the painter as an old friend and a fellow Republican. Cavaradossi, duly impressed and fully cognizant, offers to help Angelotti in the spirit of camaraderie. Two motivic fragments complement their banter. One is a nervous chromatic oscillation signifying anxiety, while the other, likewise linked to Angelotti's fugitive status, proceeds cautiously in rising and falling whole tones.

Just then, they hear Tosca, the name Mario spilling twice from her lips. Here again, Puccini's heroine is first heard but not seen, a device that he would reverse years later in *Turandot*. Cavaradossi silences Angelotti ("Celatevi! È una donna gelosa"—Go and hide! It's a jealous woman!). He promises to get rid of her, but as he says so, Angelotti nearly collapses; his escape and circumstances have taken a great physical toll. Cavaradossi, eager to deal with Tosca, sends him back to the chapel with the basket of food and wine, appropriately accompanied by the sacristan's motive.

At last, Cavaradossi responds to the disembodied voice and ushers Tosca in. She is in a panic and livid with jealousy. His attempt to embrace her is met with revulsion, as she recoils into the paranoia that has convinced her that Cavaradossi is seeing another woman. She demands to know why the door was locked and whom he had been talking to. ("Altre parole bisbigliavi, Ov'è?"—You were whispering with someone else. Where is she?) Cavaradossi calmly explains that it was the sacristan that she heard, and nothing more. Confident that her lover is telling the truth, she forgives him with flowers, which she arranges around the statue of the Madonna.

In contrast to Tosca's paranoia and extreme anxiety, Puccini embraces her in music that is at once calm and lyrical. Indeed, the music that introduces her onstage adumbrates her famous aria "Vissi d'arte," in act 2, an arching and endearing thematic cornucopia. Here, its first incarnation sails in on the wings of a lone cello and a flute astride a stream of triplets, played pizzicato by the strings, and an undulating horn that lends its support.

Cavaradossi is still eager to send her away, though not out of malice. His fraternal affiliation with Angelotti is perhaps no less important than she. Here, Tosca waxes coy and reminds him that she has a performance that very evening, and that it would be best if they meet afterward and go off to his moonlit villa outside of Rome.

A trace of Angelotti's jumpy syncopations announces itself alongside Cavaradossi's deliberately evasive banter; his thoughts are with his comrade, not with the high-maintenance Tosca. His absent-minded responses merely parry and deflect everything she says, raising her hackles, as well as her suspicions, again. Here, Tosca launches into her first arioso, "Non la sospiri, la nostra casetta" (Do you not long for our little house), an expansive ode to a happy home life, extolling the joys of intimacy and passion, country life and companionship. Why the notion of intimacy has to be broadcast *fortissimo* in wildly rhapsodic phrases is anyone's guess, but there you are; it's an opera, after all.

An important motivic tag, riding a wave of only four notes and spread out over only two bars, insinuates itself at the beginning of this arioso, on the words "pien d'amore e di mister" (full of love and mystery). The tag's thematic behavior is that of a chameleon, in that at times it takes on a jocular, playful character, while on other occasions (in "Vissi d'arte," for example) it transforms itself into a heartbreaking lament. No matter its mood, the appearance of this "devotion" motive invariably refers to Tosca's devotion to Cavaradossi.

No less moved, Cavaradossi swears he will join Tosca at his villa, but in virtually the same breath, he dismisses her, saying he must get back to work. Her mission to schedule a postperformance rendezvous accomplished, she is about to leave when she eyes his painting. Even at the sight of it, her jealousy catches afire, though Cavaradossi is careful to explain it is a portrait of Mary Magdelene, not a paramour. That reassurance doesn't quite work. "È troppo bella!" (She is too beautiful!), Tosca protests, casting piousness to the wolves. Cavaradossi, presuming she is complimenting his artistry, is delighted, until she claims to have seen Magdalene's baby blues elsewhere. But she is not all dumb bluster, as she recalls precisely where she has seen them: in the Attavanti Chapel. While Tosca is convinced it was the marchesa's footsteps and whispers she heard minutes earlier, Cavaradossi blithely attributes the similarity to coincidence, admitting he saw the marchesa in the church only a day earlier, praying to the Madonna. She didn't even notice that he was painting her.

Tosca, whose all-consuming jealousy has not quite abated, imagines that the marchesa/Magdelene is mocking her from aperch the scaffold. The painting's gaze transfixes her as it we hear a hypnotic progression of shifting whole-tone complexes entrusted to the woodwinds, then taken up by the strings ("Come mi guarda fiso!"—How intently she stares at me!). Taking her firmly in his embrace, and appropriating a mellifluous, deftly harmonized variant of Tosca's lyrical introductory motive, Cavaradossi reassures her that no eyes exist so beautiful as the black almond orbs that ornament her face. ("Qual' occhio al mondo può star di paro all'ardente occhio tuo nero?"—What eyes in the world can compare with your black and glowing eyes?) Though flattered and placated, Tosca nevertheless demands that he change the Magdalene's eye color to—you guessed it—black.

Their ensuing love duet elaborates the thematic fragment that lingered behind Cavaradossi when he first unveiled his painting. ("Si, lo sento, ti tormento senza posa"—Yes, I feel it, I torment you unceasingly.) Its magnetic upward swing in 6/4 time along the backs of quarter-notes articulated in duplets, with a languid appoggiatura set atop its apex, is nothing if not optimistic. That optimism coalesces in Cavaradossi's high B-flat on "Ah! L'alma acquieta" (Set your uneasy heart at rest), approaching a tenor's highest achievable pitch.

There is a childlike quality about Tosca that is not unlike that of Butterfly, though her oceanic temperament might suggest otherwise. Bipolarity was not a medically established condition in those days, but jealousy certainly was understood. As the two embrace, Tosca begs Cavaradossi's forgiveness, kisses him, and leaves. Here, Angelotti's theme, which is invariably an indication of his physical or psychological proximity, surfaces discreetly. Cavaradossi dashes to the door to make certain Tosca is indeed gone, then returns to the chapel and opens its wrought-iron gate. He queries Angelotti about strategy. In a demonstration of confidence, Angelotti confides his sister's participation in his escape, as well as his determination to cross the border to safety.

Peppering their dialogue are quiescent traces of the unveiling motive that attached itself originally to Cavaradossi's disclosure of the Magdalene painting. All along Cavaradossi had presumed it was merely a puerile, amorous adventure that brought Angelotti to the church, but now he understands otherwise. Familial love, he sees, has even stronger roots than love born of lust. Invoking the name of Scarpia, Angelotti credits the marchesa for saving his neck, at least so far, from the iron grip of that malevolent sot. The menacing theme that informed the opera's opening fanfare, and which Puccini associates with Scarpia, here comes to roost astride the character, or should I say the idea of the character, it represents.

Cavaradossi is only too familiar with Scarpia, "that licentious bigot who exploits the uses of religion as refinements for his libertine lust and makes both the confessor and the hangman the servant of his wantonness" (Scarpia? Bigotto satiro che affina colle devote pratiche la foia libertina e strumento al lascivo talento fa il confessore e il boia!). He swears to protect Angelotti, even at the risk of his own life.

Secret police are everywhere. Cavaradossi persuades Angelotti to flee at once, as the chapel is not safe, after all. But his villa, the very one where he is supposed to have his amorous rendezvous with Tosca, is more secure. Abundant motivic references inform their brusque dialogue, including the devotion motive at the mention of the villa, Angelotti's own fugitive theme, and a citation of the lyrical emblem of the marchesa, as well. Cavaradossi entrusts Angelotti with the key to the villa, promising to meet him there at dusk.

As the grateful fugitive gathers his sister's clothing, his comrade counsels him not to change into it for now; there is no time, and in any case, the path to the villa, which cuts through a vegetable garden, is deserted. What's more, should he be spotted, he can hide in a well in the garden, where he will find an obscure passage to a secret room. In representation of the well, a new fragment asserts itself here. It is an attenuated variant of Scarpia's motive, and though its rhythm is more straightforward than that of its cousin, its harmonic configuration over a string of descending whole tones is nearly identical. The reasons for their motivic similarity will become clear soon enough, when the otherwise safe refuge the well provides becomes a catalyst of Scarpia's demonic if temporary victory in act 2.

Suddenly, the boom of the castle's cannon shatters the silence; the authorities have just discovered that Angelotti has escaped. Cavaradossi resolves to accompany Angelotti, vowing to fight if captured. As they leave, the sacristan, accompanied by the bumptious, sarcastic ditty that represents him, comes in amid a confused crowd of students, acolytes, and choir singers. A penetration of horns and trumpets precedes his announcement that Napoleon has been surrounded and defeated by King Ferdinand's Austrian forces. That is certainly welcome news, given that the last thing the Catholic Church wants to see is the return of the French Republic. But the sacristan's naiveté will be short-lived; he has no way of knowing that, in only a few hours, Napoleon's forces will turn things on their head and claim certain victory.

Nevertheless, a torchlight parade and victory celebration have been planned at the nearby Farnese Palace, where Tosca will sing in a new cantata, just composed (we are not told by whom) in praise of conquest. The emblem of the sacristan's joy here is a spirited but deftly articulated tarantella cast in 6/8 time. The sacristan is dismayed by Cavaradossi's absence. He was, after all, looking forward to sharing the news with him, though all along, just as in Gozzi's fairy-tale play, he has been wary of Cavaradossi, whose glib manner, antireligious views, and stylish attire—an oversized greatcoat, leg-of-mutton sleeves, and a half-moon-shaped hat—were clues enough that he was a Republican sympathizer. But the sacristan now has his work cut out for him, and he shoos the choirboys into the sacristy to don their robes. The crowd, at least, is pleased, breaking into a chorus of laughter and boasting its good cheer amid shouts of "Doppio soldo" and "Viva il Re!" (Double wages! . . . Long live the king!).

Just then, the impromptu celebration is halted by Scarpia's ominous basso and his *diabolus* motive. Police and other agents of authority surround him, including the unctuous and sinister Spoletta, Scarpia's right-hand man. Scarpia scolds the choristers for their inappropriate behavior in a church and gruffly orders them to prepare the Te Deum. The chorus leaves in sheepish submission, fearful of what might come next. The sacristan turns his back, as if to join them, but Scarpia will have none of it: he commands the sacristan to stay where he is. With that, he bids Spoletta and his agents to search the church and its grounds for the escaped prisoner.

Scarpia, a rotund, elegantly coiffed figure whose pristine powdered wig and elaborate rococo attire serve only to render his evil demeanor as something socially acceptable, feigns patience but means business. His self-assurance relies on the measure of his power; like a wild animal stalking its prey, he prevaricates, hovers, and encircles his victims. With an air of civility astride an undertone of threat, he informs the sacristan of Angelotti's escape and asks him to disclose what he knows. Echoes of the whole-tone oscillation associated with Angelotti's escape persist throughout their exchange. The authorities have reason to believe that he took refuge in the church. The sacristan, now in a panic, leads Scarpia to the Attavanti Chapel, where they find the door ajar and a key.

On the way out, Scarpia expresses regret that he ordered the ringing of the castle bell, which warned Angelotti of the imminent search. In Scarpia's hand is a fan, which he considers a curious if unexpected clue. On it is the crest of the Marchesa Attavanti. Could she have been his accomplice, or was there someone else involved? And if so, who? Scanning the Sant'Andrea della Valle's expanse of marble surfaces, pews, ambos, and statuary, Scarpia's shifty, deep-set eyes alight on Cavaradossi's painting, while the marchesa's motive, easily identified by its dotted triplet, lingers in the background. Like Tosca before him, Scarpia recognizes the painting's sanctified subject as the marchesa. His curiosity aroused, he demands that the sacristan reveal the identity of the artist. The sacristan, terrified, obliges—the name Cavaradossi drips uneasily off his lips, assisted by a spray of the opening melody of the love duet.

At that moment, one of Scarpia's goons rushes in. Hanging from his arm is the basket of food that Cavaradossi gave to Angelotti. The sacristan's motive lurks precociously nearby, thus suggesting, to Scarpia at least, the sacristan's implicit involvement. In a private aside, Scarpia puts two and two together. He knows Cavaradossi to be the lover of Tosca (it's a small town, what can one say?) and brands him a suspect and a revolutionary. So much for due process. Seeing the basket, the sacristan suddenly becomes very talkative. He observes that the basket is now empty, when he himself had filled it with edibles only a short time earlier. What's more, Cavaradossi, who had no key to the private chapel, said he wasn't hungry, compelling the sacristan to set the basket aside in a safe place. Scarpia, duly informed, ponders the facts.

As if out of nowhere, Tosca appears, the love duet following her. She again calls for Cavaradossi, whom she addresses by only his first name, Mario. Hearing her, Scarpia makes himself scarce, hiding behind a marble column, in the nave of which is a basin of holy water. In a quiet aside, he compares himself, with certain pride, to Shakespeare's Iago, comparing the latter's incriminating handkerchief with the marchesa's no-less-suspicious fan.

The sacristan, en route elsewhere, informs Tosca that Cavaradossi has vanished suddenly. An extensive pastel of bells informs their dialogue, forming an appealing background ostinato that has the effect of sanctifying Tosca. She is unwilling to believe Mario would have done any such thing. If he did, from her jealous but enraptured perspective, that could mean only one thing: betrayal. Intuiting her distress, Scarpia slithers snakelike around the column, coming into Tosca's view. As he does, he slips one finger into the holy water, a gesture that, given his designs on Tosca, can only be construed as just short of pornographic. At the same time, as if to make a symbolic sign of the cross, church bells contribute their soft metallic sheen. Scarpia proffers the holy water to Tosca as if it were brandy. She thanks him and crosses herself, reminding this writer of Marlene Dietrich's real-life dictum, in Maximilian Schell's film *Marlene*, to do the same when speaking of Orson Welles.

The first order of prayers, in pious celebration of Napoleon's defeat, is set to begin. The doors open, and every manner of citizen, from beggar to bourgeois and peasant to aristocrat, walks in, their steps measured, their voices respectfully hushed. The cardinal, alongside the director of the local convent, assumes his place at the altar. Scarpia pays Tosca an insincere compliment, praising her for her artistic mastery, but does so only as a means of extracting from her both information and, soon enough, sexual favors. ("Un nobile esempio è il vostro"—It is a noble example that you give.) He praises her for her piousness and prayer. Why else would she be in the basilica? After all, women in those days, at least in Italy, were forbidden to sing in church. But then, Scarpia, true to form, twists the knife and answers his own question. Chiding her with the marchesa's fan, he alludes to the habits of unrespectable women who, unable to satisfy their proclivities elsewhere, find sanctuary for their torrid affairs inside churches and vast cathedrals. As he gestures toward the painting of the Magdalene, he implicitly indicts Cavaradossi and the marchesa in this deception. Tosca demands proof. ("Che? D'amore? Le prove!"—What? In love? Your proof!)

Scarpia obliges. Displaying the fan, and with the marchesa's motivic tag quietly compressed alongside Angelotti's fugitive motive in the orchestra, he suggests that just such a woman frequented the Sant'Andrea della Valle and that someone interrupted her in the throes of passion with her lover. Whoever startled them fled quickly and "lost her feathers in flight" (ed essa nel fuggir perdé le penne). Scarpia's manipulation of Tosca's jealous insecurity has only just begun.

Here emerges a dark new motive, which Puccini will recycle from time to time in reference to Scarpia's power and the emotional symbolism of the fan. It represents his dominion over Tosca. Tosca, heartbroken and jealous again, licks her wounds and avows her woes. Three words, "O, pressago prospetto!" (Oh, prophetic doubt!), cross her lips; which is merely an archaic way of saying that her suspicions were correct all along. Scarpia, mouthing in the shadows, congratulates himself. She had only come back to let Cavaradossi know that the royal jubilee has made her its prisoner; she might not be able to fulfill the commitment she had made to, and indeed extracted from, Cavaradossi to meet him at the villa.

The scurrilous Scarpia, relishing the "poison" (il veleno) that defines his strategy, approaches Tosca in a halo of faux sympathy. He inquires as to the cause of her sadness, though his offer to give his life in return for the chance to wipe away her tears is only a pretext for proximity. Tosca bemoans this betrayal that never was, vowing to bring her cheating lover and his mistress to justice. ("Dove son? Potessi coglieri, i traditori"—Where are they? Could I but catch the traitors.) Borrowing Angelotti's fugitive motive, she imagines a pursuit of her own. Her tears barely dry, she opines that God will forgive her.

Scarpia accompanies Tosca, who is beside herself with misery, to the door. A reminiscence of her now-forlorn love duet, the orchestration intensified and opulently rendered by the strings, recycles amid her misery. As she leaves, he returns to his station behind the column, where he summons Spoletta. Issuing another staccato order, he commands Spoletta to follow Tosca and to meet him later at the Farnese Palace. The tolling of a bell engenders a climate of severe solemnity that at once endorses Scarpia's political authority and, by virtue of the setting, coddles him as a protégé of the Church. The chorus, at cross-purposes with Scarpia's malevolent daydreaming, intones the Te Deum. As the orchestration thickens to incorporate an organ and even

cannon fire, Scarpia cannot resist the conceit that, in liberating Tosca's
jealousy, his reward will triple. He will capture his prisoner, eliminate
Cavaradossi, and take Tosca for his own lustful ends.

The cardinal passes, his pontifical gesturing a model of avuncular
reassurance. He blesses the throngs, who in turn bow to his holy presence, much like the bloodthirsty crowds would later do, in deference
to the sadistic ice princess, in *Turandot*. But the silent cardinal has no
riddles to proffer here, only reverent testimony to what he believes is
the ultimate victory of the Holy See.

Scarpia kneels and then crosses himself. Giving both dramatic and
musical weight to his Mephistophelean scheming is an extended crescendo that builds inexorably toward a powerful climax on "Te aeter-
nam," sung in unison by Scarpia and the chorus. Dreaming of a victory
of his own, he launches into one last conceit: "Tosca, mi fai dimenticare
Iddio" (Tosca, you make me forget God). A magisterial restatement of
Scarpia's *diabolus* theme brings the curtain down and thus conveys the
victory of villainy over conscience.

Act 2

Scarpia's apartment on an upper floor of the Farnese Palace

The change of location that distinguishes this act from the previous one
is startling on a number of levels. From a theatrical perspective, the
sets in *Tosca* are characters in their own right. Certainly, nothing could
be further from the ambience of a church than Scarpia's lavish lair. In
act 1, all was daylight and holiness; the notion of sanctuary ruled. Here,
darkness prevails in a suite that, though illuminated in soft candlelight,
is a minefield of elaborately wrought or carved objets d'art. Here a
dagger, there an antique pistol, while an Oriental dragon, carved in
silver, presides regally atop a mahogany commode in one corner. It is
high rococo, a room wholly consumed by its own decadent materialism.
Act 2 is hell to act 1's heaven.

In contradiction to his brutal duties, Scarpia, like the aristocrats
dancing below, cuts the figure of a fop. His lace ruffles, handsomely

ornamented in gold thread, brightly complement his campaign wig and the meticulous display of his jabot. Breeches were already beginning to go out of style, but the reactionary Scarpia wore his sky blue satins like a badge of honor. Whatever implements of small torture lurked within the equipage on his belt can never be known, as he rarely took it off.

Opening act 2 is a new motive, a descending rivulet of unison triplets that contain a hint of Scarpia's tritone-infested fragment. On its heels, several already-familiar motivic fragments make headway, including Angelotti's fugitive theme; Cavaradossi's lyrical homage, now played by a solo clarinet, to Tosca's eyes (based on her principal motive); and the love duet. A large floor-to-ceiling window overlooks the palace courtyard. On a lower floor, Queen Caroline of Naples, the sister of Marie Antoinette, is hosting a state dinner in honor of General Mélas, who is absent, but also the hero of the recent anti-Napoleon campaign at Marengo.

But Scarpia has not lost his head; on the contrary, he is ravenous, as always, and more than a little nervous. As the curtain opens, he is seated at his dining table, which is laid out with table settings for two, its array of linen napkins not of the sort used in those days to absorb exotic perfumes. He is confident that his men have apprehended the fugitives Cavaradossi and Angelotti, who will be sent to the gallows to await hanging at dawn. Time is of the essence, and he knows it. Given how often he removes, fidgets with, and looks at his monogrammed gold pocketwatch, it's a pity it's not human and doesn't sing, so numerous are its appearances. Tosca will come, and when she arrives, he will ensnare her with the ruthless disregard of a hunter whose prey is already in the trap.

Sciarrone, a gendarme, responds to Scarpia's delicately engraved Louis XIV silver handbell. He impatiently asks if Tosca has arrived, only to be told that a chamberlain has been dispatched to fetch her. To the accompaniment of his *diabolus* motive, Scarpia gestures toward the window, instructing his charge to open it. A pristine, gracious melody in 2/4 time and in the style of a gavotte rises quietly from below, where the queen's ballroom guests, a-glitter with aristocratic revelers, dance into the night. (The gavotte, incidentally, is not Puccini's, but an invention of his brother, Michele, who was also a composer, albeit a minor one.) Dispatched to the gate, where he is to wait for Tosca, Sciarrone takes with him a letter from Scarpia.

Here, Scarpia sings an ode to gluttony and lust, convinced that Tosca will bend to his will, if for nothing else than for love of Cavaradossi. ("Ha più forte sapore la conquista violenta che il mellifluo consenso"— For myself the violent conquest has stronger relish than the soft surrender.) In an outburst that is more unbridled declamation than melodious aria or busy arioso, he confesses his preference for hurtful indifference over genuine concern and for glib promiscuity over seasoned commitment. The orchestra echoes that violence as it crescendos to a vehement climax amid a flourish of horns and a tense string tremolando. ("La cosa bramata perseguo, me ne sazio e via la getto. Volto a nuova esca"—I crave, I pursue the craved thing, sate myself and cast it aside, and seek new bait. God made diverse beauties.) A terrifying plunge of the act's opening motive segues into the next scene.

Spoletta, his plumed tricorn hat in hand, knows his place, and when he arrives, he assumes it. Standing stiffly in the doorway, Spoletta fields Scarpia's agitation, spitting back staccato answers to every one of his master's interrogative barks. Scarpia, who cannot be bothered to so much as look at his lieutenant while addressing him, speaks instead to his knife and fork. He learns that the fruit of Spoletta's surveillance of Tosca led to Cavaradossi's villa, tucked discreetly away on a country road and flanked by trees. He observed Tosca as she went into the house, only to emerge abruptly a few minutes later. With his deputies in tow, Spoletta and his dogs jumped the garden wall and broke in. But once inside, Angelotti was nowhere to be found.

Infuriated, Scarpia swears that, for such gross incompetence, he will send Spoletta to the guillotine. (One can only wonder how Scarpia, transfigured into a character in a twenty-first-century setting, would react to cell phone company employees.) In an effort to assuage Scarpia's fury, he parries, assuring him that he confronted and arrested another occupant of the villa: Cavaradossi. A subtle, almost imperceptible citation of the "Magdalene" motive lurks just behind Spoletta's bright tenor. Now that Cavaradossi, who has knowledge of Angelotti's whereabouts, is in custody in the palace, there should be no problem extracting from him the information they covet. Scarpia, not entirely satisfied, concurs as he paces the room, muttering, "Meno male!" (Not bad!). Here, a significant new motive, associated with interrogation and carried ominously in a low register by a flute, makes itself known, floating perilously in 2/4 time from an F-sharp to an A against staccato punctuations in the bass that occur on the second beat of every bar.

The dulcet sounds of the new "victory" cantata, which the queen has commissioned, drift euphoniously through the window, Tosca's ardent if distant soprano at its helm. The effect is jarring, as the offstage cantata is in a wholly different key—A minor—than the music onstage, which is informed largely by the E-minor "interrogation" motive. Hearing the cantata, Scarpia stops in his tracks. He asks Sciarrone to bring in Cavaradossi, as well as a judge, a scribe, and Roberti the executioner.

Once inside, Cavaradossi refuses Scarpia's entreaty to take a seat, thus denying him whatever advantage he may be seeking. Scarpia, who has also taken a moment to listen to the cantata, continues, accusing Cavaradossi of illegally harboring Angelotti. Cavaradossi denies it vehemently, as his only objectives now are to protect his comrade and to keep his word no matter the cost. A tense tremolando patina shudders vigorously in the strings as Scarpia demands Cavaradossi's cooperation. ("Dov'è Angelotti?"—Where is Angelotti?) Here, the "well" motive rears its anxious head, but its mood is now pugnacious and its tempo swift. Though Cavaradossi discloses nothing of what he knows, this motive's very presence conveys what is on his mind.

Scarpia tries another approach, lowering his voice and addressing Cavaradossi with near-avuncular familiarity in an effort to coerce a confession. Here, Puccini introduces a new, *lamentoso* motive, an unsettling descent in hemiola emblematic of pain. Cavaradossi predictably refuses. Losing his patience altogether, Scarpia slams the window shut just as Tosca and the chorus alight on a high B-natural, and he demands that Cavaradossi reveal Angelotti's location: "Questo è luogo di lagrime! Badate!" (Beware! This is a place for tears!).

Cavaradossi stands his ground in a defiant volley of "Nego!" (I deny it!), while Scarpia presses him with merciless abandon. The trump card is Tosca herself, whose arrival is as shocking to her lover as his presence is to her. She is out of breath; whatever Scarpia wrote her, it threw her into such a panic that she ran from the queen's ballroom and flew up the stairs, not an easy feat in a wine-colored Empire-style velvet dress and a camlet. Here, Tosca throws herself into her lover's embrace, where she is warned to keep her mouth shut. ("Di quanto là vedesti, taci, o m'uccidi"—Of what you saw there, say nothing, or you will kill me.) She signals to him that she understands.

Not one to be tested, Scarpia approaches them both; Cavaradossi must testify before the judge, who is waiting in the torture chamber— where else? There's nothing like a little waterboarding, after all, to loosen a prisoner's tongue. The interrogation motive, now ablaze in the brass, punches through in a threatening *fortissimo*. Evidently, torture has its own tune, too.

A brief but plangent interlude, fashioned on the recent hemiola-rich "pain" motive, adumbrates the agony to come. Alone at last, Scarpia finds time for a private chat with his favorite actress. He inaugurates their dialogue with an exceptionally suave theme, the thematic design of which, though not identical to it, conforms to Tosca's principal motive as well as the marchesa's. The plush instrumentation sets it amid a velvet hush of flutes and muted strings. Coming from Scarpia's malignant mouth, its loveliness is marred by the unctuous incompetence of his seductive powers. ("Ed or fra noi parliam da buoni amici"—And now let's talk together like good friends.)

The pair banter quietly, Tosca pretending indifference and Scarpia pretending friendship. Slipping behind a Greco-Roman chaise, he presses her with a gentility he declined to show Cavaradossi when asking the same questions. No one other than Mario Cavaradossi was at the villa, she tells him. After all, she explains, "Nulla sfugge ai gelosi" (Nothing escapes a jealous eye). It seems that Tosca will be no easier to put off her game than her lover.

Scarpia, his laugh a reservoir of quiet malevolence, summons Sciarrone and inquires as to how things are going with Cavaradossi. Finding that he is adamant in his denial, Scarpia insists they probe further and compel him to respond. Tosca is so far unaware of the subtext; *interrogation* and *torture* are hardly synonymous for a diva. By now, Scarpia has resolved that the time has come to end Tosca's naiveté. He says, "No, ma il vero potrebbe abbreviargli un ora assai penosa" (The truth might shorten an extremely painful hour for him).

Her alarm turning to terror, Tosca is treated to her own chamber of verbal horrors; Scarpia, the male version of Turandot, swoons in sadistic pleasure as he discloses what is really happening to Cavaradossi: "Legato mani e piè il vostro amante ha un cerchio uncinato alle tempia che ad ogni niego ne sprizza sangue senza mercè" (Your lover's bound hand and foot with a ring of hooked iron at his temples that spurt blood at each denial). Here, the wailing hemiola motive adumbrated in the first moments of Scarpia's interrogation surfaces to the accompaniment of a new but no less harrowing motive, this one a slow ascent of sustained major and minor triads placed precipitously on offbeats above violas in *divisi* (that is, a musical division of labor, wherein the same instrumental group plays different melodic lines). A rumble of timpani infects it with even greater prescience. This gloomy D-minor figuration is made all the more luxurious by the simultaneous ascent, in the orchestra's tenor and bass registers, of the identical theme belted out on the strong beats, but which drift downward in opposite motion as the figure dissolves into cadence. Indeed, Puccini's manipulation of such eerie imitation is as unsettling as it is harrowing.

Cavaradossi's gurgling groans do nothing to inspire Tosca's continued silence. As Scarpia reminds her, and she knows, only she can save him. Of course, that, too, is a lie in this opera, where no one tells the truth. Here, Tosca breaks; she doesn't beg so much as order Scarpia to stop, making of herself, for one brief moment, a pale imitation of Scarpia. Scarpia keeps his word and suspends the torture. In return, he demands that she cough up what she knows. She negotiates, though not demurely, demanding to see Mario, but Scarpia refuses. Her lover's stentorian lyric tenor will have to do, instead; Cavaradossi assures her that the torture has, for the time being, ceased, but to hold her tongue in spite of it.

She does, for a moment. But it takes only a single gesture from Scarpia, in the form of a threat, to make her go prostrate. Speak, he says, or the torture will continue. Throwing herself on the entrance of the torture chamber, Tosca embodies desperation, like a silent film actress hurling herself in front of a train. A rhapsodic, chromatically inflected tag inspires Tosca's cry of "Mostro!" ("No, no! Ah ... mostro ... Lo strazi, lo uccidi!"—No, no! ... Ah, monster! Murderer ... you're killing him!), as well as Scarpia's response, which duplicates it. ("Lo strazia quel vostro silenzio assai più"—It's your silence that's killing him.) Her insults fail to move the dispassionate Scarpia; her litany of denials, buttressed by those of her lover, is not what Scarpia wants to hear.

Here, the orchestra lets loose with a belligerent ascending chromatic scale that alights on a string tremolando, as Scarpia commands Spoletta to open the door a little wider. In an uncanny fit of sadistic one-upmanship, he obliges Tosca to listen, with even greater clarity, to Cavaradossi's agonizing screams. Tosca's cries for mercy crescendo and intensify cumulatively in tautly engineered ascending sequences, culminating in an anguished melodic spiral doubled by the strings, which we can call her "anguish" motive. This expressive tag in turn owes its melodic design to Mario's lyrical ode to Tosca's eyes in act 1, which, as we have seen, is itself a variant of her principal motive. Puccini will soon enough turn to it again, embedding it within the cadence of "Vissi d'arte."

She is led to the open door of the chamber and, peeking in, sees firsthand the consequences of brutal flagellation and, no doubt, partial dismemberment. She wants to speak to Mario; fearing she may break, he responds in anger, but not desperation. ("Stolta, che sai? Che puoi dir?"—Fool! What do you know and what can you say?)

The dialogue flies by swiftly. Scarpia dispatches Spoletta back to the torture chamber to get on with business. A not-quite-broken Tosca collapses in tears onto a divan, as Scarpia stands by indifferent and in silence. As Scarpia edges closer to Cavaradossi's chamber of horrors, signaling his henchman to continue, Tosca's will evaporates altogether. "Che v'ho fatto in vita mia?" (What have I done to you in my life?), she asks, her disposition one of hopeless resignation.

Hearing anther pained gurgle from Cavaradossi, she gives up Angelotti's location in the well, alongside the well motive. ("Nel pozzo . . . nel giardino"—In the well, in the garden.) Learning this, Scarpia calls off his thugs, but Cavaradossi has already passed out. An orchestral cry of Scarpia's *diabolus* motive presses forward as he orders the torture stopped. Tosca implores Scarpia to let her see her lover, which he does. The gendarmes bring him in, bloodied and badly beaten, and set him on the sofa. The interrogation motive surfaces darkly, carried by the winds and violas, only to segue moments later into the hemiola affectations of the pain motive. Tosca is horrified but finds the stamina to go to him. Ashamed, she smothers him in kisses, her tears overflowing. A shade of the "Tosca's eyes" motive, an oasis of major tonality, briefly interrupts the snarling declamative conflicts that paint this act largely in the minor.

No longer needed, the executioner, the judge, and the scribe take their leave. At Scarpia's insistence, Spoletta and his officers stay put, if only for a few minutes. Cavaradossi, his voice rising barely above a whisper, asks Tosca if she revealed anything. She denies it, but just then, Scarpia commands his minions to the well. With this, and in the halo of the well motive, Cavaradossi recoils, bitterly accusing Tosca of betraying him. He rejects her advance and falls back onto the couch, cursing her all the while.

Unexpected news, at least on the political spectrum, suddenly energizes Cavaradossi as the tempo accelerates. Sciarrone returns to announce a military reversal: Napoleon's troops at Marengo have rallied and trumped Mélas, repulsing the Russian-Austrian forces. Predictably, the orchestra takes note of military conquest with a brazen display of brass and winds astride a string tremolando, appropriating and substantially amplifying the Magdalene motive as the fundament of its musical (and perhaps political) capital. While that may appear to be an odd motivic choice at this juncture, it may be that in choosing it, Puccini wanted to sanctify the victory in some way as a gift from God, or a supportive nod from the Virgin Mary.

Feeling vindicated, Cavaradossi lets loose with a cry of "Vittoria!" (Victory!). Like torture, victory also has its song, and Cavaradossi is ready to lend it his voice, which he does with spirited enthusiasm: "L'alba vindice appar che fa gli empi tremar!" (Thou spirit of vengeance, awake! Let tyrants and myrmidons quake!). The tune here is again not Puccini's own, but a strident confection by his brother, Michele. Obviously, Puccini was not above nepotism, and in appropriating two familial exemplars, he gained a kind of ersatz solidarity with Cavaradossi's uncompromising loyalty to his brother in arms, Angelotti. Thus, however false or inadequate either theme may ring, their inclusion was certainly purposeful.

In any case, Cavaradossi's gloating is short-lived, as Scarpia calls in his men, who drag him off to await execution. ("Braveggia, urla! T'affretta a palesarmi il fondo dell'alma ria!"—Go, shout your boasts! Pour out the last dregs of your vile soul!) Tosca, in a valiant but ill-informed move, attempts to follow but is violently restrained by the gendarmes. Accompanying this scuffle is Tosca's anguish motive, here thrown about in stretto by the orchestra with the force of a tornado.

With his men and Cavaradossi exiled to other rooms, Scarpia finds himself alone with Tosca yet again. As easily, and perhaps as cruelly, as he launched his verbal invective against Cavaradossi, he resumes the elegant thematic profusion that only a short time earlier convinced him of his seductive powers. His reptilian demeanor again at ease, he offers a devastated and nearly immobile Tosca a glass of Spanish wine as he invites her to finish the intimate dinner he had so graciously prepared.

Not amused, Tosca takes a seat at the table, just as he asks. She cuts to the quick. Staring him down, she asks bluntly, "Quanto?" (How much?). He mocks her mildly with a sinuous laugh, throwing her words back at her. Still looking to strike a bargain, Tosca asks him again: "Il prezzo?" (Your price?), she declaims (but does not sing) astride the accompaniment of a bleak tremolando played with shrill assurance by the violins.

Scarpia, not one to be outdone, assures her that he has not come this far in his career only to break his oath of office for a common bribe. In musical attendance here, in the orchestra, is a subtle variant of Cavaradossi's unveiling motive, shorn of the raised fourth scale degree, and transformed into Scarpia's "lust" motive. However, its closing tag parts ways with its earlier incarnation, outlining instead a darting lightning bolt of an arpeggio in ascent. Though he is fully aware of his reputation as a venal man, Scarpia has his standards: Tosca herself is the sum of his desires. ("Già mi struggea l'amor della diva ... Ah, in quell'istante t'ho giurata mia!"—Already in the past I burned with passion for the diva ... In that instant I vowed you would be mine!)

Tosca's tears, commingled with her hatred, have inspired Scarpia to make her his lover. Opening his arms, he begs for her embrace and slithers closer. Tosca, for her part, reviled, stands up and retreats behind the divan. The "lust" motive and Tosca's anguish motive converge as he draws near. By now the window looks a good deal more inviting than Scarpia; she threatens to defenestrate herself but changes her mind. Like a newly caged animal, not sure where to run, she makes for the door, thus implying she will attempt to appeal to the queen for mercy.

Scarpia is unimpressed, assuring Tosca that it is too late for that; the queen would "merely grant pardon to a corpse" (La Regina farebbe grazia ad un cadavere!). The evocation of death brings with it a recall of Scarpia's *diabolus* motive. As Tosca returns to the divan, Scarpia crawls back, deflecting her protest that he is nothing more than a demon ("Non toccarmi, demonio!"—Don't touch me, devil!). For his part, Scarpia remarks that there is really no difference between the "spasms of wrath or spasms of passion" (Spasimi d'ira, spasimi d'amore). At last, his patience has run out, and he attempts to seize her. She flees to another sofa, evidently her only refuge in a small room. Her cries for help, to her now-familiar anguish motive that informed her last outburst, go unheard and unanswered. Suddenly, the sound of two distant snare drums emerges, signaling the preparations for Cavaradossi's hanging. Scarpia warns that her lover has only one hour to live and that his fate has been sealed by her actions, or, more accurately, by her refusal to act. A flush of trumpets and horns, played quietly as if offstage, melts into a death march assumed by the lower strings playing pizzicato in tandem with the clarinets and bassoons.

As the woodwinds dissolve into quiescence, Tosca brings forth her most celebrated aria, "Vissi d'arte" (I lived for art) (CD Track 5). Elements of the expansive motive that introduced her, together with that of the anguish motive, combine in a string-saturated lament of unusual expressive fervor. While Scarpia stands by, she bemoans her bad luck and extols her own virtues, or what's left of them. In an attempt to make sense of her predicament, she invokes her faith in God, the kindness she has always shown others, and her devotion to the Madonna, for whose mantle she gave jewels and beneath whose statue she so piously laid flowers.

Broken and inconsolable, Tosca's last hope is Scarpia himself. Prostrating, as opposed to prostituting, herself before him, she looks upon him as her new Madonna. She intones a sad plea, a sequence of descending fifths against a syncopated pulsation in the violins. ("Vedi, le man giunte io stendo a te!"—Look at me, oh, behold, with clasped hands I beseech you!) He won't back down, again reproaching her, his lust theme in tow, for failing to give him an "instant" when she is asking for a life. Just then, Spoletta enters to deliver the stunning news that Angelotti killed himself, taking poison the moment he was apprehended; just then, a brisk patch of Angelotti's fugitive motive flies through the orchestra. The news, while encouraging for the authorities, does not satisfy Scarpia, who orders his men to string up the corpse on the gibbet. Spoletta, faithful foot soldier that he is, inquires as to Cavaradossi's fate: Will anything change? What's to be done with him? For the answer, Scarpia turns his lascivious glare toward Tosca. Her eyes brimming over with tears, she nods in consent as she buries her face in her arms. To complement her shame, a densely Wagnerian chromatic tag—but more likely a citation, perhaps, from the funereal *Crisantemi*—surfaces and, in a bit of unusual scoring, is played by a string quartet. A menacing, rough-hewn minor third expands, forming a new motivic starburst emblematic of duplicity; Puccini will put it to use again before the act is over.

Even now Tosca risks her neck and Cavaradossi's by imposing a condition. She demands Scarpia free him at once. But the devious Scarpia knows better; he deflects but does not deny her wish. The law will not allow him to grant a convicted prisoner a pardon with such capricious dispatch. The execution must at least appear to have been carried out, though it need not be. Spoletta, he assures Tosca, will take care of it, just as with Count Palmieri, whose sham execution Spoletta likewise orchestrated. Instead of hanging, Cavaradossi will face a firing squad whose weapons will hold blanks instead of their real ammunition.

As he authorizes Spoletta to carry out his orders, Scarpia gives peculiar emphasis to certain words, gesturing with abnormal specificity so that his meaning is not misunderstood. ("Simulata! Come avvene del Palmieri! Hai ben compreso?"—A sham one! As we did with Palmieri! You understand?) Tosca, convinced that his plan is plausible, concurs, having no clue just how duplicitous Scarpia can be.

Spoletta departs, leaving the way wide open for Scarpia to make of Tosca just another lurid conquest. She demands he grant her and

Cavaradossi safe conduct, so that following the false execution, they can flee the country unharmed. He agrees and retires to his desk to prepare the documents. Here a dark new motive, in F-sharp minor, leaps forward, its labyrinthine character at once sultry, mysterious, and conspiratorial; it provides a shadowy conduit into Tosca's thoughts. As Scarpia scribbles, she hovers over the dining table, where she takes a sip of wine. There she spots a knife as sharp as the fury she feels. She picks it up and discreetly tucks behind her. The document complete and sealed, Scarpia, like a hovering vulture, approaches her, eager to devour her in his sweaty embrace, to the whooshing accompaniment of his "lust" motive: "Tosca, finalmente mia!" (Tosca, you are mine at last!) (CD Track 6).

Not so fast, paysan! That is *not* in fact what she says, though it might have been had the libretto been written by Harold Pinter. Rather, the words "Questo è il bacio di Tosca" (This is the kiss of Tosca) ooze from her lips, spewing forth like venom as she stabs Scarpia in the heart. The music boils, its pace accelerating in a feverish tumble of brass and strings, jagged accentuations, and abrupt diminutions, its blistering harmonies competing for dominance in spurting viral sequences. Reeling and in shock, Scarpia, mortally wounded, stumbles toward her, his arms still outstretched. ("Maledetta! . . . Aiuto! . . . Muoio! Soccorso! Muoio!"—Accursed one! . . . Help! I am dying! Help! I die!)

Tosca, wedged between him and the table, repulses him, pushing him back to the floor. He writhes, he crawls, he slithers in agony, begging not for forgiveness but for help. Now it is Scarpia's turn to cry for aid, and his turn to be refused it. It's Tosca's turn to twist the knife, literally: "Ti soffoca il sangue? E ucciso da una donna!" (Is your blood choking you? And killed by a woman!). The scowl on her face never leaving her, she has gone mad, yet she invites our sympathy, and even our encouragement. It is Tosca now who, leaning over him and still clutching her knife, issues a command, repeating it no fewer than four times: "Muori dannato! Muori! Muori! Muori!" (Die, damned one! Die! Die! Die!). Satisfied he is dead, she forgives him, her unsung words a spittoon of crackling consonants and fruity vowels interrupted only briefly by silence as the orchestra itself expires. ("È morto."—He is dead!) Intoning, "Or gli perdono!" (And now I pardon him!) to the mysterious "conspiracy" motive, she fixes the dark eyes once extolled by her lover on Scarpia's limp body, saying in *declamato* (spoken, not sung), "E avanti a lui tremava tutta Roma!" (And all Rome trembled before him!).

Here she drops the knife. A bottle of water lying nearby becomes complicit in her guilt; in an attempt to cleanse her soul, she washes her hands. Then, finding a mirror, she fixes her hair, an irrational act, but a balmy bit of stage business. But where is the safe-conduct document? Failing to find it on Scarpia's desk, she sees it in his hand; it is the last straw he'll ever grasp. She pries it out of his cold, bony fingers, placing it ever so delicately in her bosom.

The flicker of a candle on the table distracts her, so she blows it out. But she has second thoughts; approaching Scarpia's desk with curious reverence, she takes a burning candle to relight the one she has just extinguished. The scene of two crimes thus transformed into an occasion for ritual, she carefully positions one candle on either side of Scarpia's fat, lifeless head. The Madonna, or some member of her family, is never far from Tosca in this opera; seeing a crucifix on the wall of the demon she's just murdered, she gingerly removes it and lowers it on to Scarpia's chest, just over the open wound. A flash of Scarpia's lust motive, sullenly appropriated by trombones, exhales his vanquished spirit alongside a mnemonic kernel, given over to a clarinet, of Cavaradossi's mellifluous tribute to his lover's eyes. She kneels, says a prayer, rises, and, disoriented in the now-darkened room, looks for the door. She finds it, opens it nervously, and leaves. A lukewarm ember of Scarpia's *diabolus* motive, which is all that's left of it, sputters out in the shadow of a distant snare drum. Curtain.

Act 3

The platform of Castel Sant'Angelo

The setting for the events of *Tosca*'s act 3 is the celebrated Castel Sant'Angelo in Rome. Host to the Mausoleum of Hadrian, a medieval fortress, and once a residence of popes, its sepulchral ambience is ideally suited for the ominous events of Sardou's story. It is also a historically accurate locale; executions, largely by decapitation, were indeed carried out for centuries inside its cylindrical walls. The victims' heads were displayed on poles as a warning to those who might consider challenging authority.

As the curtain opens, the stage itself strikes a pose far removed from Scarpia's elegant if sinister suite at the Farnese Palace. The light is gray, the furnishings sparse and utilitarian; the space boasts a monolithic character, as if for entry only the dead need apply. A single hardwood bench, a cushionless chair with a stiff back, and an oversized registry fill out its darkened corners. Its arid visual vocabulary conveys desolation and hopelessness, adrift in a sea that is decidedly not papal.

Elsewhere on stage, a casemate looms threateningly, its vaulted chamber giving sanctuary to a cannon. Affixed to a wall alongside it is an antique crucifix, dimly illuminated by the diminishing flame of an oil lamp. Along the wall to its right is a stone stairway that angles upward toward a precarious, if spacious, platform. The mood is grim as dawn draws near, though the view toward the Vatican and the Basilica of St. Peter in the distance, along with the hush of their matinal bells, momentarily refreshes the senses.

An optimistic fanfare, proclaimed generously by four horns in unison, serves to introduce act 3. The theme is new but contains within itself, by virtue of the rhythmic design of its triplets, the seeds of *Tosca*'s introductory motive and its rhapsodic variants (including Cavaradossi's Tosca's eyes motive). It is also a remnant of the "Latin Hymn," the thematic material Puccini originally had in mind but ultimately jettisoned for the concluding love duet. A lightly orchestrated modal sequence of descending triads, cast in triplets, drizzles hazily in *pianissimo* over a quiet ostinato drone in open fifths in the bass. A transparent symmetry of violins, clarinets, and piccolos sets a bright, carefree, and bucolic tone at odds with its visual counterparts on stage. A vague hint of Scarpia's *diabolus* motive, now reduced to a passing thought, three times infests the prevailing texture.

Offstage, a young shepherd boy, tending to his flock, gives innocent, vibrato-free voice to this haunting modal melody astride a dulcet jangle of sheep bells and quiescent timpani. The gentle patter of the bells of

St. Peter's dissolves into a lyrical profusion played by the strings. As the melody expands, an accompanying pantomime gives way to a jailer, whose job is to see that everything is in order for the execution. With a lantern in one hand, he lights the candle in front of the crucifix, and another that sits atop the nearby table. A yawn crosses his face, and he takes his seat with drowsy indifference.

He looks furtively about to see if the execution party has arrived. It has. A picket of guards, unruffled and stiffly attired, steps in with Cavaradossi, who is shackled and gaunt. Surprisingly, Puccini enshrouds his hero's entrance with a wholesale citation of the endearing theme of "E lucevan le stelle" (And the stars shone), arguably the opera's most famous aria, in full blossom and in advance of the aria itself. While it establishes right off an exceptionally bleak mood of abject melancholy and isolation, it is so carefully wrought and entwined with the dramatic elements that it does nothing to compromise the aria when it does appear. Certainly, with its string-rich orchestration and the insistent death knell, and its vibratory punctuations of trombones and a low bell (which, in the story, is supposed to be the Great Bell of St. Peter's, though in some productions, a gong has to do), the effect is as powerful as it is disturbing.

Cavaradossi follows the lead of the sergeant in charge, who directs him to the casemate, rousing the jailer. The sergeant hands a letter to the jailer, who, upon reading it, dips into the registry and, with his feathered pen a-twitter, takes note of his prisoner's answers to several relevant if bureaucratic questions. Here the action—or, more accurately, the singing—begins in earnest. The sergeant informs Cavaradossi that the execution is on schedule and that he has only an hour to live. He offers to bring in a priest, but the anti-Church Cavaradossi firmly declines. However, he inquires if he might leave behind a note for a loved one. As he does, a fragment of his act 1 love duet, its once-ebullient optimism now transformed into a heartbreaking elegy, perks up, carried aloft by a quartet of cellos in harmony. To ensure his last wish is granted, and that his letter is delivered, he removes from his finger a gold ring and gives it to the sergeant as a bribe. A trace of Tosca's anguish motive surfaces as he begins to write.

Overcome by emotion, Cavaradossi cannot continue. Memories of his life together with Tosca, and thoughts of what it could have been, overwhelm him. With this, his poignant aria commences: "E lucevan le stelle ed olezzava la terra" (And the stars shone and the earth was perfumed) (CD Track 7). Introduced by the breathy strain of a lone clarinet, it is an expansive, heartbreaking lament in E minor whose opening phrase rises tenuously from the dominant pitch (B) to its counterpart an octave higher, before descending, by way of a falling fifth, back to where it started and then rising yet again to the tonic. While there is no need, in this slim volume, to confuse anyone by moving into technical areas, there is no harm in mentioning that in this aria, Puccini's harmonic sensibility coalesces; his fondness for the prolongation of dominant and dominant-quality harmonies, as well as delayed tonic resolution, is fundamental to his compositional vocabulary. Of course, that simple explanation hardly accounts for any number of other compositionally strategic issues that define his music, but it is a fairly basic one.

Cavaradossi finishes the aria in tears, his grief unabated. Enter Spoletta, the sergeant, and, behind them, a breathless Tosca, who awaits instructions on where to find Mario. Spoletta merely gestures, pointing the way to Cavaradossi's dismal lair. A guard, ordered to keep an eye on them both, accompanies Tosca to the platform; Spoletta and his cronies, including the jailer, take their leave.

Moments later, Cavaradossi, his head buried in his arms, feels Tosca's soft touch on the nape of his neck, accompanied by a quiet recall of their love duet from act 1. Startled, but still in pain, he leaps to his feet and embraces her. Tosca is moved beyond words; momentarily unable to speak, she shows him the safe conduct. Together they read it aloud; Cavaradossi, incredulous, but seeing Scarpia's signature and seal, cannot grasp how she could possibly have coerced it. "La prima sua grazia è questa" (This is his first act of clemency), he says. "E l'ultima" (And his last), she replies.

Regaining her composure, she tells him everything; her appeal to the Madonna and the saints; her repeated entreaties that fell on deaf ears; Scarpia's monstrous behavior and unwelcome advances; her refusal to comply; his promise to spring Cavaradossi on one lurid condition, namely, that she sleep with him; his writing of the safe conduct via the Civitavecchia Road; and finally, her impromptu decision to kill Scarpia with his own knife. A bouquet of motivic reminiscences informs her appeal, among them the motives for Scarpia's lust, Tosca's eyes, and for conspiracy, the last of which compelled her, like a hidden voice, to murder.

Cavaradossi, listening carefully, takes her hands in his and, in tones as tender as a rose, extols her virtues and swears his love. ("O dolci mani mansuete e pure"—Oh, sweet hands pure and gentle.) The interjection of Tosca's conspiracy motive within the fabric of this otherwise gentle arioso is no accident; its inclusion allows Cavaradossi to participate vicariously in the killing of his enemy and torturer, thus conveying his thoughts to the observer. What's more, the musical statement here has no closure; it merely drifts off into Tosca's next vocal adventure.

In any case, the game is afoot but not up; Tosca has a carriage waiting to take them to a ship and, from there, to safety on the other side of the border. The very idea of freedom and a new life together sends them into ecstatic spasms of the sort that Scarpia himself only dreamed of. Their florid, lightly scored duet is all light and air, a refreshing aromatic breeze whose embrace of a major tonality and diatonic melodies provides a welcome contrast to the melancholy laments that have, thus far, informed so much of this act.

But first, she discloses the plan that Scarpia hatched to ensure Cavaradossi's safety, which was to be the price paid for her passions. She advises him of the sham execution and coaches him on how to effectively fake his death so that even the guards won't know. Cavaradossi listens to her as he never has before, regarding her advice as sacrosanct. Her speaking voice is ambrosia, and he longs to hear more of it. Their passion has become compassion, culminating in an exalted vocal restatement, sung in bold unison, of the opening horn fanfare. ("Trionfal, di nova speme l'anima freme in celestial crescente ardor"—Triumphant, the soul trembles with new hope in heavenly increasing ardor.) As they drift off and dawn breaks on the horizon, a distant tolling bell rings four times, signaling the hour. But its magnetic reverberance also holds them in its power, as if to sanctify their union.

The entry of the firing squad, accompanied by Spoletta, the sergeant, and the jailer, disrupts their reverie. The jailer informs Cavaradossi, as if he didn't already know, that the appointed hour has come. Taking the registry with him, he exits by the stairway. Spoletta gives his men their instructions, and they assume their appointed places in the firing line. Tosca reassures Cavaradossi and implores him to be careful. Like a back-seat driver, she again offers him tips on how to most effectively play his part. She reminds him to take a fall the moment he hears the shots and to do so naturally and without pretense, so as not to be found out. Lest he forget, she insists, with almost coy delight, that he wait for her signal before he gets up.

Their laughter pays tribute to the victory they are certain they have won. Cavaradossi is led away, as Tosca prepares herself to witness the mock execution from the casemate. Refusing a blindfold, Cavaradossi walks with grim solemnity to the firing wall. Here, Puccini insinuates a new motive, an oddly mechanical confection distinguished by a falling minor sixth and an elegant turn that wistfully recalls Cavaradossi's Tosca's eyes motive. It melts into a descending chromatic consequent that is likewise hypnotic. Its continual repetition in the background is unsettling yet dramatically and compositionally integral; though it is a melody in its own right, and not merely a rhythmic orb, its function is akin to a pedal point or ostinato. Its reiteration heightens tension as it exploits its listener's expectations.

A delay gives Tosca cause for concern. The sun has risen, and the executioner is late in taking care of business. Her anxiety dissipates the moment she sees the commanding officer lower his sword, which is a signal for his platoon to fire. They do. Cavaradossi, looking confident and straight ahead, falls, just as she asked him to. Impressed by his convincing performance, Tosca lets loose with "Là! Muori! Ecco un artista!" (There! Die! Ah, what an actor!). She smiles discreetly upon seeing Spoletta approach Cavaradossi, whom he covers in a cloak. An officer calls his platoon to attention, dismisses the sentinel, and marches off with rigid military precision, accompanied by Spoletta. Tosca is uneasy with all the ceremony, fearing that Cavaradossi may stir too soon and give away the game, thus putting them both in danger.

With the guards and firing squad gone, Tosca moves gingerly toward her lover, beseeching him not to move, at least just yet. ("O Mario, non ti muovere"—Oh, Mario, do not move.) The mechanical march motive persists, making of itself a bastion of anxiety. The platform has emptied, but just in case, she steps to the Castel Sant'Angelo's parapet and, looking over it, sees no one. She is assured now that the soldiers have returned to their barracks. She goes to Cavaradossi, who hasn't stirred. Here, the music gradually dies out, the endless repetitions of the mechanical orb having run out of steam. Silence. "Presto! Su, Mario! Mario! Su! Presto! Andiamo! Su! Su!" (Quickly! Up, Mario! Mario! Up! Come! Up! Up!) When he doesn't respond, she throws off the cloak to see his lifeless, bullet-ridden corpse. She screams, "Mario! Morto!" (Mario! Dead!) and collapses, devastated, onto his body. It seems you just can't take the cadaver out of Cavaradossi.

The duplicitous Scarpia has claimed a victory beyond the grave and is about to score another point from hell when Sciarrone, Spoletta, and his men, chattering anxiously below, reappear. They have found Scarpia's mutilated remains in his quarters, and they know who did it. Seeing Tosca, Spoletta runs toward her. But she catches him off guard, repulsing his attack and pushing him back with such tornadic force that he loses his balance. Warned that she will "pay dearly" for taking Scarpia's life (Ah, Tosca, pagherai ben cara la sua vita!), she agrees: "Colla mia!" (With my own!). Here, a robust orchestral restatement of the principal theme of "E lucevan le stelle" soars in *forte*. With that, Tosca flees to the parapet and, with a cry of "O, Scarpia, avanti a Dio!" (Oh, Scarpia! Before God!), tosses herself over the edge to her very messy death. The curtain comes down.

Madama Butterfly

Characters	Voice Type
Cio-Cio San (Madama Butterfly)	Soprano
Suzuki, her maid	Mezzo-soprano
B. F. Pinkerton, lieutenant in the United States Navy	Tenor
Sharpless, United States consul at Nagasaki	Baritone
Goro, a matchmaker	Tenor
Prince Yamadori	Baritone
The Bonze, Cio-Cio San's uncle	Bass
Yakusidè, Cio-Cio San's uncle	Bass
The imperial commissioner	Bass
The official registrar	Bass
Cio-Cio San's mother	Mezzo-soprano
The aunt	Soprano
The cousin	Soprano
Kate Pinkerton	Mezzo-soprano
Trouble (or Sorrow), Cio-Cio San's son	Non-singing role
Cio-Cio San's relatives, servants, and friends	

In two acts. Libretto by Giuseppe Giacosa and Luigi Illica. Based on the play *Madame Butterfly* by David Belasco and the short story "Madame Butterfly" by John Luther Long. Premiere at Teatro alla Scala, Milan, February 17, 1904. Second version performed at Teatro Grande, Brescia, May 28, 1904.

In January 1903, some three years after Puccini attended David Belasco's play *Madame Butterfly* at the Duke of York's Theatre in London, Puccini was en route home from a dinner party with his old friend Alfredo Caselli (a grocery store proprietor, not to be confused with Alfredo Cassella, the composer), when his driver lost control of his car. With him were his common-law wife, Elvira, and his sixteen-year-old son, Tonio. Had it not been for the intervention of a local doctor who heard the car's violent tumble as it flew over an embankment and overturned, Puccini might well have died. Fortunately, he and the other passengers were not seriously injured. Puccini retired temporarily to his vast estate at Torre del Lago, where he remained for four months to recuperate from a broken leg.

For some, including his own sister, Suor Giulia Enrichetta, the accident was an act of divine intervention in consequence of her brother's sins, and others, including his publisher, Giulio Ricordi, convinced themselves it was fate paying Puccini back for having had one too many extramarital affairs. Whatever the case, none of that stopped Puccini from continuing work on *Madama Butterfly*, which had been the focus of his attention since gaining the rights in March 1901. But if by some celestial design it was a paramour that slowed his progress, allowing him time to contemplate and work through this most innovative of grand operas, then it was certainly Madama Butterfly herself.

Indeed, Puccini fell in love with the character of Butterfly the moment he laid eyes on her in Belasco's celebrated production. A Covent Garden stage manager, Francis Nielsen, had suggested to Puccini that he see the play while in London for the premiere of *Tosca*. Though the composer didn't speak a word of English, he understood perfectly what he needed to: the spirit of a story populated with enormously rich characters shaped by destiny and thrust into situations that could lead them only, inevitably, to tragedy.

David Belasco, an American dramatist, producer, and playwright, hailed from San Francisco, where he was born in 1853. Though a scion of a Jewish family, he was raised in a Catholic monastery. Photographs invariably show him to be a pudgy and physically nondescript individual given to wearing white clerical collars, as if to sanctify himself in the public eye. His dramatic imagination and mastery of stagecraft were legendary in his day, and his subsequent influence on American and European theater proved significant. Though his theatrical interests were varied, and he fancied himself a playwright above all, he is largely remembered for the stunning effects he created onstage, resulting in productions of memorable visual beauty.

Among them was *Madame Butterfly*, a play he fashioned from the short story "Madame Butterfly," published in 1897 by John Luther Long, a Philadelphia attorney. It's a relatively simple story, though as Belasco, Puccini, and his librettists Giuseppe Giacosa and Luigi Illica proved, its substance relied on minute detail. Yet another source, and Long's inspiration, was Pierre Loti's novel *Madame Chrysanthème*, published in 1887. Loti was a seaman who, like Long's antihero, recounts his exploits, material and sexual, in late nineteenth-century Japan, where he enters into an arranged marriage with a young Japanese girl.

Belasco's adaptation of "Madame Butterfly"—and what we know today as the opera *Madama Butterfly*—concerns an American naval officer, Benjamin Franklin Pinkerton, who, stationed in Nagasaki, discovers that women are little more than chattel. He marries a fifteen-year-old geisha, Cio-Cio San, also known as Butterfly, thus entering into a contract that, in those days, was not worth the paper it was written on. Knowing full well he could annul the marriage at any time under Japanese law, he rents a home and provides for Butterfly. They wed before her family and friends and consummate the marriage that evening.

For Pinkerton, Butterfly is a plaything, nothing more; but for Butterfly, Pinkerton is her whole world. She is hopelessly in love with him, and her kindness and wholly trusting nature prevent her from seeing him for who he really is. For him she renounces both her religion and culture, bringing anathema from her family. Three years go by, and Pinkerton, who sailed off within days of their wedding, has not returned or even written her. But suddenly, he resurfaces, with a new, American wife, Kate. Butterfly has in the interim given birth to his child, whom she is asked to give up to their care. She does, but now betrayed and completely disillusioned, she kills herself in an act of hara-kiri.

The story was a good fit for Puccini, who intuited in it an opportunity to explore passion and betrayal on several levels simultaneously. His characterization of Pinkerton barely masks his implicit disdain of American culture, though he balances it with a sympathetic portrait of the wise and cultivated American consul, Sharpless. Unlike the heroines of his earlier operas, whom he cast as rather monolithic figures and edgy femme fatales, Butterfly is a victim: of male dominance, of American greed, and of misunderstanding. While fate may rule her, she is the only female protagonist in his work whose character Puccini took the trouble to develop. Unlike Manon, Tosca, or Mimì, her destiny is not preordained, nor has she put herself in a situation that would compel her to die or invite tragedy. Indeed, Puccini allows her to grow from an innocent child to a tortured woman and mother; her journey, such as he paints it musically and dramatically, is as humane as it is perilous.

Belasco's play had only one act, a novel dramatic construction that at first Puccini wanted to emulate. Indeed, at its controversial premiere at La Scala in Milan, *Madama Butterfly* was presented in two acts, the second considerably longer than the first. But the two-act structure proved too taxing on the audience, which booed and hissed its disapproval. That situation was not helped by the scurrilous machinations of Edoardo Sonzogno, an entrepreneur and publisher who had it in for his bitter rival, Puccini's friend and publisher Guilio Ricordi. Puccini was convinced that Sonzogno orchestrated *Madama Butterfly*'s failure by demeaning it publicly and through other means, given his previous tenure as La Scala's general manager.

But if there was a plot to discredit Puccini and ruin the opera, it failed. For its second production, the composer, as was his wont, scaled things back, dividing act 2 into two scenes—in effect creating a third act—though the entire opera takes place in one setting. It was a resounding success and, as history reflects, went on to productions the world over, becoming one of the most endearing and popular operas in the repertoire.

When Puccini composed *Madama Butterfly*, Japanese culture and its various artifacts had for decades been all the rage in Europe, and nowhere more so than in France. Among composers, Claude Debussy had taken a spirited interest in Japan's music and art, codifying these in his own works with extraordinary skill and sophistication. Though Debussy's opera *Pelléas et Mélisande*, with its exotic whole-tone and hexachord colorings evoking something of Oriental stasis, had its premiere in Paris in 1902, Puccini had not heard it when he penned *Madama Butterfly*; but he was intrigued by the French composer's *Nocturnes* for orchestra, whose equally remarkable compositional innovations could not have failed to influence him. It is more than likely, too, that Puccini was familiar with Debussy's exotic piano music, to which he would have had easy access for study.

Madama Butterfly is the only one of Puccini's operas in which all of the action takes place in the same location, that is, on the same set. It is also unusual, though not unique, in that it takes us inside the home of his heroine. The cultural context of *Madama Butterfly* is invested with significance that none of his other operas can claim. The character Manon Lescaut lives at the pleasure of Géronte, who is her keeper, not her husband; everything she owns, and is so eager to take with her when she tries to flee, belongs to him, including the house. Likewise, *La rondine*'s Magda is essentially a courtesan whose valuables are gifts (though absent any information to the contrary in the libretto, it is merely a presumption to say her home is not her own). Tosca is famous, well coiffed, and presumably well-to-do, if naive in other areas, but she never discusses, nor are we shown, her abode. *Tabarro*'s Giorgetta lives on a barge, and then only reluctantly, her only purpose in life being to abandon it and her husband in favor of better accommodations and a new lover. Only in the independent, quick-thinking Minnie of *La fanciulla del West* does Puccini draw a woman whose life is pretty much her own.

In Japan, as well as in the opera, a home was a character in its own right, whether in real life or on stage. A house was, in those days, an emblem of family and virtue, a symbol of collective moral values, and a sacred site of familial lineage. Butterfly's home was her own. That Pinkerton leased it for less than honorable reasons was not relevant; in her eyes, no matter her naiveté, they were a legitimately married couple bonded by legal and moral commitment.

At first, the story and the opera seem rather simple. But in fact, a wealth of detail informs it, musically and otherwise, as even the smallest transaction within it contributes significantly to the whole. Every gesture, every accompanying motivic cell, every soliloquy or vocal ensemble influences the fabric of both music and story; indeed, virtually every event is an organic consequence of what came before it.

While *Madama Butterfly* is not Wagnerian in its scope, or in its appropriation of motivic material to make a point or define, with any specificity, a character—as we have seen, Puccini puts motivic material to use contextually as mnemonic reference or prophetic anticipation—it is nevertheless unusually complex. Beyond that, and any analysis that would deconstruct it on aesthetic or technical grounds, it remains one of the most moving, communicative, and emotionally cathartic inventions in the history of music and, I dare say, theater, as well.

Act I

Pinkerton's house at Nagasaki, late nineteenth century

Often in opera, as the curtain rises, so does the dawn. But not in this case. Rising disembodied from the orchestra pit is a vigorous fugue in 2/4 time, its abbreviated, lightly ornamented subject anxiously articulated exclusively, at first, by the strings in close-quartered intervals (CD Track 8). A second phase follows the fugue, a nervous, polonaise-like two-bar fragment whose Oriental flavor is distinguished by a flash of parallel fifths and octave doublings. Here, the day has already blossomed, and standing center stage is Lieutenant Benjamin Franklin Pinkerton, who cuts a striking figure in the bleached white uniform of a United States naval officer. Fresh off the battleship USS *Abraham Lincoln*, Pinkerton has only just begun his business in the city of Nagasaki, as Goro, a marriage broker, leads him through a spacious Japanese house, resplendent for its tidiness and the view it commands over a hill and out toward the harbor, where Pinkerton's ship is docked. Though he is not a major character, Puccini associates with Goro an abbreviated, hobbling motive, a precipitous but quiet drop of octaves and open fifths against four eighth-notes that will resurface from time to time.

The terrace and garden just beyond the living room's oversized windows and rice-paper doors charm the senses with a fragrant array of cherry blossoms and delicately arranged hyacinths. Here, amid the delicate flora and the sparsely furnished angles of a home in sore need of feng shui, Pinkerton prepares for his imminent wedding to Cio-Cio San, also known as Butterfly, a fifteen-year-old geisha whose innocence will soon enough emerge as the very soul of this opera.

Pinkerton couldn't be more pleased with Goro, whose ambition is equaled only by his unctuous and prevaricating demeanor. It was Goro, after all, who, in his dual role as a marriage and real estate broker, found precisely what Pinkerton needed. While complimenting him on his efficiency and professionalism, Pinkerton marvels at the architectural innovations of Japanese construction, with its sliding doors and discreetly installed sandalwood panels. Goro is unimpressed but remains responsive to the needs of his client, who has entered into a net lease on the house for the next 999 years, give or take a few, with an option to cancel at virtually any time. With a brittle clap of his hands, Goro summons Suzuki, Butterfly's devoted maid, as well as her cook and manservant, who at one time were in the employ of Butterfly's once-prominent but no longer flush family. For geishas, arranged marriages, especially with well-to-do foreigners, were more than a convenience; they were a godsend.

Suzuki, an endearing figure whose constant expression of earnest concern never abandons her for a moment, cites a wise man, Ocunama, extolling as she does so the gods, perfume, and the gates of paradise. ("Dei crucci la trama smaglia il sorriso"—A smile breaks through a web of trouble.) That the citation is in fact hardly Japanese, but a quotation of the Irish-born English novelist-cum-travel writer Lawrence Stern's *A Sentimental Journey Through France and Italy* seemed to bother no one in the early days of the opera, least of all its audiences. Even at this early stage of the narrative, listeners were already enthralled by Puccini's oddly affecting, even exotic music and visually arresting set design. Even so, Puccini enshrouds Suzuki's sincerity, which no one can mistake for obsequiousness, with the opening fugue subject, thus imparting to her a certain gravity and complexity that at first glance her character would appear to deny.

Suzuki's stream-of-consciousness chatter succeeds only in boring Pinkerton, who has other things on his mind, not the least of which is his child-bride-to-be. Goro sends Suzuki and the other servants away, so as to counsel Pinkerton about the documentation he needs to dispatch in order to seal his commitment. Pinkerton knows nothing about Butterfly's family, which will surface soon enough for the wedding party. Here, a descending motivic fragment, articulated in an uninterrupted stream of dotted notes in consecutive intervals of minor thirds, which then transform and angle upward in stepwise motion, is at once pert and regal. As a bassoon punctuates his recitative with blurting beeps, Goro discloses who will be among the guests. As always impecunious and not a little impertinent, he then insinuates his presumption that the legacy of Pinkerton's investment will be an heir, a remark that Pinkerton merely marginalizes with another compliment about Goro's proficiency.

Sharpless, the American consul and an advisor to Pinkerton, is en route. Accompanied by music that for its marchlike countenance is at once reliable and prosaic, Sharpless, a consistently steady fellow, hurries breathlessly up the hill to the house. He is distinguished by the formality of his dress and a stentorian baritone that, in the long recitatives and slow harmonic rhythms that inform the music Puccini entrusts to him, bespeaks his honesty and integrity. To Sharpless, Puccini assigns a vivacious and cheerful tune, distinguished by a seventh chord with a lowered leading tone. Whether Stravinsky, some eight years later, either deliberately or unconsciously borrowed this motive for inclusion in "La semaine grasse" of *Petrushka* is unknown, and probably unlikely, but the similarity is sufficiently striking to consider the possibility; after all, in a filmed interview in the late 1960s, Stravinsky admitted to "stealing" motivic ideas, if only from the best.

Pinkerton boasts of his business acumen and the net lease that, like the marriage contract, is as flexible under Japanese law as the day is long. Indeed, it is precisely the lack of commitment codified in Japanese contracts that Pinkerton finds so enormously appealing; contracts of this sort are no more than an open-ended license to do what he pleases, when he pleases. His marriage contract includes an option to annul at any time, and thus he has nothing to lose but only to gain. For Pinkerton, the Japanese people are little more than chattel or pawns in a game to be won.

Indeed, we can only surmise, in addition to the literary source material for this opera, if Puccini might also have had in mind Commodore Perry, who in 1853 landed in a Japan that for centuries prized its isolationism and that more often than not decapitated anyone, friend or enemy, who dared to challenge its autonomy. Perry and his American forces, ignoring all that, simply took what they wanted and bulldogged their way into the country with gusto.

In contrast to Sharpless's brutal honesty tempered throughout by his taste and diplomatic savoir faire—making him the only sympathetic American character in this opera—Pinkerton shows his true colors, which Puccini, who never failed to criticize American culture, equates with red, white, and blue. Here, the orchestra, in a heavy dose of brass and woodwinds, slips into a self-serving rendition of "The Star-Spangled Banner," giving voice to only its first dozen notes.

On its heels comes the deliciously lyrical "Dovunque al mondo lo Yankee vagobondo si gode e traffica sprezzando i rischi" (Everywhere in the world the roving Yankee takes his pleasure and profit, indifferent to all risks) (CD Track 9), wherein Pinkerton extols the glory of conquest and the pleasures of capitalism, no matter who or what, in the embrace of power unchecked, these might compromise. Two memorable thematic fragments inform this aria, one a rather comfortable melodic descent, given over solely to the orchestra, from an upbeat A-flat to D-flat below, and the other an endearing diffusion in the same key (G-flat major) that allows Pinkerton's bright tenor to soar above the orchestra, much in the manner of Strauss's tenor in the first act of *Der Rosenkavalier*. As if echoing the sentiments of nostalgic imperialism, Pinkerton's remarks take on a certain prescience as the aria continues: "Affonda l'ancora alla ventura . . . La vita ei non appaga se non fa suo tesor i fiori d'ogni plaga" (He drops anchor at random . . . He's not satisfied with life unless he makes his own the flowers of every shore). When Pinkerton gives proud voice to these words, infused again, as the aria draws to a close, with fragments of "The Star-Spangled Banner," the effect is more than jarring; it's frightening. Even if contemporary audiences take it for granted and dismiss it as mere entertainment, its undercurrents remain unnerving.

Meanwhile, Goro, his mercenary character intact, offers Sharpless a selection of young virgins for only a hundred yen, a bargain accompanied by echoes of the motivic melisma that has infused the act thus far. But even here, as Sharpless sarcastically challenges Pinkerton's sanity for having arranged it all, a musical hint of Butterfly, yet to be seen onstage, emerges: It is a brief, nearly parlante descent that falls gently away as it leaves behind precisely the psychological impression Puccini hoped it would.

But Pinkerton is a charmer; in an extended aria ("Amore o grillo—dir non saprei"—Love or passing fancy—I couldn't say), he confesses his feelings for Butterfly proceed more from lust and infatuation than anything else, and his willingness to reify her as a either a thing ("vetro soffiato" and "lucido fondo di lacca"—blown glass and glossy lacquer) or a bug ("farfalletta"—butterfly) paints him unmistakably as a sociopath. In spite of its attendant lyricism, Pinkerton's aria sails forth astride an ascending and descending vocal arpeggio, accompanied by pizzicato strings, only to sputter every now and then as he spins out his thoughts in a periodic string of repeated notes.

Sharpless, whose broad culture and erudition have positioned him well to dismiss such xenophobic machismo as anathema to a civilized people, cautions Pinkerton about his betrothal; after all, the girl will take the union seriously, even if Pinkerton does not. A commitment made in bad faith could lead to unforeseen and perhaps tragic consequences. Indeed, only a few days earlier, Butterfly, true to her name, alighted at the American Consulate to take care of business, and the sound of her voice, mysterious and sincere, found its way to Sharpless's savvy ears, touching him immeasurably. Sharpless persists in his warning with "Sarebbe gran peccato le lievi ali strappar e desolar forse un credulo cuor" (It would be a great sin to strip off those delicate wings and perhaps plunge a trusting heart into despair). The music codifies his concern in a passionate motivic ascent in stepwise motion, which is then distinguished, in its second bar, by an expansive reach of a major sixth.

Thus, in their first duet, Pinkerton and Sharpless square off at cross-purposes, the former wholly unconcerned with Butterfly's future, and the latter, assuming the tone of an errant Tiresias, more than a little uneasy with the lieutenant's callous indifference. With that, Pinkerton, dismissive of Sharpless's anxiety, proposes a toast to his "real American" wife, a future trophy he has yet to acquire.

The entrance of Butterfly, the defining moment of act 1, is as much an introduction to the opera's heroine as it is a more general, if abstract, portrait of incorruptible innocence. Here, just as Goro announces the arrival of the wedding party amid a dim offstage chorus of female voices, Puccini introduces the first of several Japanese themes, and it becomes a chilling emblem of Butterfly's culture and her ultimate fate. This theme's importance, both musically and dramatically, cannot be underestimated, in that Puccini refers to it several times throughout the opera. An angular construction that tosses its pitch material back and forth in a ruminative exchange delicately colored in the context of a pentatonic scale, it is drawn from a popular Kabuki theater dance, "Echigo-jishi" (Echigo Lion Song). Though a satirical ditty played most often on a solo koto, it is not exactly a folk song, but an original composition of Kineya Rokuzaemon IX, an early nineteenth-century Kabuki musician.

As she approaches, Butterfly's offstage voice is aflutter with pride and given to an ethereal yet intensely ardent melody in 4/4 time that moves forward in ascending sequences. Puccini makes this theme of love all the more magical by bringing Butterfly's voice into focus amid the distant women's chorus as it intones a picturesque vision ("Quanto cielo! Quanto mar!"—What an expanse of sky! What an expanse of sea!), a rhapsodic solo violin, and the delicate sprinkling of a celeste. Her words here ("Io sono la fanciulla più lieta del Giappone anzi del mondo"—I am the happiest girl in Japan, or rather, in the whole world) merely support, rather than enhance, the power of the music, which represents the fullness of Butterfly's abundant love and infinite trust in others.

The second phase of the music, which Butterfly so passionately intones, is a ravishing melody in 6/4 time that curves upward on the wings of elongated eighth- and quarter-notes. Here, another Japanese traditional tune, a variant perhaps of the "Sakura" (Cherry Blossom Song), set amid a thin but pristine patina of flutes, bells, quiescent strings, and a harp, emerges with exquisite delicacy. When she reaches the top of the hill, she does so in full traditional costume, attired in the embroidered ceremonial robes of her ancestors. Her face is that of a painted porcelain doll, and her manner is at once grateful, timorous, and uncertain.

Her demeanor suggests neither pretense nor fear, but excitement. Though she is eager to engage Pinkerton in conversation on their wedding day and is entirely susceptible to his flattery, Butterfly first pays her respects to Sharpless, who, like Pinkerton, represents America and its way of life. With his customary gentility, Sharpless probes for answers, inquiring about her family. He learns that her mother is present but her father died long ago; though she doesn't reveal it just yet, her father was a samurai who committed *seppuku*, that is, Japanese ritual suicide invariably inflicted over matters of honor. Wise beyond her age, Butterfly freely admits without shame, and to the strains of the aforementioned Echigo lion song, her past as a geisha. Over a playful pattern of whole tones, the flutes and woodwinds, in a mood of mischievous abandon, proffer a playful Oriental dance more Russian than Japanese in its musical demeanor. Here Butterfly, chirping like a bird, teases Sharpless with mercurial coyness, challenging him to guess her tender age. She does, of course—"Quindici netti, netti . . . Sono vecchia diggià!" (Just exactly fifteen. I'm already old!)—thus disclosing a material fact that, in light of her circumstances, was no less shocking to Western ears in those days than it is to anyone now, no matter their origins.

With the arrival of the imperial commissioner and registrar, the wedding party expresses its cynicism in chorus, indicting Pinkerton as shallow and unattractive. Butterfly's inebriated uncle Yakusidè searches in vain for another bottle of wine, while Pinkerton and Sharpless, on the choral periphery, congratulate each other. Perhaps in deference to his earlier appropriation of "The Star-Spangled Banner," and as a matter of cultural balance, here Puccini avails himself of the "Kimigayo"—the Japanese national anthem originally set to the words "May our gracious emperor reign." But its inclusion here, unlike the American anthem, is neither cynical nor mocking, but entirely ceremonial. The registrar, too, is assigned another Japanese popular tune, "Takai-yama" (High Mountain), a humorous song that, in its original Japanese incarnation (but certainly not here!), extols the loveliness of cucumbers and eggplants. Pinkerton, again bored, dismisses the formality and the curious sight of Butterfly's family and friends as nothing more than farce. ("Che burletta"—What a joke.)

As the guests and relatives break into a lively chorus, Puccini reintroduces the jaunty dotted motive that accompanied Goro's first mention of the wedding party. As their banter crescendos in a canonic tumble, Goro entreats them to quiet down. Sharpless intones an earthy arpeggio ("O amico fortunato"—O fortunate friend), a reflection on Pinkerton's good fortune in finding such a charming girl, while Butterfly's mother and friends gently chide one another over the sincerity of the groom. Pinkerton himself contributes to the patter, boasting in quiet asides his self-satisfied conviction that Butterfly is no more than a trifle, a flower petal to be plucked. Here Sharpless again cautions his charge to take his responsibility seriously, but his words fall on deaf ears.

Where Goro fails, Butterfly succeeds. Calling everyone together, she persuades her guests to sit quietly while she has a word with Pinkerton, from whom all the festivities have thus far succeeded only in separating her. Astride the ravishing theme of love that accompanied Butterfly's arrival, Pinkerton asks if she is satisfied with their new home. She is, but asks his permission to set aside a few mementos and possessions of her own. One by one, she removes from the bulbous sleeves of her extravagant kimono a number of items, which, to Western eyes, might appear to be merely objets d'art. First, a handkerchief, then a sash, followed by a mirror, a fan, and an unwanted jar of rouge. The orchestration, reduced to a whisper of strings and clarinets, accompanies her tenuous, even tedious adventure. Here a bit of Japaniana of Puccini's own invention is hardly uninspired; it is a reference to a Ha-uta, a genre of Japanese vocal music from the Edo period, where song "leafs" or pages were assembled into a larger collection. Puccini's motive is certainly atmospheric; its slim progression of whole tones and a minor third pivoting atop an open fifth suggest something at once mysterious and seductive. But just as that tune vanishes, the oboes and strings whisper a familiar Japanese melody, the "Sakura" (Cherry Blossom Song). As these delicate flora have long been associated with love, and the bloom that wears off of it, Puccini's use of it here rings appropriate and touching.

Suddenly, and with some consternation, Butterfly takes out her most treasured possession. ("Cosa sacra e mia"—This is sacred to me.) She declines to show it to Pinkerton, as its meaning for her is even more private than the love she has for him. As Butterfly is neither willing or prepared on this, the happiest day of her life, to impugn her happiness or worry her new husband with sad thoughts, she steps aside momentarily. Here, the music darkens, as the strings survey, with brusque intensity, an augmented fourth in descent—our old friend from *Tosca*, the *diabolus in musica* (the devil in music). Goro, as always on the ready whenever there is opportunity for intrigue, pulls Pinkerton aside, explaining that the mikado sent this mysterious object to Butterfly's father; it is a sheath containing the dagger he used to commit hara-kiri. Goro demonstrates in mime, drawing an invisible knife to his own gut.

Finally, Butterfly brings out her *ottoke*, which are miniature statuettes representing the spirits of her ancestors. It is a solemn moment, because, as she does so, she discloses an act of humility and devotion born of the deepest affection, an affection totally lost on the callous Pinkerton. In an arioso, "Io seguo il mio destino" (I follow my destiny), she sings poignantly of her clandestine visit a day earlier to the Christian mission, where she renounced her religion and, in an effort to become as American as Pinkerton, swore to cut the familial ties that bind her to her loved ones and homeland. (In an earlier edition, Puccini had Butterfly dispose of the statuettes rather than set them aside, thus giving greater emphasis to both the gravity and finality of her action.) To the troubled strain of Puccini's own Japanese-inflected motive, and looking at Pinkerton, she intones, "Amore mio!" (My dearest love!); but the pentatonic inflection of the figure, combined with its sudden dynamic intensity, here conveys fear and even horror, rather than mystery.

Goro again demands silence, as the official ceremony is about to begin. The commissioner, in quasi parlante, proclaims the contract valid and the pair to be wed. Soft bells and woodwinds color the commissioner's prosaic recitative, and the prevailing mood and music drift momentarily into a kind of languor. At this point Puccini introduces a new Japanese tune, "Oedo-Nihonbashi" (The Nihon Bridge at Oedo). Oedo, or Edo, is an ancient name for Tokyo, and the Nihon Bashi bridge, made of stone, was the last conduit out of the city going south. The text of the original folk song has some resonance here, as it describes the journey of a feudal lord to pay homage to his emperor at Kyoto. If there is any royal imprimatur suggested here, it is that attributed to the imperialism of the Americans, in the person of one B. F. Pinkerton.

The commissioner congratulates the couple, as the registrar gives Pinkerton his blessing to have "many descendants" (Posterità). Sharpless takes his leave on the same joyful motive that announced his first appearance. Now eager to get rid of the guests and get on with the business of his new concubine, Pinkerton proposes a toast. But just then, the name of Cio-Cio San spits forth from the menacing lips of Butterfly's uncle, the Bonze, a Buddhist priest. The hollow sound of a Japanese gong bellows out from behind, as the orchestration thickens and the music grumbles into a conflict of syncopations and dissonances. Strings turn to brass as an overbearing figure attired in traditional garb, the Bonze, discloses that he has learned of Butterfly's visit to the Christian mission. Gesticulating wildly, his spindly fingers pointing in accusation, he denounces Butterfly over a tense tremolando pedal point in the strings and condemns her to damnation, entreating the wedding guests to do the same. ("Ci hai rinnegato e noi ti rinneghiamo!"—You have renounced us, and we renounce you!) They do, enraging Pinkerton, who then throws the lot of them out. The innocent, dotted-rhythm motive, which accompanied Goro's first announcement of the wedding party, now transforms itself into something sinister and compulsive, its whole-tone progressions harmonized in thirds by the winds and brass and ornamented by an uncertain trill. It becomes, in short, a motive of rejection and condemnation. The voices of the now-disenchanted wedding party fade in the distance, as does the orchestra, its haunting oboes diminishing the motive to near-moribund quiescence. What had begun so joyously has turned into a scene of bitter reproach.

Butterfly, reduced to tears, finds comfort in Pinkerton's assurances that all will be well, and with that, she kisses his hand. To a now somewhat uncomfortable Pinkerton she explains that, from what she has heard, Americans view such gestures as an expression of respect. The orchestration is again diaphanous, the accompanying music having been reduced to a placid wash of strings recalling earlier motives. ("Davver?

Non piango più"—Really? Then I won't cry anymore.) Suzuki, always faithful but fearful for her mistress's safety, intones a quiet prayer, its patter unintelligible to the impatient Pinkerton.

With the guests gone and the servants offstage, the two lovers at last have time for themselves. Here, a less skilled composer might have found himself in a compositional quandary, given the dramatic circumstances, which, if the storytelling is to succeed, must suspend the disbelief of the observer. But Puccini knew precisely how to sustain tension and exploit dramatic contrasts. All the bustle of the first three-fourths of the act, with its myriad themes equaled only by the sheer number of characters, has evaporated. We are left with the two principals on their wedding night, their voices entwined in a duet that becomes increasingly passionate. Butterfly has blossomed into a woman, her frequently coy asides and girlish chirping now a thing of the past. She is transformed musically, as well, as Puccini envelops her in music that is exceptionally rich and rhapsodic, and thus appropriate to the status of an operatic heroine.

Here, as Pinkerton looks on in genuine admiration, if not lust ("Viene la sera"—Night is falling), Butterfly prepares herself for her first night with her new husband, when her romantic dreams will be consummated. Even here, Pinkerton's demeanor is suspect; he smokes a cigarette as his bride disrobes, setting aside her wedding dress for a simple white nightgown. The mood is sotto voce as the music pulsates to a gently ascending and descending melodic wave played repetitively by the strings in 6/8 time. Butterfly, still shy and insecure, at first expresses her wish to hide, uncertain if Pinkerton will find her as attractive as she hopes. Now a recollection of the Bonze's ominous reinvention of the dotted motive—the "condemnation" motive— temporarily disturbs Butterfly. ("E ancor l'irata voce mi maledice . . . Butterfly rinnegata . . . e felice"—And still the angry voice is cursing me . . . Butterfly renounced . . . and happy.)

Assuaged by Pinkerton's flattery, her doubts melt away. With his tender entreaty, "Bimba dagli occhi pieni di malìa ora sei tutta mia" (Dear child, with eyes full of witchery, now you are all mine), Pinkerton sets the stage for their ephemeral, nocturnal romance. The melody he so shrewdly performs here, marked "Andantino calmo," is suave and affecting. As her inhibitions vanish, Butterfly compares herself to a moon goddess but is still unsure if she is ready. Pinkerton, giving voice to yet another gorgeous theme, this one exuding comfort and consolation, promises her, "L'amor non uccide, ma dà vita, e sorride" (Love does not kill, but gives life and smiles), a pronouncement that, in this case, could not be more wrong. The impressive sincerity of passion that informs their love duet is nothing if not a lie on Pinkerton's part. Perhaps that is why, when Butterfly recalls their first meeting ("E mi piaceste dal primo momento che vi ho veduto . . . Siete alto, forte"—I liked you from the first moment I set eyes on you . . . You are tall and strong), the music shudders with an archaic recall of the Bonze's condemnation motive. On the heels of her optimistic refrain "Or son contenta" (I am happy now), a brief motivic tail, carried by the oboe, comes to prominence. Though the motive is short, Puccini will put it to significant use in act 2.

Beneath the gentle strain of a solo violin, Butterfly's naiveté, bolstered by her innocence and kindness, holds in its embrace a resplendent new melody in E-flat. Its simplicity is complemented by its metrical organization in 4/4 time, "Vogliatemi bene, un bene piccolino, un bene da bambino" (Love me with a little love, a childlike love). Borrowing this expansive theme, Pinkerton again flatters, as he opines that her name suits perfectly her fragile beauty. Butterfly momentarily recoils, to the accompaniment of the now-familiar Bonze threat motive, confiding in him her terror of an old myth, to wit, that in the West, butterflies are routinely impaled by those who catch them. Pinkerton admits that, while there may be some truth in it, it is only because those who love butterflies don't want them to fly away.

Butterfly's theme of love, with its exotic harmonic coloring and noble sentiments, surrounds the lovers, swelling to an impassioned climax in cumulative rising sequences that find ecstatic expression in music of utterly ravishing and incomparable beauty, culminating in a blazing high C. "Vieni, vieni" (Come along, come), Pinkerton implores her, as they both sing in unison of things celestial and infinite: the stars, the enchantments of evening, the expanse of the sky, and the desires of the heart. And indeed, it is directly to the heart that this glorious music goes so movingly and with such unerring assurance.

Act 2, part I

Interior of Butterfly's house

Three years have passed since Pinkerton left Japan soon after his wedding night. Suzuki, trusting and patient, has been waiting for his return ever since, always hopeful and never doubting his sincerity. Unaccompanied flutes usher in a brief orchestral introduction that is a bareboned reference to the fugue subject in act 1, with the occasional hint. The violins follow suit, echoing the identical fragment before it is picked up with ominous regard by the basses. A patch of Wagnerian chromaticism empties into a restatement of the condemnation theme, wholly consumed by the woodwinds.

Ringing her supplication bells three times, Suzuki, kneeling before an image of the Buddha, intones another of her prayers. Why Puccini sets it to the registrar's banal "Takai-yama" (High Mountain Song) is anyone's guess. If he did so deliberately—and insofar as he researched Japanese folk music while composing *Madama Butterfly*, that seems likely—then its inclusion in this context appears to be a cynical nod toward a religion he may have viewed, from his Catholic perspective, as primitive.

Butterfly, having invested herself entirely in an ideal image of Pinkerton, rather than the man he actually is, finds herself in stasis. She is frozen in time, her only objective to reunite with the man she loves. She spends her days staring out at the harbor, her gaze affixed on every ship that enters it. Worse still, she is again impoverished, thanks to Pinkerton's selfish neglect and failure to fulfill his obligations. Complementing her anguish is a motivic fragment, significant for the role it will continue to play throughout the act, which is articulated by a descending diminished arpeggio and which we will henceforth refer to as the "anguish" motive. Echoes of earlier motives are mnemonic references; a trace of the opening fugue, for example, surfaces when the thrifty Suzuki shows Butterfly a few coins, which are the extent of her meager savings. In the same breath, Sharpless's friendly fragment coincides with Butterfly's defense as she reminds Suzuki that Pinkerton has taken care of the rent, an arrangement assured by Sharpless's intervention; finally, the theme of love comes into hearing as Butterfly protests that Pinkerton's intentions were honorable, in that he provided for her security.

Suzuki, who has misgivings, expresses her doubts that Pinkerton will ever return. Infuriated, Butterfly berates her and, in an unusual outburst of psychical violence, even threatens to kill her. She refuses to accept any such assessment. Distraught but not defeated, Butterfly recalls Pinkerton's promise, made as he was leaving: "tornerò colle rose alla stagion serena quando fa la nidiata il pettirosso" (I will return with the roses in that happy season when the robin builds his nest). Here, a tender new motivic fragment, as if to codify Pinkerton's promise, peeks out from under, its slow sequence of four eighth-notes punctuated by rests before descending, at double the pace, in sixteenths. Butterfly, her innocence crumbling, compels Suzuki to echo her words: He *will* come back.

As Suzuki dissolves in tears, Butterfly alights on one of the most famous arias in the history of opera. In "Un bel dì" (One fine day) (CD Track 10), Butterfly envisions, with picturesque clarity, the arrival of Pinkerton's ship in a distant plume of smoke, followed by his eager arrival, the sound of her name on his lips, and the bliss that comes with union renewed. This most expansive of cantilenas, in the unusual key of G-flat major, is wistful yet redolent with regret, its mood at once conciliatory and resigned. In its second period ("E uscito dalla folla cittadina un uom, un picciol punto s'avvia per la collina"—And from the midst of the city crowd a man, a tiny speck, will make his way up the hill), the aria avails itself of Butterfly's "tornerò colle rose" theme, as well as the truncated motivic tag that followed her paean to Pinkerton at the conclusion of act 1 ("Or son contenta"). Not coincidentally, Puccini shrewdly weaves in just a touch of another Japanese song, "Jizuki-uta" (Workman's Song), just as Butterfly wraps her lips around the words "s'avvia per la collina," which suggests that if Pinkerton wants her, he'll have to earn it. Exploiting a stratospheric tessitura, the wrenching climax, as an expression of her "unalterable faith" (sicura fede), bleeds into a searing orchestral codetta that recycles the aria's principal theme in full tutti.

A reservoir of familiar motives associated with Sharpless and Goro yields to the former's entrance, though the latter, given the musical innuendo, is not far behind. An attenuated strain of "Oedo-Nihonbashi" (The Nihon Bridge at Oedo), played by the clarinet, adumbrates Sharpless's diplomatic mission: to deliver Butterfly a letter from Pinkerton. She declines to be addressed as Butterfly, instructing Sharpless to address her as Madam Pinkerton. But in her excitement, she hardly lets Sharpless get a word in edgewise. If her nervous chatter is a desperate attempt to deny the truth, then her delusion is complete. Indeed, in the midst of her idle patter with Sharpless, she breaks into a busy Japanese tune as yet unheard in the opera, "Miyasan" (My Prince). "Miyasan" was originally a propaganda song set to the words of a Samurai, Count Yajiro Shinigawa in 1868, urging the invasion of Korea. ("Io son la donna più lieta di Giappone!"—I am the happiest woman in Japan!)

Her curiosity aroused, Butterfly parries and deflects Sharpless's invariably polite entreaties, inquiring as to when robins make their nests. Astride the *tornerò* motive a sparse accompaniment offers sound effects—a spattering of triangles and string pizzicatos—in a light mockery of her naiveté. In perhaps an inadvertently comic bit of stage business, Sharpless protests that he knows nothing about "ornithology," a word Butterfly neither understands nor can even pronounce. She is not in the least perturbed when she discloses that, shortly after Pinkerton had left for brighter shores, the ever-manipulative Goro had offered her a new, Japanese husband, the wealthy Yamadori. Goro, who has been standing quietly nearby, growls to the accompaniment of the condemnation motive that Butterfly couldn't do better, given her sorry circumstances and impending poverty.

No sooner is Yamadori's name invoked than he arrives, carried aloft, by servants, on a golden palanquin. His reputation for bloated pomposity precedes him; he, like Butterfly, is a devotee of all things Western. Here Puccini pays homage to his golden stature with the "Miyasan" (My Prince) theme in tandem with a wash of arpeggios, played by the violins and woodwinds, and complemented by a crash of cymbals. Butterfly is neither intimidated nor angry, but amused; her pride, as the American she now believes herself to be, persuades her that derision of old customs and compatriots is perfectly all right. As Yamadori brags of his multiple marriages and multiple divorces, trumpets give way to the "Echigo-jishi"; the tune's original, pre–*Madama Butterfly* incarnation as a satirical parody is well placed, and here serves as a send-up of everything Yamadori stands for.

Sharpless has not anticipated the array of distractions, nor Butterfly's disinclination to face reality. Faced with a moral dilemma that is Pinkerton's duty to resolve, Sharpless wrestles with his obligation to disclose the truth versus his inborn civility that intuitively dissuades him from causing her more pain. Along with Yamadori, Goro returns her taunt, along with a cynical aside addressed to Sharpless: she still thinks she is married to Pinkerton. Desertion, they tell her, is reason enough under the law to dissolve a marriage. But Butterfly, her pride unbroken as her heart resists breaking, only perpetuates her illusions when she sarcastically informs them that in America, the country to which she now owes allegiance, men of their low character are routinely jailed at the very mention of divorce. As if to drive home the point, a perceptible rumble of "The Star-Spangled Banner" lingers timorously in the background.

As Butterfly languishes in her dream world, the three men huddle in an effort to exchange the facts. Goro discloses that Pinkerton's ship, which is in the area, has been signaled. Sharpless, charged with breaking the news that Pinkerton has no desire to rekindle his relationship, pledges to disavow Butterfly of any illusions. Butterfly makes no secret of her distaste in Goro's presence, and that of Yamadori, too. As Suzuki pours tea for them both, Butterfly dismisses them as tiresome ("che persone moleste"), signaling her desire that they make themselves scarce. Both leave, though Yamadori, in a suave yet unctuous melodic refrain distinguished by the absence of anything even remotely Japanese, makes a final appeal: "Addio, vi lascio" (Farewell, I leave you). She turns him down flat, and he, with Goro in tow, leaves as pretentiously as he arrived.

Sharpless, surrounded in the glow of his motivic tag, now turns to the task at hand as he begins to disclose the contents of Pinkerton's letter. Butterfly takes it from his hands and presses it to her heart; she cannot read English, and thus the document itself becomes for her a conduit to Pinkerton's soul—or lack of it. The orchestration thins to a slim *pianissimo* patter of gentle arpeggios played by the violins in pizzicato in tandem with a bassoon. The strings expand and thicken the orchestration as Butterfly's anticipation mounts; she hangs on every word, and so does the music. But Sharpless has read to her only the opening of Pinkerton's letter, which merely hints at his intentions. Still faithful, Butterfly hears only what she wants to.

Setting aside the letter, Sharpless improvises *a cappella*, the music having dissolved into silence. "What would you do," he asks, "if he were never to return?" A pause between his final word and Butterfly's response precipitates the menacing hammer blow of the timpani with a scratch of strings behind it. Here, the mood turns from one of frenetic anticipation and hopeful ebullience to inevitable terror. As the truth begins to sink in, Butterfly responds that she would have only two choices: entertaining with her simple geisha songs, or death. With that, the clarinets and bassoons pulsate eerily with a repetitive chromatic oscillation above a persistent pedal point. Sharpless, sympathetic and sorrowful, recommends she marry Yamadori but succeeds only in offending her. At first she asks him to leave, then changes her mind, but not without disclosing the extent of the pain Sharpless has caused her.

The theme of love returns, entirely transformed now into a proud and brilliant processional. Its tone is no longer intimate, but public. With this Butterfly reveals the fruit of her long night three years earlier with Lieutenant Pinkerton: a child. ("E questo? E questo? E questo egli potrà pure scordare?"—And this? And this? Can he forget this, as well?) Although his is a wordless role, there is scarcely a production of *Madama Butterfly* that has not turned this two-year-old into a child of at least six or seven; perhaps there's something about Japanese cooking. Alas, this is really due to pragmatic considerations, not the least of which concern child employment laws and the attention span of toddlers. In any case, in the midst of this and an echo of "The Star-Spangled Banner" is a new Japanese melody, "Kappore-Honen" (Harvest Dance of Love), that will henceforth be associated with the child. Puccini's choice of song was hardly inappropriate; "Kappore-Honen" was a popular song that extolled a bountiful harvest.

Taking the boy in her arms, Butterfly addresses him directly in an earnest and melancholy aria. Here she bemoans the fate that Pinkerton's behavior would bring about. "Do you know what that gentleman had the heart to think?" she asks the boy, pointing to Sharpless, as she prepares to launch into one of her richest arias, "Che tua madre": "That your mother would have to take you in her arms and in all kinds of weather walk the city streets to earn you food and clothing." Elements of two other Japanese themes disclose themselves in this heavily pentatonic confection: the work song "Jizuki-uta" (which Puccini exploited earlier in "Un bel dì") and "Suiryo-Bushi" (Foreboding Tune), a well-known ode to regret, popular in the nineteenth century, that was a reflection on both the joy of meeting and the sorrow of parting.

Certainly it is no accident that in "Che tua madre" Puccini cumulatively embraces so many Japanese elements simultaneously, as if making an effort to invest the child with everything Butterfly has lost: her heritage, her religion, her family, and perhaps her soul, as well. The inclusion of these melodies also provided Puccini and his librettists a way of indicting Pinkerton and what he stood for: the selfish indifference and greed of American culture. Butterfly has allowed herself to be deceived, but she is not about to allow anything of the sort to happen to her son.

At Butterfly's insistence, Sharpless, who is saddened but also strangely overjoyed, reaches out for the child as he asks him his name. His mother answers that his name is Sorrow (Trouble, in some translations, but that is in part because of the "true" story that Long claims to have inspired him; in that case, Trouble was indeed the name of the geisha's son), and that, when Pinkerton returns, his name will be Joy. That Puccini declines to use here the "Foreboding Tune," given its reference to joy and sorrow, is surprising; this may perhaps be an example where a composer felt that less is more and that a little Japaniana goes a long way. However, with the horns blaring a vivid recall of the principal theme of "Un bel dì," Butterfly's disposition, though still forlorn, suddenly brightens.

Sharpless leaves, taking Pinkerton's letter with him, as Goro, who has been lurking just outside the door, enters. Butterfly berates him for spreading vicious rumors that no one knows who the child's father is. By now, if we are to take the libretto seriously, Butterfly's rage, represented musically by tense tremolandos in the strings and pungent dissonances, punctuated by the brass, in jagged descending sequences, has already turned into psychosis: She threatens to kill Goro, just as she threatened to kill Suzuki earlier. ("Vespa! Rospo maledetto!"—Serpent! Accursed toad!) In most productions she removes her father's dagger from its sheath and tackles Goro to the floor as the orchestra churns up, with the strings and oboes, a variant of the condemnation theme. Suzuki, taking action, restrains her. As this bit of stage business amounts to little more than a denouement that threatens, in its own right, to attenuate by adumbration the final scene, it is left to the most imaginative directors to discern a more convincing approach that at once maintains dramatic tension as it visually conveys Butterfly's rage. But certainly in words and gesture, and perhaps more so than is reflected in the musical accompaniment, Butterfly has murder very much on her mind.

As Goro leaves, coldly evicted by Butterfly, a burst of cannon fire is heard in the distance. A moment of silence ensues, framing what follows. Butterfly imagines she has reason for renewed hope as she discerns, from the lens of her telescope, that it is the *Abraham Lincoln* sailing into the harbor. The entire first half of her soliloquy, beginning with "Bianca ... Bianca ... il vessillo Americano delle stelle ... " (It's white ... white ... the American flag, with the stars), is essentially delivered parlante. As her heart fills to the brim with hope, she inaugurates an optimistic arioso, "Scuoti quella fronda di ciliegio" (Shake that branch of the cherry tree), where thematic reminiscences flood the scene. Melodic drafts, supported by the flute and strings, quietly whisper the mnemonic winds of "Un bel dì," which soon burgeons forth in a crescendo to a voluminous *forte*. Echoes of "The Star-Spangled Banner," as well as thematic fragments of her love duet with Pinkerton from the end of act 1 likewise find favor as Pinkerton's man-of-war comes into view.

Convinced that she was right all along, Butterfly, with Suzuki's help, harvests the cherry trees of their fragile blossoms, sprinkling them around the house in anticipation of Pinkerton's arrival. The orchestration intermittently complements the women's playful dialogue in diaphanous sequences amply colored by the woodwinds. Their chatter blossoms as surely as the fragrant flowers to which they pay tribute and concludes with a languorous duet in thirds. ("Gettiamo a mani piene mammole e tuberose"—By the handful let's scatter violets and tuberoses.)

In a moment that evokes the palest dramatic, but not musical, shadow of Strauss's Marschallin in *Der Rosenkavalier* (which is only coincidental, as Strauss had not even composed it when *Madama Butterfly* was published), Butterfly takes a look at herself in a mirror and is shocked to see her worn and pale reflection. Against a hush of horns, a harp, and muted strings, Butterfly prepares herself with Suzuki's able help, adding rouge to her cheeks and combing her long locks. She calls for Sorrow, whom she needs to ready in advance of meeting his father. Then, to the strains of Yamadori's "Miyasan" (My Prince) theme, and a touch of the ominous condemnation motive, Butterfly wonders what her estranged relations and acquaintances will think when she proves them wrong. ("Che ne diranno!"—What will they say now?)

Perhaps in an effort to recapture it, Butterfly revisits her past as she puts on her wedding dress. They punch three small holes in the soshi screen so that each of them can hold vigil in expectation of Pinkerton's arrival. Night falls and the full moon rises, bathing the room and its occupants, who sit in still silence, in a pale glow. The suave orchestral intermezzo that ensues provides an eerie patina of motivic recalls, not the least of which is the anguish motive from the opening of act 2.

Emerging offstage is the delicate and all-too-famous "Humming Chorus" (CD Track 11) sung wordlessly by sopranos and tenors. Set against the same pallid pizzicato arpeggiations that made their first appearance when Sharpless intoned Pinkerton's letter, this is a unique moment in this opera and, indeed, in the history of opera. This is true not only for the sheer invention of it all, but also because of the form it assumes: it is in essence a lullaby masquerading as cantilena.

Act 2, part 2

Here the curtain falls, but not for long. An orchestral interlude anticipates part 2 of act 2; given its formal construction, and in spite of the fact that the stage setting is the same, it might as well be a third act.

Some productions call it just that, inserting an intermission at this point. The intermezzo opens with the oscillating second period of the "Echigo-jishi" (Echigo Lion's Song), a wash of major thirds and whole tones, now broadened into an impassioned *forte* and played by the strings. As the music exfoliates, Puccini interpolates the principal motivic material of the previous two acts, culminating in an opulent reminiscence of act 1's love duet.

As the curtain opens, so does the dawn. A quiet chorus of sailors' voices wells up alongside the twitter of birds and bells in the distance. A solo horn gives voice to a bucolic melody, played *pianissimo*, that bears a vague resemblance, if only by virtue of its rhythmic design and pitch trajectory, to the "Miyasan" (My Prince) theme. Butterfly is still awake, her vigil no more than an expression of her determination to get the first glimpse of Pinkerton in three years. Suzuki wakens to Butterfly's tender lullaby to Sorrow, "Dormi amor mio" (Sleep, my love), sung against a sheen of muted strings and a harp. Here, Puccini again recycles the child's theme, "Kappore-Honen" (Harvest Dance of Love). Suzuki, who begs Butterfly to get some rest, discloses her concern with periodic asides of "Povera Butterfly!" (Poor Butterfly!). Exhausted, Butterfly takes her advice and leaves the room with Sorrow in her embrace.

As if by stealth, Pinkerton, wearing the same white uniform, approaches the house with Sharpless and Kate, his new American wife. The absence of Butterfly, as he does so, is itself a dramatic articulation of a particularly intense moment. Suzuki, perhaps no less disillusioned than her mistress Butterfly, opens the door to a new theme that is decidedly Western, it is a stately sarabande that imbues Butterfly's home, more than the visitors who have just arrived, with a certain dignity that even they cannot compromise. The theme itself, at once hopeful and sad, is distinguished in its fourth bar by the inclusion of a lowered seventh, which lends its broad melisma a touching pathos. Suzuki brings the men up-to-date on Butterfly's disposition: her long wait, her nightlong vigil, and her infinite devotion to and confidence in Pinkerton. With this, she offers to rouse Butterfly, but Pinkerton, coward that he is, hesitates and asks her to wait. Spotting Kate in the wings, Suzuki, terrified to have confirmed what she already knows in her heart, asks Sharpless to disclose her identity. "È sua moglie" (She is his wife), he mutters sotto voce.

With this commences an ardent terzetto, which Puccini molds with considerable elegance from the touching sarabande theme. ("Oh! L'amara fragranza"—Oh, the bitter perfume.) Sharpless has the welfare of the child in mind, while the self-serving Pinkerton can do nothing more than sing of his own woes with faux remorse. Suzuki is mortified by these developments and is hardly reassured when Sharpless, in the midst of the terzetto, asks her to bring Butterfly in. Pinkerton's conceit flowers at the top of his tenorial tessitura as he eyes a photograph of himself.

Sharpless reproaches Pinkerton for his behavior and reminds him that he had been warned. ("Vel dissi? Vi ricorda?"—I told you! Do you remember?) Whether Pinkerton's remorse is genuine is a matter of interpretation; indeed, here is an example where the written word and the music do not necessarily correspond, insofar as Pinkerton's actions—his refusal to face the woman he has scorned and so brutally hurt, his audacity in bringing with him his new wife, and, not least, the disdainful arrogance he has shown all along toward both Suzuki and Sharpless—all testify to a man whose character is hardly ambiguous but entirely false. His expression of regret matters little underneath music that he merely shares with the others in the room. He is a mediocrity, and the only real remorse he demonstrates is that of a man whose only regret is having gotten himself into a bit of a social mess. Though Puccini may very well have intended to make of Pinkerton an authentically remorseful and sympathetic character as *Madama Butterfly* drew to its close, even he could not rescue such a despicable man from himself.

Pinkerton, his only hope for absolution from responsibility being the holy dollar, presses money into Sharpless's hands. In the lushly orchestrated "Addio, fiorito asil di letizia e d'amor" (Farewell, flowery refuge of happiness and love), Pinkerton sings his heart out, what's left of it, above an expanse of horns and violins. But Sharpless is merciless in his admonitions and, supported by motivic fragments from "Amore o grillo" (Love or passing fancy), continues to lay blame.

Pinkerton, as if to confirm his status as a coward, beats a hasty retreat so as to avoid coming face-to-face with Butterfly. As he leaves, he passes Kate, who assumes his place; she has come for Pinkerton's child. Her demeanor is that of a kind and caring woman; she means no harm but, under the circumstances, is powerless to prevent it. She assures Suzuki, who ushers her inside, that she will care for the boy as if he were her own. Here the music becomes unusually tense and uneasy, swelling in chromatic sequences astride a pedal-point pulsation of strings. These in turn are punctuated by a shadowy reference to the opening fugue subject, now ominously pointed up by a lone oboe and then a spattering of clarinets.

Butterfly's hoarse cry for Suzuki, the only friend she has left, now becomes an emblem of her desperation. Suzuki begs her to stay where she is, but Butterfly, with a hint of the condemnation motive afire in the background, refuses and rushes in. Her only thoughts go to Pinkerton: "È qui . . . è qui . . . dove è nascosto?" (He's here, he's here . . . where's he hidden?). Just then she spots Kate, and the game is up. She doesn't want anyone to tell her who this strange woman is, for she already knows. For Butterfly, this is an existential moment; she now not only understands the truth, but also has come to accept it. Indeed, in some ways this can viewed as the climax of the entire opera, or at least a negative climax. The texture dissipates, dwindling into an unnerving quiet punctuated by a bass clarinet. Butterfly's song is no longer a song at all, but an abstract of idealized resignation. Her voice, reduced to a pathetic whisper, pays little more than lip service to Giacosa and Illica's words; there is nothing left for her. ("No, non ditemi nulla . . . nulla . . . forse potrei cader morta sull'attimo"—No, don't tell me anything . . . I might fall dead on the spot.) And just as she intones that morbid thought, the music stops altogether for what seems an eternity, though it is only a few seconds.

As if a veil had been lifted, but not a weight, Butterfly queries Suzuki, asking her questions to which she intuitively already knows the answers. Her innocence now nearly devastated, she has become impatient with her maid's wishy-washy prevarications and wants only the facts, no more. Is he alive? Did he arrive the day before? Suzuki's

affirmative response, buttressed by her confirmation that Pinkerton
will not in fact return, serves only to seal her fate. Kate, who stands
quietly to the side, frightens her; but Sharpless's assurance that Madame
Pinkerton is an innocent victim of the entire debacle does nothing to
diminish Butterfly's terror. In wrapping her lips around the words "È sua
moglie!" (She is his wife!), Butterfly's edgy soprano drifts momentarily
downward from a scream to a quiescent string of repeated notes above a
prescient pedal point in the winds: "Tutto è morto per me" (Everything
is finished for me). Here, the final appearance of Sorrow's theme, the
"Kappore-Honen" (Harvest Dance of Love), is invested with poignancy
that it perhaps had not acquired in earlier incarnations, as it accompanies Butterfly's last thread of hope: "Voglion prendermi tutto! Il figlio
mio!" (They want to take everything away from me! My son!).

Even more disturbing is Sharpless's response—"Fatelo pel suo
bene il sacrifizio" (Make the sacrifice for his sake)—which is cruelly
ironic, thanks to the accompanying recall of the "Duvunque al mondo,"
Pinkerton's delicious if self-absorbed aria from act 1. In assigning him
this mnemonic fragment, which was once the exclusive domain of
Butterfly's lover, Puccini essentially entrusts the boy to Sharpless in
both musical and psychological categories.

Though touched, Kate is hardly ready to give up. She is on a mission,
now charged with the responsibility her husband has declined to live up
to. Kate's role is small, confined largely to recitative pronouncements
on a single pitch, so as not to compromise or overwhelm the passions
of the principals. The extent of her participation is limited to begging
Butterfly's pardon and taking care of business: "E il figlio lo darà?" (And
will she give up the child?). Butterfly recoils, unable to look at Kate,
content to merely congratulate her, in song that is both pious and sad,
for having co-opted the happiness that should rightfully be Butterfly's.
("Sotto il gran ponte del cielo non v'è donna di voi più felice"—Under
the great dome of heaven, there isn't a happier woman than you.)

Butterfly agrees to surrender the boy, but only if Pinkerton himself
comes to fetch him in a half hour. A thrust of propulsive syncopations,
set to the nervous, concluding motivic tail of Butterfly's "Or son contenta" (I am happy now), undulate in the lower strings and woodwinds,

followed by a citation of the broad, matinal motive that opened the second part of act 2. Butterfly complains that the room is too bright; she is already looking forward to a permanent night. She instructs Suzuki to find Sorrow, who is playing outside, and keep him occupied. Suzuki, perfectly aware of what Butterfly is about to do in her absence, leaves in tears.

A burst of timpani pounds sullenly, like excited heartbeats, in a crescendo of hollow open fifths, which saturate the theater with a palpable sense of foreboding. As the sound of the drums recedes, the cellos swell up in lament from below, complementing a recall of the condemnation motive. Preparing for the end, Butterfly lights a Japanese version of a votive candle, bows before the Buddha, and removes the dagger from her father's sheath. Inscribed on the blade are precisely the words she is obliged to intone: "Con onor muore chi non può serbar vita con onore" (He dies with honor who cannot live with honor). This might have spelled the end of the opera right there, but Puccini twists the knife, so to speak, before it even touches her. Just as she raises the dagger to her throat, Suzuki pushes Sorrow inside. Butterfly abandons her weapon, if not her commitment to hara-kiri, and runs toward her son, whom she embraces and smothers in kisses. Whether he is old enough to understand what she tells him, namely, that she is about to die ("muor Butterfly") doesn't matter as much as the dramatic gesture.

In "O a me, sceso dal trono dell'alto Paradiso" (Oh, you who have come down to me from high heaven), Butterfly's voice pierces the prevailing tutti. She bids farewell, entreating her boy never to forget her face, even as he goes away beyond the sea ("andar di là dal mare").

As the opera draws to its tragic close, Butterfly gives her son a doll and an American flag, neither of which he can see, insofar as she has also blindfolded him. Thus does she part with Sorrow. To the grim and solemn funereal beat of a processional, a complement of timpani, trumpets, and strings thunders around her in chromatically inflected sequences. As they do, she recovers the dagger she had dropped only moments earlier, retreats behind a screen, and plunges the dagger into her heart. The pace quickens as the strings lead, and the fatally wounded Madama Butterfly staggers bloodily toward Sorrow, collapsing and dying in front of him.

Pinkerton and Sharpless arrive, just in time to see Butterfly expire. The "Or son contenta" (I am so happy) tag, ablaze in trumpets and trombones, surges underneath Pinkerton's cries of "Butterfly." The "Suiryo-Bushi" (Foreboding Song), already familiar from "Che tua madre," brings down the curtain. The ending is unusually abrupt but hardly illogical; the final chord is not that of the tonic B minor, but an altered chord on the sixth degree of the scale, and thus colored by a G-natural. This not only creates an impression of irresolution, but establishes as compositional fact that the music simply stops, rather than draws to a gradual close. It is as if to say that, with the death of the heroine, from whose perspective we have been persuaded, in this opera, to filter our own, there is nothing left to say. Life has come to an end, in darkness, and that's it. Perhaps this is the operatic equivalent of *point of view*, a strategy more common to cinema, where a character's perspective can be conveyed, if so desired, without ambiguity. Whatever the case, the story and music of *Madama Butterfly* reverberate long after the curtain comes down, and will continue to do so for a very long time indeed.

La rondine

Characters	Voice Type
Magda de Civry	Soprano
Lisette, her maid	Soprano
Ruggero Lastouc, a young man	Tenor
Prunier, a poet	Tenor
Rambaldo Fernandez, Magda's lover	Baritone
Périchaud, a guest at the salon	Baritone/bass
Gobin, a guest	Tenor
Crébillon, a guest	Bass/baritone
Rabonnier, a guest	Baritone
Yvette, a guest	Soprano
Bianca, a guest	Soprano
Suzy, a guest	Mezzo-soprano
A butler	Bass
A voice	Soprano

A comedy in three acts. Libretto by Giuseppe Adami based on a libretto by Heinz Reichert and Alfred Maria Willner. Premiere at the Théâtre de l'Opéra in Monte Carlo, March 27, 1917.

The year 1913 was nothing if not significant to the history of music. In Paris, the premiere of Stravinsky's *Le sacre du printemps* (The Rite of Spring) caused riots, to speak nothing of the controversy it aroused among critics. Puccini, accompanied by his then common-law wife, Elvira, was in the audience, and though he was oddly inspired by it, his critique was not exactly complimentary. "An absolute cacophony," he opined. "It's all the work of a madman."

Given the raucous public climate that accompanied *Le sacre*, along with the fascination it held for the intelligentsia, you might think that the furthest thing from the mind of one of Europe's leading composers would be operetta. Even so, the enormous continental success of Richard Strauss's elegant if elaborate *Der Rosenkavalier* only two years earlier held a certain fascination for Puccini, whose world renown was by then firmly established. Though *Der Rosenkavalier* is indeed a full-fledged opera, its ingenious construction as a string of elegant waltzes lends to it, at least superficially, something of the ambience, though not the formal structure, of Viennese operetta. It is a work at once musically substantive but implicitly entertaining, not only as a matter of its physical decorum and the rococo charms that informed its story, but for its essential optimism. *Der Rosenkavalier*, then, is a through-composed work that simultaneously celebrates complexity, rejects tragedy as the principal capital of its subject matter, and avoids cliché, both dramatic and musical, as it exploits the comedic dimensions of farce.

Puccini could not resist the temptation when, on a promotional tour for *La fanciulla del West*, Siegmund Eibenschütz (the intendant of Vienna's Karltheater) and the publisher Emil Berthe offered him what was then a small fortune to compose an operetta. Introduced to them by Franz Lehár, a leading composer of lighthearted operettas whose commercial success was so brilliant as to attract, some years later, the attention of a nascent Hollywood, Puccini envisioned opportunity. As far as a story, Eibenschütz and Berthe had something specific in mind, a book by Alfred Maria Willner.

As usual, Puccini was demanding and fussy. After the death of Giulio Ricordi in 1912, his relationship with the Casa Ricordi, now under the direction of Giulio's son Tito, began to crumble. Puccini was a careful, deliberate, and thorough man who never entered into any negotiation casually and without aforethought. Tito, who had only profits in view, failed to understand or even tolerate, as his father did for so many years, Puccini's point of view.

Thus when Willner sent him the first sketch of a libretto for the proposed operetta, Puccini didn't bother to consult Tito Ricordi. He was now on his own, and he could also afford to be. In any case, he found Willner's libretto entirely unsatisfactory, calling it "slipshod" and "banal." There was not a chance Puccini would enter into a contract, no matter how much was at stake financially, if the libretto failed to meet his high standards. What's more, the subject matter had to appeal to his instincts as much as it did to his musical intellect; Puccini thrived on a challenge, but never for its own sake.

Even so, there was a silver lining behind the cloud of Willner's sketch, in that it convinced Puccini that operetta was not a form to which he was at all well suited. As he confessed to his appointed agent in Vienna, Angelo Eisner, "An operetta is something I will never do; a comic opera, yes, like *Rosenkavalier*, only more entertaining and more organic."

Willner did not give up hope, even in the face of Puccini's by-then-widespread reputation as a particularly difficult composer to collaborate with. A few months later, in April 1914, Willner sent Puccini another story outline and called it *Die Schwalbe*, German for *The Swallow*, or in Italian, *La rondine*. The sketch was more succinct and thought out, a consequence, perhaps, of Willner's collaboration at this point with another writer, Heinz Reichert. Although the story bore only a superficial similarity to Verdi's *La traviata*, the ambience was lighter, and for all appearances, at least at first, it was material well suited to comedy.

This time Puccini liked it or, at the very least, trusted his intuition to pursue the project. Gathering his forces, he brought in Giuseppe Adami, a thirty-three-year-old journalist, to render it in Italian and arranged a meeting in Vienna so that the three of them could discuss the project in detail. Two months later, Puccini was at work on the score, telling his friend Sybil Seligman that it was to be a "light, sentimental opera with touches of comedy . . . agreeable, limpid, . . . with lively and fetching tunes . . . a sort of reaction against the repulsive music of today."

The outbreak of World War I in July 1914 put things on hold. As he was contractually committed to an Austrian firm on enemy territory, Puccini found himself in a quandary. He was far too clever to burn bridges, which is precisely what would have happened had he taken an official, public stance against Germany. Had he done that, he would have severely compromised his own and his publisher's relations with central Europe, and that in turn would have cost him prestige as well as revenues. Though he would never be able to avoid altogether the appearance of impropriety, in light of his cordial business relations with the Austrians, he resolved to extricate himself from the contract. To this end he met with Berthe, the Viennese publisher, in Zurich. Negotiations proved to be in his favor, as only fragments of Willner's libretto remained intact; Adami's adaptation had by then become an entirely new animal. Berthe reserved the rights to the premiere of *La rondine*, which he agreed to make contingent upon the war's ending.

While Puccini never severed his ties with Ricordi, *La rondine* became a casualty of the bad faith between them. Following its completion in 1916, Casa Ricordi declined to purchase and publish *La rondine*. And so it fell to the Casa Sonzogno, which was Richard Strauss's publisher, to make a deal with Puccini. To sweeten things, Casa Sonzogno purchased Berthe's rights to the premiere, thus leaving the door wide open on the question of where that event would take place. In Monte Carlo both the Casa Sonzogno and Puccini found the ideal opportunity, and they awarded the premiere to the distinguished opera house there. The decision was not without detractors, however; Puccini found himself accused in some quarters, notably that of Léon Daudet, the son of composer Alphonse Daudet, of cooperating with the enemy, which, in his view, owned the opera. To produce it, then, in France, or with of an ally of France, was tantamount to treason.

Puccini deflected this criticism admirably and successfully through the media. The first performance, on March 21, 1917, was a resounding success, though its reception was considerably cooler on Italian soil, at least among the critics.

Never satisfied, Puccini penned several versions of *La rondine*, each with a different ending. One of these had its premiere on April 20, 1920, in Palermo. He revised the opera again for a third edition but did not live to see it performed. What's more, the Allies bombed the Casa Sozogno's headquarters during World War II, obliterating the autograph and orchestral parts. While a surviving vocal score includes several pages of music that were not part of earlier editions, any reconstruction would be merely speculative without either sketches or a written memorandum in Puccini's own hand.

Act I

Magda's salon

As the curtain opens and a lush suite of rooms comes into view, a wash of glamorous music with strings, harps, brass, and triangles a-flutter forecasts more than one of the principal themes to come. The jaunty opening subject divides into two parts: an irresistible dance in 2/4 that hurls a robust syncope downward toward two bars of heavily accented downbeats. The second part, which will come to represent the idea of love, is an elegant four-bar fragment that holds its own in a fluid progression of close-quartered, chromatically inflected chords. While one production may differ from another, the quality and nature of its props wholly depends on the opera company's budget, so savvy set directors will spare no expense on authenticity; at the very least they will do their level best to respect Puccini's and his librettist's wishes.

For the moment, then, let us imagine such an ideal production. Here, in the soignée Parisian salon of Magda de Civry, a kept woman who dares not admit her past as a courtesan, every corner is sumptuously appointed. On one side is a bright winter-garden conservatory where floor-to-ceiling windows, their rococo moldings visible in the shallow light, look out onto the expansive formal gardens of the Tuileries, which in spring are awash in roses, tulips, and, in late summer, chrysanthemums; reverberating with the sound of children at play, they offer sanctuary for the discreet whispers of young paramours. Velvet drapes enrich the salon, which abuts a partially hidden entrance to Magda's upstairs boudoir. Hanging atop a large salt-and-pepper marble fireplace is a decorative Louis XIV mirror, its coiled wooden brocade delicately ornamented in gold leaf as it lavishly frames the opulence it reflects.

An ideal apartment for entertaining, this exquisitely appointed maisonette sports a few pristinely placed chaise longues, a generous number of turquoise-hued Queen Anne chairs boasting embroidered floral patterns, a delicately upholstered, serpent-shaped his-and-her loveseat, a bird's-eye maple armoire, and a Biedermeyer table, all expertly arranged. The myriad, nearly transparent panels of a Japanese rice screen neatly accentuate the elaborate wall hangings, which, in their eclectic depiction of seraphims and biblical themes, bear less of a resemblance to the Old Masters at the nearby Louvre than they do Bataille's and Poinçon's mercurial Tapestries of the Apocalypse at the Chateau d'Angers. Enveloped in blue and white Chinese porcelain, an abundance of fresh-cut yellow and red roses, carnations, and lilies peer from every available surface, their fragrance mingling with a vague scent of lavender. A rosewood Pleyel grand piano, draped in a decorative silk brocade, its cracked, eggshell-colored ivories faded from years of exposure to the southern sun, is complemented by taffeta-shaded lamps that, from underneath their drooping tassels, gently illuminate in candlelight a patch of English landscape paintings in ornate gilded frames. Elsewhere, a lonely brass samovar, a memento from Saint Petersburg and polished to perfection, presides regally atop a walnut-lacquered bloodwood commode, its cabriole legs delicately ornamented with caryatids and vitruvian scrolls.

Within this plush and colorful environment Magda, a woman of taste, if not always means, holds court for a coterie of her closest friends, among them her lover and benefactor, Rambaldo Fernandez, and the poet Prunier, who, for all his wit and arrogance, proves a clever and amiable companion. Six others—Crébillon, Yvette, Bianca, Périchaud, Gobin, and Suzy—make small talk as they sip pear brandy and absinthe from diamond-shaped crystal. Here the music is conversational, a reservoir of fragments drawn from the principal melodies of the opera's introduction and tossed liberally among the guests. As Lisette, Magda's coquettish if somewhat overbearing maid, serves white chocolates and pours coffee from a familial silver service, the guests gather around the piano, which, like virtually every other objet d'art onstage, becomes a character, albeit a nonsinging one, in its own right.

Prunier cynically condemns the virtues of romance or, more accurately, romantic love, which he assures the guests is alive and well in the City of Light. Lisette, her dark eyes beaming in a fit of one-upmanship, dismisses Prunier with a vulgar aside. While her cutting remark "Storie! Si vive in fretta. 'Mi vuoi?' 'Ti voglio.' È fatto!" (Rubbish! Life's too short. "You want me?" "Yes, I do." That's it, then!) amounts to only the briefest motivic fragment, set forth by the woodwinds in a high register, it is an important one and will resurface frequently as an emblem of her impudence. Offended but hardly ignoring her, Prunier, his French armor ever so slightly dented, blithely confronts Magda so as to register his formal objection to Lisette's odious remarks. But Magda, amused and even impressed by Lisette's audacious insolence, is deferential and asks her to get on with her work.

Prunier, now free to engage his braggadocio, turns to the other guests, who, hanging on his every word, playfully flatter his ego and feign to take him seriously. Romance is a fad, a sickness, a kind of madness, he says, to which women are most susceptible. Meanwhile, Crébillon, already bored, has turned his attention to an article he spots in a newspaper that, until this moment, has merely languished on a table beside him. News of a catastrophic market crash seems a good deal more worthy of contemplation than the romantic prevarications of a fop. Indeed, Prunier, who is concerned only with showing off, pays no attention. "No one is immune, not even Doretta," he opines.

But Doretta is merely a creature of his imagination, the heroine of his latest lyric, which he has set to music. Prunier's exaggerated claim to have immortalized her in a song that no one has yet heard compels Magda and her female guests to press him into service. The subject of the song is, naturally, love, a subject that Rambaldo can only sniff at and indict as a cliché. As daylight dissolves into the crepuscular amber of dusk, Prunier, eager to oblige, accompanies himself at the piano. In a display of pianistic éclat worthy of a virtuoso, he preludes with a stream of widely arpeggiated chords. He sings of Doretta's dream—"Chi il bel sogno di Doretta pote indovinar" (Who can interpret Doretta's lovely dream?)—wherein a nameless king beseeches a young virgin to yield to his will, with a promise to lavish her with riches if she does. Enveloped within the quiescent strain of a violin, a harp, and a celeste, Prunier elaborates tenuously, his song at once supple, affecting, and largely diatonic, its refrain defined by the drooping descent of a major third set against pulsating syncopes below; the girl of Doretta's dream proves stoic and firmly declines the king's dubious offer, convinced that money cannot buy happiness.

As Magda, oddly touched by this tale of woe, draws closer to a now-befuddled Prunier, he stops playing, confessing he has been unable to devise an ending. Magda, her face gently irradiated in the dim glow of candlelight, takes Prunier's place at the piano, assuming the air of an ancient bard. However, Puccini, who was not one to beat a dead drum, refrains from turning Magda into a pianist; the strings surround her earnest soprano throughout. Indeed, in this arioso, Magda reiterates the verse ("Chi il bel sogno di Doretta") (CD Track 12) as a lush cantilena, but she finds a resolution: enlightened Juliet-like by the kiss of a young man, Doretta discovers the real meaning of passion, if not love. Her creative moment an inspiration to herself as well as her guests, Magda pauses with a thought: "Che importa la ricchezza se alfine è rifiorita la felicità! O sogno d'or poter amar così!" (What does wealth matter after all, if happiness blossoms! What a golden dream to have a love like that!).

Impressed by such eloquent poetic sentiments, Prunier helps himself to the nearest bouquet of roses and showers Magda with their aromatic petals. Likewise impressed, Rambaldo congratulates her on her sincerity, only to be met with Prunier's haughty pronouncement that a "romantic demon" dwells within each of us and that we are powerless to exorcise it. But Rambaldo, not amused, comes to the defense of machismo, declaring himself immune from such sentimental detritus. As if to rebuff Prunier, as well as Magda's exordium to selflessness, he pays homage to the glory of materialism by producing a pearl necklace, which he promptly places in his lover's hands. The accompaniment, in spite of its oboe coloration, is uneventful and prosaic, as if to indict Rambaldo for a lack of imagination. Magda gladly accepts the pearls, though not without protest that she cannot be bought. She says, "Ho una sola risposta: Non cambio d'opinione" (I've only one thing to say: It doesn't change what I feel). With that string of words, the orchestra launches into a subtle, nearly imperceptible waltz in E-flat that avails itself of an unsteady hemiola, reflecting an undercurrent of uncertainty. That Magda's fundamental hypocrisy, as a woman who, on the contrary, does nothing *but* sell herself, does not go unnoticed by Prunier, who irreverently but softly reminds her that *his* Doretta would never consider any such thing.

As was the custom in those days, male visitors in search of admittance to a respectable home or club were expected to present their calling cards. Lisette, agitated and out of breath, returns uninvited, to inform Rambaldo, in a tense string of rapid-fire eighth-notes, that an impatient young man has been waiting hours to see him. With Magda's permission, Rambaldo invites him in; he is the son of an old friend. As Rambaldo excuses himself en route to the winter garden, Prunier urges Magda to dismiss her maid, who has become, like a buzzing mosquito, a source of annoyance for him. That he does so in the aura of a suave, wholly contented new waltz tune in stepwise motion and in the bucolic key of B-flat is puzzling, in that it appears to convey precisely the opposite of anger. The reasons for this will become apparent soon enough. Yet for all her pettiness, Lisette's energetic enthusiasm brings "a ray of sunshine" into Magda's quotidian existence, or so she says. But her guests presume that Magda, as a woman to whom much has been given, leads a life sufficiently fulfilling as to need neither the cheer nor support of a servant.

Here, Magda makes her first and only reference to a *grisette*, a sometimes pernicious attribution that, in nineteenth-century Europe, referred to a flirtatious and emotionally dependent female hanger-on who indulged not only artists, but the well-to-do, for personal pleasure and also as a personal avocation. Lurking behind the moniker *grisette*— a word that, to untrained ears, might sound as if it were a culinary regimen of shellfish in butter and garlic—was inevitably the agenda of a groupie at best, and a prostitute at worse. "I believe you are like me," Magda opines, to the distant accompaniment of the love motive, her tone awash in sorrow, "and often regret the little grisette who was so happy with her lover!"

As custom had it at dinner parties in those days, and actually still does in certain circles, the men and women segregate after dinner, moving into separate rooms to enjoy their cigars and aperitifs, respectively. Thus Prunier, bowing to social convention, has joined his comrades, leaving the members of the fair sex to fend for themselves. With her guard down, Magda discloses a private, bittersweet memory of long ago when, as a young woman, she ran away from an elderly aunt who looked after her, eventually landing at a popular Paris nightclub, Chez Bullier. Her extended arioso, "Può darsi! Ma che non si dimenticano più!" (Perhaps, but I can't ever forget them!), emerges in the embrace of a thin, even veiled accompaniment; the orchestral texture is at once ethereal and rarefied. Here she waxes eloquent about a handsome young man she met there, whose maturity finds only superficial expression in his pristinely trimmed mustache. All a-swoon, Magda held out every hope that he would sweep her off her feet. He didn't, but in an effort to impress her, he ordered two lagers and rewarded the waiter with an extravagant gratuity. His inhibitions loosened, he enjoined Magda to inscribe her name on the table next to his. His eyes met hers, and they held each other's gaze in silence. After that, her memory of her magical moment fades into a vague recollection of a distant song warning her of the dangers of love: her aria, "Fanciulla, è sbocciato l'amore! Difendi, difendi il tuo cuore! Del baci e sorrisi l'incanto si paga con stille di pianto!" (Child, love is in bloom! Take care, take care of your heart! Kisses and laughter must be paid for with teardrops!), intones and codifies her memory in the form of a lilting, cheerful waltz in A major.

Her heart swimming in the languorous memory of her irretrievable youth, she pines to find such magic just one more time. Suzy, Bianca, and Yvette, enchanted by Magda's not-so-tall tale, marvel at her resilience. Prunier returns, only to be caught in the cryptic headlights of chattering women who, in the context of the earlier E-flat waltz, tease him with threads of Magda's story. But in referring to Magda's aging aunt and her mysterious young suitor's mustache in the same breath, the ever-sly Prunier pretends to misunderstand, as if Magda's aunt was the victim of a glandular disorder: "Curiosa! Non m'attira!" (Curious! She doesn't attract me!).

Prunier has aroused Magda's curiosity. Just what sort of woman *does* he find attractive, she asks. His response is neither sarcastic nor vague, but predictable. "To win me over, a woman must be refined, elegant, wayward . . . in a word, worthy of me! Galatea, Berenice, Francesca, Salome!" Here, Puccini, paying tribute to Richard Strauss (whose *Rosenkavalier*, as we have seen, was to some degree a model for *La rondine*), cites a tiny motivic fragment from *Salome*. It's a delicious moment that, given voice by a lone clarinet, vanishes almost as quickly as it appears; though brief, the citation is that of *Salome*'s most memorable motive, an exotic, serpentine minor third that permeates that remarkable work. But Prunier has no fear of seeing his head served on a platter; on the contrary, Prunier wants Magda's hand, but not in marriage or even out of affection. Now suddenly a self-styled seer, Prunier reveals that, in order to determine if a woman embodies the special qualities he demands, he must read her palm; thus does he add the role of carnival barker to his repertoire of manipulations. (Keep in mind, it's precisely moments like this that remind us, when all is said and done, that the clear, cold wind of logic is anathema to opera, which, though hardly on the order of surrealism, somehow makes absurdity seem acceptable). Prunier obliges when the ladies beg him for a reading; reaching for the Japanese screen, they gather around Prunier, now a faux Svengali, at the foot of the piano.

Attention shifts suddenly to a frenetic Lisette, who returns with the calling card of Ruggero Lastouc, the impatient young son of Rambaldo's old friend. Here, Puccini reintroduces Magda's earlier waltz tune, "Fanciulla, è sbocciato l'amore" (Child, love is in bloom!), the anthem of amorous passion unfulfilled. Rambaldo greets Ruggero cordially as Prunier forecasts Magda's future, which he augurs with deliberate ambiguity and with the first reference to the opera's title: "Forse, come la rondine, migrerete oltre il mare, verso un chiaro paese, di sogno, verso il sole, verso l'amore" (Perhaps, like a swallow, you will migrate beyond the sea, to a bright land of dream, toward the sun, toward love). Prunier's melodic line here is unnaturally calm and pontifical, not unlike (though only coincidentally) Russian Orthodox chant, as it proceeds upward in diatonic sequences over a dominant pedal point. Whether Prunier's prediction bodes well or ill is anybody's guess, and Magda, perturbed, ponders her fate.

Lisette offers Ruggero a glass of champagne, which he welcomes heartily. Engaging Ruggero's attention, Rambaldo inquires if it his first time in Paris. Here, the provincial Ruggero gives voice to his aria "Parigi! È la città de desideri" (Paris! It's the city of desire), wherein he extols the bewitching enchantments of the City of Light. There is something of an Italian country song about this aria, which soars in two strophes above a droning bass pedal point and the lush harmonization provided by the strings and oboes. The lilting triplets that tie up its successive phrase periods likewise impart a certain elegance befitting its subject matter.

Prunier, still preoccupied reading the ladies' palms, resurfaces when Rambaldo inquires as to which nightspot might be the most suitable one to send Ruggero to for a good time. Eager to give his young charge a taste of Paris *soir*, Rambaldo gently chides Prunier, who, in a sarcastic aside, assures Ruggero that the very notion of finding magic on one's first night in the city is nothing more than superstitious rubbish. Lisette, again speaking out of turn when she has not been spoken to, riles Prunier with a firm objection to his cynical encomium. A brief but glaring trumpet fanfare offers only a patriotic hint of "The Marseillaise" as she assures Ruggero that it is hardly nonsense, but the truth; Paris is nothing if not "il regno della donna" (the kingdom of women). Prunier will have none of it, and he spars with the impetuous maid in spitfire banter that is as crusty as it is belligerent. Fed up and no longer trying to conceal his anger, Prunier demands her dismissal, but is calmed by a newly sympathetic Magda as they take off for a private tête-à-tête in the conservatory.

With Prunier cooling off in another part of the house, it is left to the women to decide where to send Ruggero. Lisette gains the upper hand as the ladies spurt the name of one club after another. Perhaps familiar with her mistress's lonely-hearts history, she recommends Chez Bullier, an idea that meets with the approval of everyone, including Ruggero himself. Magda returns, nervously fidgeting with her pearl necklace, and is given to a fit of nostalgia at the very mention of Bullier's. Like the darkening shadow of an eclipse, a certain indifference engulfs her; she tosses her new necklace to one side and drifts into a daydream born of old memories and newly aroused desires.

But Prunier, having regained his composure, cannot resist making one last obnoxious wisecrack, saying that the air smells of Lisette, whose lavender perfume has left a disembodied trace of her behind. Rambaldo bids good-bye as his prosaic, stepwise theme again raises its head, and, along with the other guests, he takes his leave. To the accompanying lull of the hemiola-rich waltz that followed her acceptance of the pearl necklace ("Ho una sola risposta"), now delicately dispersed by the violins and a harp, Magda ponders what to do with the rest of her evening.

Once everyone is gone, Magda asks Lisette to call for a carriage, as she, too, wishes to experience the night in ways that she perhaps has not done in years. Lisette obliges her but reminds Magda that it is her night off. Magda agreeably dismisses Lisette, and then, finding a slip of paper left behind by Ruggero, surveys the names of the nightclubs the ladies had brought to his attention. With Prunier's prophetic words about a migrating swallow, the sea, and new love still reverberant, she resolves to go to Chez Bullier herself, as if in search of her destiny. On the heels of her abbreviated thoughts, which come to a close on the words "verso il sole" (toward the sun), the orchestra dissolves into a prolonged but ethereal cadence, thus emphasizing her reflective demeanor as it fore-shadows regret yet to come.

Magda wastes no time and swiftly retreats to her boudoir, closing the door firmly behind her in such a way as to suggest she is also closing the door on her current, unhappy situation. For the singer in this role, this detail presents an acting challenge all by itself; while something as fundamental as closing a door may seem relatively unimportant, it can, if thoughtfully and imaginatively executed, fill out a character and color a scene. A resourceful actor will use such stage business to convey intent as much as a state of mind. Indeed, this undercurrent, or subtext, is made all the more emphatic by the subsequent silence that momentarily empties the stage. One thing is certain, and that is her determination to make herself ready, by whatever means necessary, for a new adventure, and in a manner commensurate with the seductive charms of the lively grisette she once was.

Meanwhile, Lisette has slipped back into the salon; she had retreated only into the conservatory but, unknown to Magda, has not yet left the house. In her hand is a decorative if somewhat ostentatious hat, while draped across her arm is a silk cloak, both of which belong to Magda. Careful not to make sound, lest she draw Magda's attention, she hurries back to the conservatory, where Prunier, his collar stiff, his umbrella furled, and a white carnation in his *bouton*, as befits a gentleman of that era, awaits her. Evidently his prickly hostility toward Magda was all an act; a man of his reputation, he explains, must keep up appearances, and the concealment of his long affair with Lisette was merely de rigueur. Puccini codifies their intimacy with a gentle if oddly static theme in E-flat that oscillates in stepwise motion, in ascent and descent, over four bars, only to be repeated ad infinitum throughout their entire scene.

Again the pair bickers, but this time out of the sight of anyone else, in playful affection. Prunier swears his love, but evidently that isn't quite enough; he insists Lisette find a more attractive hat and another cape; now fully enshrouded in the attire of a grisette, Lisette has fulfilled Prunier's secret fantasy. Sentimental asides fill up operatic space as Lisette applies her rouge and lipstick, and their small talk dissolves into cutesy-wootsy banality. They kiss and take off.

The stage empties for a moment before Magda, decked out in the plain and simple gear of a classic grisette, emerges. Though a white camellia might have been more appropriate, she takes a red rose from the piano and ties it in her hair. Where less than an hour before Prunier had strewn rose petals at her feet in deference to her poetic vision, now a full bulb in bloom, eviscerated of its thorns, complements her reinvented appearance. A hastily thrown shawl embraces her slim figure as she congratulates herself on having successfully rendered her persona with the guile of a great actress; no one, she sings, will recognize her. Combining speech with song, she poses to herself a question more pragmatic than philosophical: "Chi mi riconoscerebbe?" (Who would recognize me?). Reminiscences of the principal themes—Doretta's dream and the A-major waltz that informed Magda's tale of romance ("Fanciulla, è sbocciato l'amore!")—mingle effortlessly. With that, she dashes out of her luxurious home in search of a new adventure, and the curtain falls.

Act 2

The ballroom at Bullier's

Scenic, but not musical, echoes of the Café Momus from *La bohème* surface as things get under way in this no-less-bustling act 2. In a typical Pucciniesque crowd scene, artists, students, grisettes, merchants, passersby, and ladies of the night mingle in a frothy confection of after-dark revelry. The music is raucous, presenting a tense and jumpy theme in 4/4 time that is doubled in octaves and characterized by pushy syncopes. Chez Bullier is a spacious locale, ornamented by an elaborate staircase that dominates the design and overlooks all the activity. Waiters in black tie and crumpled vests crisscross en route to the coterie of lovers, tourists, and the occasional ne'er-do-wells who populate Chez Bullier. There is no dearth of tables scattered about, playing host to those who, immersed in conversation, enjoy one bottle of cabernet after another. This club plays host to patrons who know it only too well. They blithely commingle but eventually glide toward a large veranda abutting a garden, where oilpaper lanterns burn brightly, throwing off a musty odor of day-old wax. The elaborate gilded staircase that leads to this veranda is Bullier's centerpiece, providing as it does a broad perspective of the interior as well as the comings and goings of the patrons. An abundance of flowers, mostly roses, proliferates, throwing off a heavy scent that mingles harshly with the scent of wax and the suffocating, smoke-infested air.

The banter is as breathless and deafening as the various individuals, couples, and groups, loosely organized into packs and bands, engage in the cheerful but inebriated chitchat that informed Parisian night life and its bohemian subculture as much then as it does today. Puccini entrusts to these various individuals and small groups a vigorous tumble of polyphony, largely doubling the orchestra's boisterous thematic material, as their choral cooperatives swell and diminish in stride. A pack of randy grisettes surreptitiously survey Ruggero, and, as they do, their chorus blossoms into an expansive, lyrical, and lightly ornamented sirens' song.

Yet another anonymous group of students, their champagne flowing freely from decorative magnums, spots Magda on the stairs; she is announced musically with an orchestral reference to the love motive of act 1. Though unimpressed by her shabby attire, they discern in her hesitant demeanor something of a charmer; for some reason Magda, a new face in the crowd, fascinates them, and after some prodding, she confesses, as a matter of deflection, that she is awaiting someone. She says so at first only as a means of dissuading their precipitous advances but then spies Ruggero, who is surrounded by a group of flirtatious young women eager to make his acquaintance. The students observe her furtive glances in Ruggero's direction and lead her to him.

It should surprise no one familiar with or even new to opera, given what we have learned thus far, that he fails to recognize her, even though he left her home not even an hour earlier. He compliments her with a remark that flatters her distinction from the other women in the room, indifferent to her apologetic attempt to explain her sudden and unexpected presence. "Scusatemi, scusate" (Forgive me, I'm sorry), she mutters nervously astride Prunier's chantlike prophecy motive from act 1.

But her tension dissipates when Ruggero, at once restrained and courteous, as befits his naiveté, tells her she reminds him of the modest provincial girls of his hometown, Montauban. Already smitten, and in an effort to endear herself to Ruggero, Magda expresses her desire to dance with the gusto of the provincial girls of Montauban. The pair, intoxicated by desire, join hands and saunter onto the veranda and into the swirl of dancers. Their voices now one, Magda and Ruggero enter into their first, altogether too brief love duet, "Nella dolce carezza della danza chiudo gli occhi per sognar" (In the soft caress of the dance I close my eyes to dream), wherein they imagine themselves as inhabitants of a carefree world.

Here a women's chorus, symbolic of springtime and assuming the dramatic patina of a Greek chorus, edge the pair on with a cozy new waltz, proceeding in minor thirds and in descending stepwise motion. If the women's chorus has any specific agenda, it is to articulate the fruits of the couple's passion in song. Magda and Ruggero's voices, now in tandem and at a distance, pour out from the garden with the ecstatic tones of those in the throes. ("Dolcezza! Ebrezza! Incanto, Sogno!"—Sweetness! Madness! Enchantment! Dream!)

The dance is over for Magda and Ruggero, but their affair is only beginning. Resuming their places at the table, sweat pouring down their brows, each becomes the object of the other's fantasy. Magda, grabbing the opportunity to re-create the unrequited events that first led her to Bullier so many years before, asks Ruggero to tip the waiter generously, just as her mustachioed near-paramour of yesteryear once did. He obliges, though without grasping what has motivated her to ask him to do as much. Never mind; a toast is in order, and gazing into each other's eyes, they toast to each other and to fidelity.

By now, if we are to throw ourselves willingly into the libretto's given circumstances, we could easily accept Magda's infatuation as something far more serious. After all the professions of love and devotion to a man she met only a few hours ago, she seems surprised when Ruggero, who still doesn't recognize her, tells her he doesn't even know her name; perhaps he's just nearsighted, but for dramatic purposes, that is one rationalization that just won't do. As if on cue, she traces the name Paulette—a clever but necessary deception that at once throws her suitor off track and also fulfills her earlier fantasy—and Ruggero does the same. A circumspect Ruggero gently dismisses such an adolescent exercise as merely ephemeral, adding that Magda's real place is in his heart and mind, where she will remain for eternity.

In a touching arioso, "Perché mai cercare di saper ch'io sia e qual'è il mio mister?" (Why ever do you want to know who I am and what my secret is?), Magda embraces Ruggero in words and music, assuring him that fate is responsible for their meeting. Her song poses a gracious and endearing melody in widely spaced, slow-moving intervals in contrasting motion, accompanied by muted strings and a harp, and colored with woodwinds whenever the themes move toward cadence. Admitting how little he knows about her, but confiding the depth of his feelings, Ruggero echoes the melody in "Io non so chi siate voi . . . Sento che tu non sei un'ignota, ma sei la creatura attesa dal mio cuor" (I feel as if you are not a stranger, but the creature my heart has been waiting for). Their dialogue then burgeons into an impassioned musical climax sealed by a drawn-out kiss. A small group of onlookers sigh approvingly in a lyrical extension built on fragments of the new lovers' melody.

Certainly, Ruggero's choice of words, which can be attributed only to the fancy of the librettist, is nothing if not odd. For a man who so freely admits he has been awaiting a "creature," Ruggero may have overstepped his bounds; perhaps this is one Puccini character that would have been better suited to wearing a lizard suit in a grade-B horror movie. But again, it's opera, and thus anything goes.

Elsewhere, Prunier and Lisette, not far behind, dawdle among the revelers. Prunier, perhaps unaccustomed to such public displays, questions Lisette's excitable comportment; even on this less auspicious occasion, he prefers she behave like a lady, with dignity and restraint.

She objects to his stuffy and inappropriate formality, which serves only to compromise her freedom of association, though she admires him, or so she says, nevertheless.

How it is that the drably dressed, essentially disguised Magda catches Lisette's attention remains unexplained. With characteristic indiscretion, Lisette points a spindly finger in her direction and alerts the astonished Prunier to Magda's presence. Prunier dismisses her claim, insisting she has had too much to drink, and dares her to prove it. But as he takes a closer look, he realizes that Lisette has got it right. Magda silently signals Prunier to hold his tongue, which indeed he does, signaling back to her his consent in the deception. Acknowledging that Ruggero is indeed the young man they had met earlier in the evening, and playing along with Magda's ruse, he slyly inquires as to Magda's identity. "Paulette" asks Lisette, still unconvinced, why she is staring at her; Lisette responds, but not to Magda-Paulette, explaining to Ruggero just how much his new girlfriend resembles her mistress. Indeed, seeing Lisette all decked out in her own (that is, Magda's) clothing, Magda cannot help but make a cynical remark with regard to the elegance of her wardrobe, which is now illegitimately wrapped around her maid. Naively, now convinced the woman is not Magda, Lisette smugly admits to having stolen the clothing. Amused by the exchange, Prunier chuckles, only to be chided by Magda, who throws his earlier remarks about an ideal woman back in his face. "Is this your Salome or Berenice?" she asks, making of Prunier's arrogance an occasion for mirth.

As the champagne flows, Ruggero proposes a toast to love: "Bevo al tuo fresco sorriso" (I drink to your fresh smile) (CD Track 13). Puccini appropriated its tune from a lullaby, "Sogno d'or," that he penned in 1912 for a magazine, *Noi e il mondo*. But for the operatically inspired, theatrically amorous purposes he sought to convey in this scene, however, Puccini develops its friendly, pastoral melody into a *brindisi*—a drinking song—and thus into something considerably richer. Here, as the two couples drink to each other and to their respective paramours, this once-simple tune, now richly harmonized and contrapuntally elaborated by the soloists and a chorus of onlookers, expands cumulatively to a climax of magisterial proportions. Magda, dizzy and jubilant, sings of fulfillment, while Prunier and Lisette praise each other, as if love itself were no more than a competition. From above, the jubilant throng of onlookers celebrates the burgeoning romances that unfold before them and smothers the two couples in flowers and garlands.

Without warning, Rambaldo appears in the rafters. The old stoat, seeing the woman he loves, or thinks he loves, on the arm of another, glares at them both with the wizened grimace of a hovering hawk. An alarmed Magda appeals to Prunier to help her hide Ruggero, but Prunier's cooler head prevails: he enlists Ruggero to take Lisette to the garden, where they get lost in the crowd. Although she cannot be certain if Rambaldo has recognized her beneath her evidently ineffective disguise—a fact that miraculously seems to escape her just as surely as Puccini and his librettist had persuaded themselves that audiences would accept it—she refuses to budge when Prunier urges her to leave. "Chi ama non pensa!" (When you're in love, you don't think!), she cries.

As Prunier attempts to shield Magda from Rambaldo's view, Rambaldo, now on the threshold of lost love, firmly demands that he leave them alone. Holding on to the pearl necklace he gave Magda earlier that evening, as if it were an emblem of his commitment, he confronts her: "Che significa questo?" (What is the meaning of this?). Magda is hardly intimidated but, on the contrary, emboldened to take a stand as she admits she is in love with Ruggero. Wrapping her throaty soprano around "Ma voi non lo sapete cosa sia aver sete d'amore . . . ?" (But don't you know what it's like to be hungry for love . . . ?), Magda begs Rambaldo's forgiveness for hurting him and tells him that whatever there once was between them has flown. While Rambaldo's brazen machismo dissuades him from publicly disclosing his emotions, it doesn't prevent him from taking his leave of Magda with a caustic and perhaps prescient remark: "Possiate non pentirvene!" (I hope you don't regret it), he tells her as he turns his back and leaves, perhaps for good.

Magda is stunned but relieved as she is left alone to contemplate what she has just done. Here, the music thins out into a sequence of descending scales, carried *pianissimo* by the bassoon against a patch of quiet syncopes radiating sotto voce. The throngs of revelers have already left, and the hour has grown late or, more accurately, early; as dawn breaks, and the ancient Parisian buildings reflect sunlight in the pale and peculiar manner that has always colored the city as an oasis of dreams, a certain sadness lingers. Chez Bullier has become no more than a shell reverberant with the messy memories of a dazzling evening. Absent the legions of students, lovers, onlookers, drunks, and waiters, the stage, like Nietzsche's unforgiving abyss, stares back at the audience from beneath an ocean of broken glass, empty bottles, wine-stained tablecloths, and dying flowers. A strange female voice, accompanied by a piccolo and representing the dawn, beams its way in from offstage with a prescient caution that the charms of night are an illusion and that love cannot be trusted. Elsewhere, the sounds of commerce and quotidian life add to the ambience and rouse Paris from the hazy dreams that, only hours earlier, it had so effectively manufactured.

Ruggero and Magda reunite at the table. Prunier and Lisette are long gone. The now-lonely Bullier is their private sanctuary as the orchestra and the lovers give voice yet again to the "Sogno d'or" *brindisi*. Even after all this, Ruggero, who is either wildly unobservant or simply dim-witted, still has not recognized "Paulette" as Magda, who reasserts her love lest Ruggero think it was all in jest, a consequence of varied wines. Magda's predictable "Ti amo, ti amo!" (I love you) draws the act to a close and brings down the curtain.

Act 3

A seaside inn

Time has flown, and Magda has eloped with Ruggero to a seaside cottage—a countryside inn, really—on the Côte d'Azur. It is a bucolic setting, where wide sloping hills give way to warm, fragrant breezes, steep and winding roads, and patches of rust-colored tile roofs, which adorn the Mediterranean shore as if a giant hand had painted them there. As the curtain opens and the footlights brighten, a small garden, dotted with tables and featuring a rustling brook comes into view. The string-rich orchestral introduction recycles fragments of the previous acts' waltzes, but now serenely expanded into a pastoral embrace. Abutting the property is an ivy- and rose-covered partition, beyond which is a well-worn path that leads to the sea in a gently descending slope. Olive trees, the aroma of their flowers a permeating presence, ornament the landscape, as does a colorful variety of flora.

The lovers are blissfully happy, or so it seems. The endless compliments they paid each other at Chez Bullier hardly stopped there; here, they have made of it a virtual condition of their affair, attaining to flattery so sentimental as to make sick anyone but the most neurotic. Seated at one of the garden tables, Magda sings of her picaresque new surroundings as a distant celeste punctuates her arioso. ("Senti? Anche il mare respira sommesso. L'aria beve il profumo dei fiori!"—Do you hear? Even the sea breathes quietly. The air drinks in the perfume of the flowers!) Over a cup of jasmine tea, which Magda delicately pours for him, Ruggero boasts an endearing sentiment: "Tutto, mio amore, mi piace di te!" (My love, everything about you pleases me!). Magda already has reservations, but not for opera seats; on the contrary, it is young Ruggero's tolerance for boredom that concerns her. But he reminds her that, so long as she is by his side and in his heart, he is not alone, nor can he ever be. The breadth of his naiveté is nearly as grand as the opera itself.

The pair have somehow managed to make their home in the most expensive community in the world, but now their money has run out. Ruggero has written home to mother to ask for a few francs. Feigning annoyance but hardly astonished, Magda protests that it is not her fault that the funds have flown. Roberto makes light of her chiding and then reveals something even more troubling: he has asked his mother for permission to marry Magda. She is shocked to hear it but conceals the extent of her dismay. "I didn't know, I didn't expect it". She begs Ruggero for more information, but none is forthcoming; there is nothing more to say. His response is merely pat: "Tu che non sei l'amante, ma l'amore" (You are not just a lover, Magda, you are love itself).

Here, in a placid arioso in E major, "Dimmi che vuoi seguirmi alla mia casa" (Tell me you want to go with me to my home), he launches into a description of his modest family estate, which, not unlike their current domicile, is a countryside affair that sits atop a hill overlooking an orchard. That Ruggero's arioso is not a waltz, but a simple diatonic melody in 4/4 time, suggests his weariness with the bubbling revelry that had until now informed his love of Magda. Having sown his wild oats, which were never that wild to begin with, Ruggero wants to settle down, and his song is sufficiently peaceful to augur as much. But money is not the only thing running out; time is, too, as Magda's biological clock is ticking faster than a Sentex bomb.

Ruggero, his hopes not yet dashed, kisses Magda and leaves, throwing her into a panic as the faintest trace of the warning waltz from act 1 drifts by. In the deft chromatic surges of "Che più dirgli? Che fare? Continuare a tacere, o confessare?" (What more should I tell him? What shall I do? Keep silent, or confess?), she wrestles with her conscience, knowing that, to Ruggero, she is still "Paulette." Amid a nearly Oriental patch of parallel ninths recalling the opening sequences of *Madama Butterfly*, Magda has reached a defining moment of the sort that, in the real world, Jean-Paul Sartre would later call *existential nausea*: pride and desire battle for supremacy with moral responsibility. Should she disclose her sordid past, not only as a grisette, which would come as no surprise to Ruggero, but as a kept woman and thus, essentially, a prostitute?

Her thoughts are interrupted, as they so often are in this opera, by the entrance of Lisette and Prunier. The colorful orchestration barters familiar motivic fragments in a bright and fast-paced 2/4, making light of their argument with a patter of woodwinds in a high register. As usual, the fast-talking, belligerent Lisette is no mood for mirth. Here, she lashes out at Prunier, who, in an ill-fated attempt to mold her to his ideal vision of a woman, encouraged her to become a chanteuse. Because an artist, in Prunier's view, makes a more respectable companion than a maid, what better idea than to transform one's working-class lover into an arbiter of good taste and a model of aesthetic contemplation? Even in an operatic libretto, snobbism is alive and well, particularly where a composer and his team of writers have an opportunity, as they did here, to implicitly criticize it. In any case, evidently no one advised Prunier that transforming someone into a singer is easier said than done.

Humiliated by her failure onstage, Lisette holds Prunier responsible. In deference to her failure, Prunier has made amends, or at least pretends to, given that his real agenda is something rather different. He has promised Lisette to give her back her life, restoring her to the domestic bliss of a domestic.

Prunier, clever as always, has traced the couple to this seaside resort, but taking pains to ensure the accuracy of his information, he confirms with the butler the presence of Magda and Ruggero. Lisette still has her doubts and is weary of being dragged all over France in an effort to find Magda. When Prunier learns the pair is indeed in residence, he asks the butler to formally announce him. After all, even aging grisettes in the throes of illicit passion deserve a little warning, if not respect. Still fuming and about to go into a meltdown of conceit, Lisette disavows her naiveté, saying only, in a pronouncement worthy of Marlene Dietrich at the height of her fame, "All my illusions are gone."

In the midst of their internecine quarrel, Magda surfaces and is delighted that Prunier and Lisette would not only remember her, but travel such a great distance simply in order to see her. She learns that, since leaving Paris, she has become a subject of idle gossip and that the majority of those she once numbered among her friends can hardly believe she has abandoned her cushy urban life for an impoverished hopeless romantic.

Prunier gently admonishes Magda as Lisette looks on, reminding her that the lifestyle she has embraced is inappropriate. "This isn't the life for you" forms the extent of his blunt commentary, and it hurts Magda deeply. Though she tells him as much, she ultimately accepts his assessment with quiet dignity. In an effort to deflect his critique, Magda makes small talk, inquiring as to the reason for his visit. Prunier, who by now has made plain throughout the opera that behind every word he utters is a hidden agenda, entices Magda with half the truth. Only the night before, Lisette had made her singing debut in nearby Nice, an elegant city where the air is nearly always redolent with garlic and lilacs, while its streets play host to tourists who, embarrassed to admit they can afford only meager accommodations, pretend to be guests of the magisterial Hotel Negresco. Perhaps in a bid to spare

Lisette's feelings, Prunier, himself the Addison DeWitt of opera, discreetly avoids repeating what the critics had said but admits that her performance was not exactly to the public's liking. As the experience marked the end of her very short-lived career, she would like to have her old job back. Magda, her generosity spilling over when she no longer has a cent to her name, is delighted to welcome Lisette yet again to her fold.

Even so, Prunier cautions Magda that a similar fate awaits her and that she would be well advised to follow Lisette's pragmatic example. "She's a happy woman ... You, too, must abandon the illusion you believe to be life itself." Ouch! But it becomes apparent soon enough that Prunier's real agenda is that of a broker; he admits that he is visiting on a mission, and on behalf of someone else. He doesn't mention Rambaldo by name, but the implication is obvious.

With mocking indifference, he turns to Lisette and bids a permanent good-bye to the accompaniment of the static E-flat waltz theme that likewise served to disclose his liaison with Lisette at the conclusion of act 1. History repeats itself, because only moments later, taking her aside, he inquires as to what time she will be free that evening. "Ten o'clock," she says. He assures her that Lisette he will be waiting. Eager to get started, she dons her maid's apron and promptly returns to her domestic duties.

A breathless and excited Ruggero, with a letter in hand, enters the diminishing fray, though Prunier has already left, his dignity intact. His mother has consented to the marriage, and he implores Magda to read her letter aloud. Here, Puccini reintroduces the pulsating love theme from the beginning of act 1. But in her reading of the letter from Ruggero's mother, an extended arioso that avails itself of a dignified new theme in F major ("Essa sia benedetta se la manda il Signore ... ch'essa sara la madre dei tuoi figli ... Donale il bacio mio!"—May she be blessed if the Lord has sent her ... she will be the mother of your children ... Give her a kiss from me), Magda softens the prevailing mood. The music, too, melts into a reverent hush, evoking the tender affection of a mother whose love for her children is unencumbered by limits or conditions.

Moved but still resolved, Magda is mortified and, in rejecting Ruggero's proposal, and his mother's acceptance, confesses her unworthiness as a consequence of her torrid past. Ruggero protests that it doesn't matter, saying further that there is no need for elaboration. But Magda cannot bear the thought of deceiving the man she loves and begs him to understand: "Trionfando son passata tra la vergogna e l'oro!" (I have passed in triumph between shame and gold!). Even her implicit offer to remain his lover, if not his wife, is met with resistance; Ruggero's values are those of a provincial conservative, no match for Magda's roving cosmopolitanism.

Melodrama prevails as a distraught Ruggero, now reduced to a bundle of insecurities, launches the final duet between them, "Ma come puoi lasciarmi se mi struggo in pianto?" (But how can you leave me when I'm riven by tears?). The melodic material here, marked "Andante mosso appassionato," is new and, with the exception of the descending pattern in its first bar, proceeds largely upward in whole tones and minor thirds. Cast in 4/4, it resists both the substance and spirit of a waltz, as no such inference at this point would be either appropriate or acceptable; there is neither time nor reason for a dance when magic has flown. Ruggero pleads with Magda not to break his heart as she confesses that no other solution is possible. Magda is not unmoved, but simply resolved in her determination to take flight so as not to bring shame and ruin on Ruggero.

Unlike Manon Lescaut, who wore her real feelings and ambitions very much on her sleeve, Magda clings to an ersatz morality, all the while deluding herself into believing that, by abandoning a lover to whom she has made a commitment, she has not already brought him ruin. From this perspective, though she has convinced herself that she has taken the moral high road, she is no different than any other femme fatale. With this, Magda's audacity allows her to reinvent herself; stroking his hair, she compares herself to a mother addressing her son. On the surface, Magda's entreaty is a model of familial sincerity, as if she were merely attempting to persuade Ruggero to see things her way. But a darker, perhaps more lurid interpretation is also possible. That Puccini left this disclosure to the final moments of the opera is stunning indeed, in that what promised to be a comedy has in fact been transformed to the most dismal sort of tragedy, where death is not even a factor. What is worse, after all, than life without hope, or living a lie? True to his ambiguous feelings about women, Puccini twists the knife, indicting Magda for what she really is, cannot escape, and is destined to remain. Bells toll as she alights on an ethereally high A-flat and walks off into the crepuscular shadows on the arm of Lisette, leaving an inconsolable Ruggero to wail the curtain down.

Il trittico: Il tabarro, Suor Angelica, Gianni Schicchi

Il tabarro (The Cloak)

Characters	Voice Type
Michele, a barge owner	Baritone
Giorgetta, Michele's wife	Soprano
Luigi, a stevedore	Tenor
Tinca ("tench"), a stevedore	Tenor
Talpa ("mole"), a stevedore	Bass
La Frugola ("the ferret"), Talpa's wife	Mezzo-soprano
Stevedores, a ballad seller, midinettes, an organ grinder, two lovers	

In one act. Libretto by Giuseppe Adami, based on Didier Gold's play *La Houppelande*. The first performance of the three one-act operas of *Il trittico* (The Triptych) took place at the Metropolitan Opera House, New York, December 14, 1918.

The opening scene of *Il tabarro* will strike a familiar chord with anyone who has been to Paris. The Seine, that vast urban waterway that has long been an emblem of romance, serves as the background here, and like so many other Puccinian sets, it is a character in its own right. Along the banks, artists and merchants hawk their paintings and rare books, while passersby and lovers, taking in the sunset, breathe in the hovering scents, which in the spring and summer haunt the city. Here aromas mingle effortlessly, as the scent of espresso mixes with that of freshly baked bread and a hint of garlic. The dull laps of the Seine mimic breaking waves, their persistent pulsations in turn complementing the prevailing fragrance. The flying buttresses of

Notre Dame articulate the skyline, while rows of plane trees in bloom vibrate in the breeze that embraces them.

The opening is an extended prelude of sorts, a lyrical barcarolle set in 12/8 time that represents the quiescent but powerful undulations of the Seine. An ascent of chords played by the strings proceeds in *pianississimo* above a gentle stream of staccato triplets, creating the impression of that majestic river's perpetual ebb and flow. As the sonority expands, a car horn and siren impart to the prevailing serenity a site- appropriate realism that is authentic verismo.

Dotting the Seine are innumerable barges, which, though securely anchored, seem to linger precariously, as if they might float away at any moment. Most of them double as businesses and private residences, a style of living favored by the both the working class and the bohemian-minded rich. The barge at the center of *Tabarro* is a neat but rugged affair, if not exactly a model of haute-bourgeois decorum. Geraniums and other potted plants peer out from every corner, that is, when not obscured by a string of laundry wavering to and fro on an improvised string of ropes. The boat's flat roof doubles as a terrace, where two caged canaries, their matinal song already the day's history, coo to each other.

On the bank an aging workhorse, already exhausted from hauling a heavy load, stands stoically. Large bags of cement surround and even abut the horse cart as sweating stevedores come and go, their backs burdened by the weight of their dusty cargo. The gangplank that links the quay to the barge is the conduit of their labors, as they fill up the hold. In this opera, all gangplanks lead to their employers, the gruff Michele, who is the barge's proprietor, and his coquettish wife, Giorgetta.

As Michele admires the sunset, Giorgetta busies herself with quotidian chores: watering plants, taking down the laundry, and looking after the canaries. His pipe having gone out, Michele asks Giorgetta for a kiss, but her cool response is to offer one cheek, not her lips. Bored with her life and with her husband, her sympathies drift instead toward the three hard-working stevedores, whom Michele, at Giorgetta's urging, invites onboard for a drink. The barcarolle motives are richly amplified and exfoliate in the background. The boorish Tinca and Talpa accept gladly, as does the handsome and strapping Luigi, who summons a nearby organ grinder. Giorgetta dashes inside for the wine and returns just about as quickly.

Luigi toasts his mates to the accompaniment of a brisk oscillation in 3/4 time, which is then appropriated by Tinca and Talpa. ("Eccola la passata! Ragazzi, si beve!"—Here's the round! Lads, we're drinking!) As the wine flows, so does a dance, but Tinca and Talpa are all left feet. Giorgetta claims to understand only dance music; here, a sparse string accompaniment harbors an odd "hobbling" motive, carried by the strings in staccato. It is only four bars long and is periodically punctuated with quarter-rests. Its context here is a bit inebriated, as if unsure of itself. But its later incarnations become something duplicitous and sinister. The organ-grinder's waltz supplants it, a curious bitonal melody that sounds out of tune, played by clarinets, flutes, and an organ, which flesh it out in an unsettling pastiche. Indeed, the music here looms like a happy moment for a sad clown. Luigi steps in with deft assurance to sweep Giorgetta off her feet, but no sooner do they begin their fateful tango than Michele returns, moody and indifferent.

Michele dismisses the organ grinder. Giorgetta barely hides her annoyance with Michele. Within a few days they will leave the quay, but will the stevedores, particularly Luigi, accompany them? No, says Michele, his demeanor already showing the strain of jealous mistrust. Just then, a song peddler emerges on the opposite side of the Seine. Following the song peddler is an odd little man with a small harp strung across his back. He sings of spring and those who died for love ("Primavera, primavera"), which he buttons up with an abbreviated citation, in both music and text of Mimì's "Mi chiamano" from *La bohème* ("È la storia di Mimì"—That's the story of Mimì). A small chorus of dressmakers echoes the song in thirds. As he sings of an ill-fated lover affair, Michele returns from the hold to the barge, deaf to his wife's entreaties for attention. As the song peddler intones his weary song in the distance, Giorgetta asks Michele what is bothering him. Her declines to respond, instead turning away.

With the arrival of Talpa's wife, Frugola ("Se tu sapessi"—If you knew), the mood darkens. Her name, which is Italian for "ferret," is nothing if not an operatic leveler of her character; Frugola is a scavenger, an operatic bag lady. Her music is edgy, fast-paced, roughly accentuated, impatient, and even vulgar; the exaggerated consonants and sputtered R's lend to her voice the veracity of a virago. Her laugh is no less lusty. She boasts her jealousy that her husband inspires, and has come to take him home. On her arm is a large, tattered old bag into which she has thrown all kinds of objects, some useful, some not. She offers Giorgetta a comb as she sings to distraction about laces and velvets, discarded relics, and her tabby cat in a transitional piece in 3/8 time that avails itself of parallel chords and modal harmonies. There is a jagged, overbearing quality to Frugola's music; it is as if she is Puccini's antidote to lyricism.

Talpa, Tinca, and Luigi resurface, accompanied by the opening barcarolle motive, car horn and all. Talpa initiates the dialogue with a cynical disparagement of his wife. ("To'! Guarda la mia vecchia"—Ho! Look at my old woman!) Michele, drawn in by the camaraderie, changes his mind and asks Luigi to work for him again the next day, then leaves again without saying a word to Giorgetta. Citing the insistent gyration of Luigi's earlier drinking song, Tinca bemoans his lot, paying tribute to the glories of drink; there is no better place to drown one's misery than in spirits. His dialogue here is enriched, too, by a horn that sounds as drunk as he is. It's better not to think, says Tinca before emptying his glass and emitting a round of razor-sharp laughter. Luigi agrees, his ensuing arioso a tribute to the inequities and hardships of a laborer's life. ("Hai ben ragione; meglio non pensare"—You're quite right; it's better not to think.) Though a citation of the lyrical second half of the Seine (barcarolle) theme informs its middle section, it is nearly all declamation, as if to impart to this particular dockworker a hard and cynical view of life's vicissitudes.

Two daydreams coincide when Frugola throws herself into an image of domestic bliss, envisioning a house in the country ("Ho sognato una casetta"—I've been dreaming of a cottage), in rapid staccato declamation over a sparse patina of pizzicato strings, harp, and woodwinds. Just as Frugola concludes, Giorgetta takes over, her earthy soprano giving voice to a vigorous ascending figure as she pines for suburban life far away from the barge ("È ben altro il mio sogno!"—My dream is quite different!). Indeed, the "flight" motive she intones here won't be grounded, nor will it settle for oscillation; instead, it soars upward and away the moment it begins. Here, Luigi and Giorgetta find common ground as their voices join, astride Giorgetta's flight motive in a brass-heavy paean to provincialism: it seems they both hail from the same Parisian suburb, Belleville. Frugola and Talpa, perhaps inspired, leave arm in arm singing airily of their dream home, to the accompanying patter of Frugola's "cottage" theme.

Here, an offstage soprano and tenor voice intone wordless vowels. This moment more or less divides the opera in two, as if it were about to introduce a second act. And although its transitional function is assured, it does not rise to the level of an interlude.

While Luigi and Giorgetta proclaim the arduous passions that they've secretly enjoyed with each other long before the opera began ("O, Luigi! Luigi!"), Michele lurks nearby. The hobbling motive takes on new significance here, alluding to the secrecy and tension that link the pair in their grand deception. Arriving on deck, Michele is astonished and perhaps dismayed to see Luigi is still onboard. But Luigi, fearing he will be unable to hide his feelings for Giorgetta much longer, asks Michele to let him off at Rouen. Common sense dissuades him when Michele informs him there is no work to be found there. Luigi reluctantly agrees to stay on the barge as Michele bids them good night ("Buona notte") and retires to the cabin. As he does, a new motivic fragment announces itself in the brass: it is nothing more than a rising minor scale, yet it remains an unnerving undercurrent that is a thematic emblem of Giorgetta's fear of Michele.

With her husband gone, Luigi and Giorgetta again avow their love and their determination to flee together to a better life. Luigi agrees to return in an hour. A sheen of string tremolos, punctuated by timpani, serves to heighten the tension here. Indeed, the hobbling motive that was once merely an invitation to a dance now assumes a dangerous character as it rumbles below. To signal that Michele is asleep, Giorgetta will light a match and stand watch. A piccolo stands in for the flicker of a flame here.

Luigi expresses his impatience and jealousy of any man that would touch Giorgetta, including Michele. ("Folle di gelosia"—The madness of jealousy!) In support of his passion, a richly orchestrated hint of the ascending minor scale indicative of Giorgetta's fear pushes through, followed by a restatement of the hobbling motive, now inflated into a menacing *fortissimo* by the trombones.

No sooner does Luigi leave than Michele reappears, lantern in hand. A perturbed and puzzled Michele, wondering why Giorgetta has not retired for the evening, asks her why she no longer loves him. An ominous new motive, a placid variant of the hobbling motive, now transformed into a rolling 6/4, informs their duet. She demurs, saying she does, but that she can no longer bear being holed up in their little cabin. Only a year before, their lives together were happy. And then came their infant son, the emblem of their devotion to each other, who died prematurely. Here Michele recycles the new variant of the hobbling motive with renewed passion and earnestness. ("Ora le notti son tanto fresche"—The evenings now are so cool.) He reminds her of the warmth she felt, huddled with him together in his large cloak. Here a prescient forecast of an ominous motive, representing the cloak, surfaces quietly; whether coincidentally or not, it bears a striking resemblance both in design and harmonic construction to the torture motive of *Tosca*'s act 2. And doesn't she remember how warm he kept her, bundled in the warmth of his cloak?

But the boy's death is not something Giorgetta cares to discuss. Their voices swell together in a brief but impassioned variant of the Seine motive, now given to the soloists and sung astride a fluid stream of eighth-notes in 6/4 time. ("Ora che non c'è più i miei capelli grigi mi sembrano un insulta alla tua gioventù"—Now that he's no longer here, my gray hair seems like an insult to your youth.) Distraught but not ready to give up, Michele draws her close and tries to embrace her. He implores her to come back to him, to love him again. But Giorgetta cannot be bothered; she is repulsed by his touch, saying simply, "Che vuoi! S'invecchia. Non son più la stessa" (What do you expect? People get older, and I'm not the same). She feigns fatigue, bids him good night, and goes into their cabin.

Michele is already livid. As he mutters, "Sgualdrina!" (Slut!) (CD Track 14), bitterly under his breath, a shadowy omen appears, in the form of two lovers walking by. The haunting refrain of a distant bugle call penetrates the silence atop a long and persistent pedal point. Though its nocturnal song to dim the lights is nothing more than the dutiful call of a sergeant at arms at a nearby barracks, it augurs something darker for Michele and Giorgetta. Setting the lamps in place, he returns to the cabin but doesn't go in. Instead, he peers through a crack, only to see Giorgetta waiting for something or someone. He wonders who it might be. Not Tinca, because he is a drunk. Not Talpa, because he is too old. And how could it be Luigi, who asked to be let go in Rouen? Here the "cloak" motive rears its head, intensified by the brass and supported by a recurring river of descending chromatic scales in the lower strings. ("Nulla! . . . Silenzio"—Nothing! . . . Silence!)

Michele lights his pipe as he sinks into a quiet rage. For Luigi, who cannot make out Michele's figure from the bank, that is the signal he has been waiting for. He rushes to the quay, along the gangplank, and onto the barge. Michele grabs him, seizing him by the throat. He confronts him, daring him to admit his affair, but Luigi denies it. Luigi counters with a knife, but Michele overpowers him ("Giù il coltello!"—Drop the knife!). As he strangles Luigi, Michele compels him to admit his love for Giorgetta. Four times he says it: "L'amo" (I love her); they are his final words as Michele twists the last breath out of him. He wraps Luigi in his cloak.

Giorgetta, sensing something is wrong, comes up on deck, where she sees Michele. String tremolandos rumble uncomfortably as she begs his forgiveness. He invites her to come closer and to take shelter under his cloak as she once did. Just then he opens it to reveal Luigi's limp, dead body. And as she does, Michele seizes her, pressing her face, flesh to flesh, against the limp corpse that, only minutes earlier, had been her lover. Giorgetta's scream pierces the prevailing horror, and in a *fortissimo* blast of brass, strings, and winds, the cloak motive, now made the sound of murder itself, brings the curtain down.

Suor Angelica (Sister Angelica)

Characters	Voice Type
Sister Angelica	Soprano
The princess, her aunt	Contralto
The abbess	Mezzo-soprano
The monitress	Mezzo-soprano
The mistress of the novices	Mezzo-soprano

Sister Genovieffa	Soprano
Sister Osmina	Soprano
Sister Dolcina	Soprano
The nursing sister	Mezzo-soprano
The alms sisters	Sopranos
The novices	Sopranos
The lay sisters	Sopranos and mezzo-sopranos

Offstage chorus of women, children, and men

In one act. Libretto by Giovacchino Forzano.

Sanctuary is the calling card of *Suor Angelica*. As the curtain opens, a chapel and a cloister come into view, and bells ring in a hazy hush. Beyond the cloister is a cemetery, which abuts a garden. A lonely fountain, surrounded by flowers, articulates the prevailing tranquility, its waters streaming joyously into its stony basin. The stage is empty save for a single shard of sunlight that penetrates the mist coming off the fountain. Giving voice to the overall quiescence is a wispy celeste, supported by a diaphanous halo of muted strings. Offstage, a choir of nuns sings the Ave Maria to the accompaniment of an organ. Two lay sisters join this blissful mix, entering the chapel from the courtyard. They are late for the Liturgy of the Hours but stop for a few minutes amid the cypresses to listen to the fading birdsong, which is delicately conveyed by piccolos as the sun sets.

On their heels is Sister (Suor) Angelica, the convent's resident gardener, who quietly throws open the chapel door and does the requisite penance for her tardiness. Closing the door behind her, she intones the prayer to the Madonna, which, in the household of Catholic ideology, will let her off the spiritual hook. The sister monitor, seeing that the two lay sisters had failed to follow Angelica's pious lead, roundly scolds them for the sin of hubris, or lack of humility, her nearly monodic admonitions quietly accompanied by woodwinds. ("Sorelle in umilità, mancaste alla quindena"—Sisters in humility, you failed to keep quindene.) In an act of imposed contrition, the lay sisters confess their sin and say a prayer, twenty times, for sinners and the afflicted.

As they leave, the sister monitor finds another victim to admonish, accusing Sister Osmina of stealing roses from the garden. She denies it, but to no avail, and is sent to her cell. As she leaves, six of the sisters intone a prayer, "Regina virginum, ora pro ea" (Queen of Virgins, pray for her). The motivic fragment that informs it, an emblem of the Virgin Mary, is a procession of triads in a dotted rhythm set astride muted trumpets.

The mood shifts as the sister monitor tells the sisters to enjoy themselves. Just then, Sister Genovieffa draws attention to something of a celestial sign, an event that is explained by the mistress of novices: Three times a year, in the evening, the sun casts its light on the fountain in such a way as to turn its waters the color of gold. Her brief arioso is a lighter-than-air confection, spun out over alternating pizzicato chords colored by high woodwinds. ("O sorelle, sorelle, io voglio rivelarvi"— Oh, sisters, sisters, I want to tell you.) For reasons left unexplained, this atmospheric event throws the sisters into silence, bringing to their collective mind a memory of a fallen comrade, Sister Bianca Rosa, whose tomb lies in the convent. Together, they resolve to sprinkle her tomb with this holiest of holy waters. A brief but supple new motive, embodying the fluidity of the water, surfaces within the ensuing dialogue; it is a sequence of eighth-notes followed by two sixteenths.

Here the nuns touch on forbidden fruit: desire. Angelica reminds all that the sublimation of desire is the provenance of the Virgin Mother, who nips it in the bud before it can even begin; this alone gives her every reason to extol death as life made more beautiful. Her mellifluous arioso elaborates a sentiment of benevolence, with a consequence that evokes, with its steady dotted rhythms, the Virgin Mary motive. The monitor rejects desire altogether, whether in life or in death. All but two deny they harbor so much as a single desire; Sister Genovieffa dissents, claiming she has a simple wish, and that is to see and stroke a lamb, while Sister Dolcina likewise pipes up. But the other nuns have already guessed: Sister Dolcina wants only food. The music remains playful, throughout, its lightly scored motivic profusions punctuated by amiable choral interjections.

Querying Angelica on her position, they are greeted with another resounding denial. Suor Angelica brusquely but firmly denies having any such feelings. The nuns are not pleased; surely, Angelica has lied. After all, she has not seen or heard a word from her family in more than seven years, and it is precisely their absence that compels her to desire. She wants to see them. Thus in denying her disposition, Angelica has sinned. Huddling together, the other sisters speak among themselves of her privileged past as a proud and wealthy aristocrat, and her exile to a convent as punishment for an offense to which they are not privy.

Enter the infirmary sister, whose hastiness is equaled only by her hysteria and panic. She reports that Sister Chiara has suffered a minor but painful catastrophe; a swarm of wasps has attacked her. The infirmary sister begs Angelica to fashion an herbal remedy, and she complies, whipping up a brew with exceptional rapidity and prescribing its application. ("Ecco, quest'è calenzola"—Here, this is spurge.)

As she does, two alms-collecting sisters, their benevolence all aglow, come through with a donkey, its rough gray rump made the bearer of all manner of chattel. Here, Puccini proves that Mendelssohn was not the only composer capable of codifying a donkey's neigh; a patch of screeching strings and woodwinds imitates its hee-haw. If the "alms sisters" sound like a 1950s pop group, they are not; their purpose, other than serving the poor, is to supply the convent with what it needs or, should we say, desires. These all-too-giving women assuage the sisters in goodwill, passing among them oils, currants, flour, hazelnuts, cakes, and lentils, and thus sending them into a frenzy of—well, of *desire*. The musical invention that informs Sister Dolcina's mention of currants ("Un tralcetto di ribes"—A little bunch of currants) sports a bizarre but highly decorative interjection of a dotted figure, segregated from orchestra and singers and distinguished by a solo flute, oboe, and violin.

One of the alms bearers has left along with the donkey. But the other inquires as to whose gilded carriage is waiting outside the convent. Angelica is beside herself; she suspects she may have a visitor and that the carriage belongs to the family that has abandoned her. The musical pace quickens. A bell signals that a visitor has arrived, sending Angelica into spasms of anxiety. Here, Angelica introduces a lengthy new thematic figure in A minor, though the key signature, with one flat, suggests something entirely different; its eighth- and double dotted eighth-notes ardently expressing her burgeoning agony.

Here, the abbess enters, a model of asceticism in her own right; she is the female version of the Emperor Altoum in *Turandot*. Angelica, her

nerves on end, implores the abbess to give her information, telling her
how long she has waited for this moment and how she has sacrificed so
much to the Virgin by way of penance. ("Madre, Madre, parlate!"—
Oh, Mother, Mother, speak!) But her entreaty succeeds only in drawing
down the abbess's stern disapproval for behavior that the Church looks
upon as both selfish and impertinent. The other sisters offer up a prayer
for Angelica to the suave and consoling accompaniment of the "water"
motive. Even so, the *abbessa*, intoning a single pitch with a focus as
heartless as Turandot's introduction of the riddles, goes on to announce
the visitor as the princess, Angelica's aunt. (Can it be a coincidence that
she lands with such rigid assurance on the word "Principessa," spitting
it out with no less authority?) As she does, a haunting but significant
new motivic fragment both anticipates the princess's entrance and will
come to be identified with her. It is an ascent of two minor thirds and
a fourth in eighth-notes that hemorrhages mysteriously into a mysterious foreign tonality and stays put there on a single chord, played by the
horns, for some six and a half beats.

   In this convent, every sister has her duty, be it sacred or mundane.
A porter sister—that's the nun whose sole job is to open doors for
others—ushers Angelica into the visiting room. Here, a tall, autocratic
woman breezes in as if she were the mother superior herself, but her
function in life is entirely sectarian. She ambles toward Angelica only
with difficulty, all the while currying the support of her ebony cane.
She stops, as if surprised by the sight of her niece the nun. She petri-
fies Angelica in her icy gaze. But Angelica holds her ground, at least for
the moment, given that she is under the surveillance of the abbess. The
princess holds out her hand, not in friendship or reconciliation, but as
a gesture of haughty defiance, and with no little repugnance; Angelica
kisses her hand and once again falls to her knees. Though Angelica, her
big doe eyes by now a reservoir of foolish tears, looks imploringly and
with sympathy at the princess, it does no good. Her aunt could care
less and fixes her own stare straight ahead.

   The issue is money, naturally; the princess, portrayed by a robust
contralto, prevails stubbornly upon Angelica to sign away her inheritance; Angelica's sister, Anna Viola, is about to be married, and as
executor of the estate of their parents, who died twenty years earlier, it

is up to the princess to divide the spoils. ("Il Principe Gualtiero vostro padre"—Prince Gualtiero, your father.) The princess, who cuts a figure far more stony and repressed than any nun, is adamantine; her real agenda is vendetta. She demands that Angelica atone for the disgrace she has brought on her family's honor and twists the knife by telling her that she envisions the laments of Angelica's long-dead mother. A succession of rising fourths, set to a relentless rhythm in dotted eighths, here forms a new motivic fragment that delineates the princess's own brand of lament, stony though it may be. Accompanied by a spate of soft woodwinds, the princess's severe admonition is largely declamation on a single pitch that migrates upward and downward into an expressive melodic contour en route to its conclusion.

A humbled Angelica confesses, to the woodwind accompaniment of the Virgin Mary motive, that there is only one concession she cannot make: to entirely forget about the son she bore those seven years ago. What does he look like now, she asks? How is he? Here Puccini introduces yet another motive, a chromatically inflected funeral march that proffers as a dotted motive preceded by a rush of sixteenths, which are rhythmically organized as a group of six notes within a single beat. ("Tutto ho offerto alla Vergine, sì, tutto"—I have offered everything up to the Virgin, yes, everything.) The princess responds in silence, as the music, too, is momentarily extinguished; the boy became ill with fever two years earlier and died. Devastated, Angelica collapses in heaving, inconsolable sobs. The princess declines to help her up, but lowers her head instead in prayer.

Here, the sister porter, as if on cue, enters the room with an oil lamp, which she sets down. She leaves but returns only moments later with the abbess, a pen, and a writing table. As Angelica signs the legal papers, the sisters take hurry off. Only now does the princess approach her niece with a modicum of warmth, but Angelica sees fit, at that moment, only to return the cruel patina that accompanies her aunt's austerity. The princess raps on the door with her cane and is ushered out by the sister porter. She looks back one more time at Angelica, her face a mixed palette of pity and contempt.

Her world of pious sacrifice now made little more than an ocean of regrets, Angelica bemoans her child's fate and that he had to die without the comforts of his mother—or even knowing that she loved him. She imagines his presence, endowing it with a visceral intensity. Her poignant but lengthy aria here ("Senza mamma, o bimbo, tu sei morto"—Without your mother, my baby, you died) elaborates the "agony" motive that greeted the princess's arrival at the convent. The orchestration is pure Puccini: a ravishing penetration of soft strings, augmented by a harp, and the emergence of a solo violin that wails plaintively at climactic moments. The coterie of sisters has not forgotten her; coming in from the garden, they surround and comfort her. Together they sing the praises of celestial paradise to the strains of a simple, ascending diatonic progression and then, one by one, retire to their respective rooms.

By now dusk has turned into night, and Angelica's room is filled with moonlight that is only dimly disturbed by the rows of cypresses visible from her windows. An expressive intermezzo ensues, its musical capital informed by a melodic sequence from Angelica's "agony" motive, here introduced by a solo cello. She leaves her cell and, with shrewd discernment, gathers some stones and dry twigs, places them in a bowl, and fills it with water from the fountain. These she boils over a crudely made fire, adding to its bubbling mixture a few special herbs, each of them poison. In her melancholy "Aria dei fiori" (Aria of the Flowers) (CD Track 15), she pays homage to her beloved flowers, which will now kill her. ("Suor Angelica ha sempre una ricetta buona fatta con fiori"— Sister Angelica always has a good recipe made with flowers.) She bids a silent farewell to her sisters and to the chapel, all the while thinking of her dead son. For this, Puccini again issues the noble dotted motive that augmented her paean to the ills of desire early on in the opera ("I desideri sono i fiori dei vivi"—Desires are the flowers of the living), now poised over tensely over a dominant pedal point. Leaning against a cypress, she drinks the poison but, as she does, is jarred by her own actions. Echoes of the funeral march, associated with her dead son, give way to a recall of the Virgin Mary motive. Suicide will surely condemn her to hell, if not of her own making, then one imposed by Christian ideology, and thus separate her from spending eternity with her son.

In soulful prayer, she begs forgiveness, imploring the Mother of God to embrace her in salvation. An offstage choir pours in while Angelica looks for a sign. With that, a miracle occurs. A piano and trumpets complement the offstage evocation of the Virgin Mary motive: a mysterious light illuminates the chapel, and angels, their bilious wings aflutter, materialize in droves. The Virgin Mary, described in the libretto as the Queen of Solace, comes into view, just behind a small blond child dressed in white. As the child moves toward the dying Angelica, the choir extols the glory of the Virgin. Angelica dies, the light fades, and the curtain closes.

Gianni Schicchi

Characters	Voice Type
Gianni Schicchi	Baritone
Lauretta, his daughter	Soprano
Zita, cousin of Buoso Donati	Contralto
Rinuccio, Zita's nephew	Tenor
Gherardo, Buoso's nephew	Tenor
Nella, Gherardo's wife	Soprano
Gherardino, their son	Soprano or treble
Betto di Signa, Buoso's brother-in-law	Bass
Simone, cousin of Buoso	Bass
Marco, Simone's son	Baritone
La Ciesca, Marco's wife	Mezzo-soprano
Maestro Spinelloccio, a doctor	Bass
Ser Amantio di Nicolao, a notary	Baritone
Pinellino, a cobbler	Bass
Guccio, a dyer	Bass

Opera Buffa in one act. Libretto by Giovacchino Forzano based on "Commentary of the Divine Comedy by an Anonymous Florentine of the Fourteenth Century" (first published in 1866), inspired by the thirtieth canto of Dante's *Inferno*.

In this comedy of errors and buoyant music, the finale of *Il trittico*'s three one-act operas, we find ourselves in thirteenth-century Florence. The year is 1299, and it is nine o'clock in the morning. Poor old Buoso Donati, a wealthy Florentine aristocrat, has just died, and his bedroom,

which is bathed in sunlight and candle smoke, is the centerpiece of the
stage. To the left of the bedroom is a large door, and beyond that, an
elaborate staircase leads to a landing. Looking farther, a pair of glass
doors opens onto a broad wraparound terrace that abuts a wooden
trestle. Another picture window overlooks Arnolfo's Tower. The bedroom and its adjoining space is a minefield of hidden crevices; there is
a hatch under the stairs and, to its right, another staircase, yet another
door, and a gallery. Surrounding Donati's canopy bed are candles, while
a set of heavy velvet drapes hang glumly, obscuring the body, which is
covered in a blanket.

As his greedy (but not immediate) family of nine gathers around and
offers prayers in faux-pious supplication, their shallow facades disclose
their insincerity. Their indeterminate moans and wails are heard on
the heels of a brusque and brass-rich opening fanfare in 3/4 time that
is defined by a descending sequence of slurred duplets. This motive,
insistent and pedestrian, serves as a kind of ostinato through much of
the opening scene. Meanwhile, the seven-year-old Gherardino, the son
of Buoso's nephew Gherardo, has spread himself languidly on the floor.
He is bored and, instead of paying his respects, plays a game of marbles.
Elsewhere, Marco, the son of Buoso's cousin Simone, along with his
wife, La Ciesca, and another cousin, the sixty-year-old Zita (also known
as La Vecchia), noisily mourns Donati's passing while snickering under
their breath. A brief motivic oscillation of slurred descending duplets,
successively played by a flute, an oboe, and the strings, insinuates itself
periodically, as if to offer a caustic commentary on the unfolding events.
A fragmentary consequent, comprising two sixteenths slurred to a
quarter-note, followed by a dotted-eighth duplet, rises and falls over
a bar and a half. This quiet fragment will likewise prove motivically
valuable, as it carries within itself the character of a private thought,
like an impassive observation by some unseen observer.

Betto of Signa, Buoso's brother-in-law and a poor relation, cuts a
sordid figure in his wholly apocryphal consternation, while Gherardo
and his wife, Nella, vie for their own place as the most persuasive
mourners. Zita's nephew Rinuccio is likewise a bundle of bad intentions. As their collective—though ersatz—sadness turns into a comical

competition, Gherardino knocks over a chair, interrupting their litany of phony prayers with a rude thud.

Amid all this, Betto of Signa circulates a rumor, in a buzz of indiscreet whispers, that Buoso hasn't left a penny to any of them but instead bequeathed his estate to the friars of a local monastery. Suddenly, all their tears run dry as mourning turns to panic. What can they do? Here, everyone turns for counsel to the seventy-year-old Simone, who was once the mayor of Fucecchio and thus is the most politically savvy among them. A man of facts but not flight, he sees things in black and white; if Buoso gave his will to a lawyer, it is too late, and there is nothing anyone can do to change it. If, on the other hand, his will is in the house, there is still a chance that something could be done, albeit illegally.

Their futures in peril, they turn the house upside-down in a desperate effort to find the will. Rinuccio, in a tenuous aside, mutters that his amorous plans with Gianni Schicchi's daughter Lauretta depend on the will. Here the opening fanfare motive takes flight, in a swift but light tumble representative of urgency as the family begins its scramble to find it. ("No, non è"—No, it isn't there.) Meanwhile, on another side of the room, Betto eyes a silver serving dish and surreptitiously extends his hand to steal it and the various items on it. No one notices, but he drops it when it Zita claims to have found the will. It is no more than a false alarm; she has not, so the chaos intensifies. This coterie of avaricious ne'er-do-wells ransack the room, running amok and into each other as they empty cabinets, turn over drawers, and throw books and papers quite literally to the wind. Just as they passed the rumor, one to the other, in rapid succession, and then hurled the detritus and chattel of the rooms into the air, now they embroil themselves in one false alarm after the other.

At last, Rinuccio finds the will tucked away in a drawer upstairs. Confident that they will all be rich, he asks his aunt Zita for permission to marry Lauretta on May 1, also known as May Day. This he bellows forth to an expansive new theme in 6/8 time, representative of his love for Laura. ("Mi sembrerà più dolce il mio redaggio potrei sposarla per Calendimaggio"—My inheritance will seem sweeter if I can marry her on May Day.) Zita's response, as she grabs the will from his clasping hand, is terse: He can marry whomever he pleases so long as things proceed as everyone now expects them to.

Here, Rinuccio sends Gherardino to fetch Gianni Schicchi and his daughter Lauretta. Zita cannot find the silver scissors to open the scroll containing the will, as Betto looks away. Giving up, she tears the ribbon from the scroll, only to find another parchment surrounding it. Accompanied by the lightly scored, bleating fragments of the two aforementioned motives, she unveils the will. The family members surround her in breathless anticipation, reading it to themselves in stunned silence. A stately, even reverent new motive of descending sixteenth-notes asserts itself in a conventional progression from tonic, to subdominant, to dominant, and back to the tonic. ("Zitti! È aperto!"—Quiet! It's open!)

As the strings vibrate in tremolo, thus heightening the tension, the family's faces pale. A solo oboe, its caustic oscillation spanning the two thirds that also complemented the opening motive, rears its head. Here it is repeated in ascending sequences. Buoso has left nothing of any lasting value to anyone in his family. If the bulk of his estate, which includes his house in Florence, his mills in Segna, and one stubborn mule, is the real prize, then no one has benefited. But as their eyes linger on the document, they discover the rumors were true; Buoso has left the friars his fortune.

With that, Simone extinguishes the candles, while everyone else contemplates what to do next. Rinuccio, dejected and confused, sees his one hope of living in luxury with the woman he loves go up in smoke. They complain bitterly that the friars' good fortune will become their undoing. A blistering bluster of individual complaints intersects, becoming a cacophony of bitter reproach. Their anger culminates in a raucous yelp attuned to a bright new motive, a swift descent of slurred quarter-note duplets blared out in unison by the brass and followed up by the strings, to which Puccini entrusts a slew of rapidly progressive, if disjointed, eighths. Just then their collective idea that it might be possible to alter the will in some way takes hold, but even the savvy Simone can find no solution.

But Rinuccio has already sorted it out. He recommends engaging the services of Gianni Schicchi, who is a provincial businessman well known for his astute sensibility. But the rest of the family demeans him and his daughter Lauretta as bumpkins and commoners unworthy of the attentions of the Donati family. Zita wants nothing to do with Schicchi. Rinuccio knows better. In an extended aria ("Avete torto. È fine, astutuo"—You're mistaken. He's crafty, astute), he reminds them of what a cunning and clever fellow Schicchi is and claims that he is their only hope; here Schicchi's confidence and winning ways are represented by Rinuccio, in anticipation of his future father-in-law's appearance, by a broad succession of major and minor chords in triplets. He expands into a broad and effusive tribute to Florence itself, in the form of a soaring *stornello*, a traditional Tuscan song ("Firenze è come un albero fiorito"—Florence is like a tree in flower), lightly ornamented by an abbreviated forecast of Lauretta's celebrated aria "O mio babbino caro," her endearing avowal of love for Rinuccio. Despite his entreaty, his relatives reject the idea out of hand; Schicchi is nothing more than a peasant, they protest, and hardly a man in their collective aristocratic league.

Here, Gianni Schicchi and Lauretta arrive, their presence surrounded in the subtle halo of the "O mio babbino caro" motive. Taking a look around, Schicchi is astounded by the sour expressions on everyone's faces. While Rinuccio and Lauretta engage in small talk, Schicchi makes his way into the bedroom. To the accompaniment of the tendentious opening motive in gasping duplets, Schicchi eyes Buoso's unattended cadaver surrounded by candles. Even so, he encourages the deceased's greedy entourage to look on the bright side. ("In questo mondo una cosa si perde, una si trova."—In this world you lose one thing, you find another.) That hardly amuses Zita, who now must admit to being disinherited along with the rest of the family. Her tone is shrill and set astride the boisterous sixteenth-note motive that earlier bespoke the will. She demands that Schicchi leave at once and that he take his daughter with him; after all, she has no dowry, so what good is she to her nephew Rinuccio? Lauretta objects, telling her father in earnest that her feelings for Rinuccio are sincere, while Schicchi himself sneers at Zita for her selfishness and accuses her of sacrificing the young couple for mere material gain. ("Brava la vecchia! . . . Vecchia taccagna! Stillina!"—Well done, old woman . . . Old skinflint! Miser!) Lauretta and Rinuccio swear their love for each other while Zita holds firm in her refusal to see the union through, so long as no one has any money.

In a spirited quartet, Zita and Schicchi continue to argue bitterly as Rinuccio and Lauretta, refusing to let this bump compromise their happiness, give voice to their young dreams to the intermittent melodic strains of Rinuccio's earlier stornello. The family chirps in, rising up in a chorus of voices, which urge everyone to think of the will. Schicchi has had enough, and he darts for the door with his daughter in hand. Rinuccio stands in his way, begging him to help. But Schicchi, pointing his finger at Zita and the rest, refuses ("A pro di quella gente? Niente, niente, niente!"—For these people? No, no, no!). Only his daughter Lauretta's intervention convinces him to reconsider, with an arching but tender entreaty that became one of Puccini's most celebrated and beloved ariettas. ("O mio babbino caro, mi piace, è bello"—Oh, dear Daddy, I like him, he's handsome.) (CD Track 16) With the strings and a harp providing a gentle, diaphanous accompaniment to an exceptionally rich, sympathetic, and opulently harmonized melody—its entirely symmetrical phrases lending to it something Puccini denies all the other arias in the work, that is, the autonomy of an independent song—Lauretta threatens to throw herself off the Ponte Vecchio and into the Arno River if she cannot marry Rinuccio.

A moved and sympathetic Schicchi, giving way to his daughter amid a marchlike progression of bassoons, horns, and strings that echo the uneasy oscillation in thirds of the opening, demands to see the will. He reads it, evaluates it, and contemplates its efficacy and consequences. "Niente da fare!" (No way out!), he sings against an abbreviated punctuation of trumpets and to the desolate looks of his daughter and Rinuccio. The lovers, losing hope, soar upward in unison with a reminiscence of their love theme, the original incarnation of which was earlier entrusted solely to Rinuccio in "Mi sembrerà più dolce." But here the words melt into quite a different sentiment: "Addio, speranza bella, dolce miraggo!" (Farewell to our bright hopes, our sweet mirage!). But a moment later, things change with Schicchi's utterance of a most portentous "Però!" (However!); with that single exclamation, Lauretta and Rinuccio see their renewed hope for a May wedding burgeoning on the horizon, their song palpitating with expectation as the tempo accelerates. ("Forse ci sposeremo per il Calendimaggio!"—Perhaps we shall be able to marry on May Day!)

Sending Lauretta out on the terrace to feed the birds (represented here by a bright if swooping flute), so as not to make her privy to his labyrinthine plot, Schicchi gathers the Donati family around him and breaks into a wicked smile. He queries everyone as to the disposition of the body. If no one has been told that Buoso has died, then keep it that way, he tells them. Everyone pledges silence. Still, he expresses some concern about the servants. Haven't *they* seen the body? Zita assures him they have not and that no one else other than family members has even entered the room since Buoso's death.

His confidence restored, Schicchi instructs Marco and Gherardo to move the body to the next room. But just as they get under way, Spinelloccio, Buoso's doctor, knocks on the door. With the corpse now removed, the women hurriedly make up the bed. The family delays the doctor, telling him that Buoso is resting, opening the door only a bit. Meanwhile, Schicchi makes himself scarce, hiding behind the drapes. To darken the room, Betto closes the shutters. Informing all this convivial tension and uneasy repartee is a melodyless rhythmic pulsation of darkened strings and a side drum. The ruse now in play, they admit the doctor, who asks to see his patient. At first, everyone stands in his way. But suddenly, to everyone's astonishment, Schicchi speaks up; he has taken up position on the bed, behind its lavish drapes, and responds to the doctor in a perfect imitation of Buoso. Betto is so shaken that he drops the silver tray he lifted. Against the perpetual rhythmic patina of the strings, now lightly colored by the woodwinds and slightly expanded into mysterious, if intermittent, harmonic progressions, Schicchi-cum-Buoso assures Spinelloccio that he feels just fine. He just wants to take it easy. The doctor, his wizened voice a lightly accented, comedic nasal drawl (an exaggerated affectation of the Bolognese way of speaking), is impressed with his patient's progress and, thus satisfied, leaves.

With the coast clear, Schicchi emerges from behind the drapes. Light pours in as Betto reopens the shutters. "Era uguale la voce?" (Was my voice like his?), Schicchi asks. Though they assure him it was, as the succession of major chords echoes the earlier motive of Schicchi's success (given voice by Rinuccio in "Avete torto"), no one in the room understands what the point was. An impatient Schicchi explains it to a roomful of expectant onlookers who he deems to be little more than idiots: if the doctor fell for his fraud, so will the notary, who will be told that Buoso has taken a turn for the worse, is dying, and needs to draw up a will. ("Ah, che zucconi!"—Oh, what blockheads!) Here, Schicchi's exasperated parlante relies largely on a single rather unremarkable motivic six-note fragment that oscillates upward in eighth-notes toward a sustained quarter-note on A-natural and then falls just as quickly back, again in eighths, to a sustained quarter-note on D.

Into this otherwise mundane motivic mix, which serves to emphasize Schicchi's crafty, schematic deliberations, Puccini interjects a recall of the breathless duplets that opened the opera. Continuing, Schicchi explains that the notary, upon his arrival, will find Schicchi enshrouded in dim light; and just as he did earlier, when the doctor came in, he will be in Buoso's bed, wearing the dead man's nightcap. This plan augurs a coy new arioso, emblematic of scheming, in a minor key that is defined by a tepid descent of eighth-notes sporadically separated by rests and accompanied in unison by delicate wisps of the woodwinds. It is also a melody that, for its sly humor and café-society ambience, is nothing if not reminiscent of the celebrated film music, composed decades later, of another remarkable Italian composer, Nino Rota. Satisfied that Schicchi is indeed Buoso, the notary will then sign off on the new will, Schicchi opines, and will find nothing in the least suspicious.

With this, the Donatis, impressed by Schicchi's ingenuity and seeing their wealth assured, embrace him, honoring him as they would a pope by kissing his hands. Their excitement is palpable in a flurry of staccato exhortations that praise Schicchi while nervously pressing Rinuccio to fetch the notary. But then from Simone's lips comes one especially pertinent question: How will the spoils be distributed? Schicchi nods in assent to the familial consensus that the estate be divided equally. The Donatis, with uninhibited self-assurance, now boast one to the other about the goods that will now be theirs; each lays claim to the parcel to which he—or she—believes he is entitled. Here Puccini codifies the interpersonal tension in a sequential pattern of stacked major and minor thirds, astride a sustained open fifth, that drifts downward and upward in 2/4 time. Simone boasts his seniority and claims the house, the mule, and the mills should, by default, go to him. No sooner do the words slip out of his mouth than his relatives, with Zita at their helm, shout him down in favor of their individual needs. ("No, no, no, no! Un momento"—No, no, just a moment!) Schicchi takes a certain wicked pleasure in their behavior, as it serves only to confirm this view that the Donatis covet goods more than love.

Like a bad omen, a funeral bell tolls in the distance. But how could anyone know of Buoso's death? Gherardo investigates, only to find out that it was merely coincidence: it tolled for someone else. ("Requiescat in pace"—Rest in peace.) Lauretta returns to the bedroom, but Schicchi promptly dispatches her back to the terrace with instructions to give the birds something to drink.

In a gesture of equanimity, Simone nominates Schicchi to determine how the estate will be divided. Everyone concurs as Schicchi puts on Buoso's nightclothes in anticipation of the notary. But here, each of the family members secretly tries to bribe him, to the accompaniment of Schicchi's humorous scheming motive, promising riches if he gives them what they want. "Sta bene!" (Very well!) he says, in mock assent. His words, convincing all that their assets are safe, give way to a harmonious lullaby of sorts, sung in Schicchi's honor by the three women, Zita, Nella, and Ciesca. ("Spogliati, bambolino"—Get undressed, baby boy.)

But just as he is about to take Buono's place on the bed, he issues a warning. The penalty for publishing a fraudulent will is exile and worse, dismemberment; the guilty will have a hand chopped off. ("Prima un avvertimento"—A warning first.) To the strain of a breezy, folksy new tune, a stornello in its own right, he taunts them with wicked words: "Addio, Firenze, addio, cielo divino, io ti saluto con questo moncherino" (Farewell, Florence, farewell, heavenly skies, I bid you adieu with this stump). Schicchi lets it sink in that they are all complicit and at risk. To demonstrate their solidarity, this gang of nine merely echoes his words.

Schicchi, a clever fellow, quickly takes his place in bed. To an echo of the "will" theme, Amantio, the notary, arrives with two witnesses, Pinellino and Guccio, in tow. He begins to avow Schicchi, whom he believes to be Buono. To make his impersonation even more convincing,

Schicchi offers a trembling hand while sheepishly protesting that it is the onset of paralysis, which makes it impossible for him to move. As the notary intones the preliminary Latin ("In Dei nomini, anno Dei nostri Jesu Christi"), Schicchi adds a codicil annulling any and all of Buono's preexisting wills. What's more, he allows only two florins for his funeral and bequeaths only a few lire to the friars, a decision that the notary questions. Thinking quickly, with the music reduced to a whisper and again set to the will theme, Schicchi says only that leaving a larger sum to the Church would only lead to suspicions that his wealth was no more than ill-gotten gain and would thus damage his posthumous reputation. So far, Buono's selfish relatives couldn't be more relieved and overjoyed. They nearly go into rapture when he orders his gold be divided equally among them and bequeaths the smaller estates at Fucecchio and Figline to Simone and Zita, respectively.

For the pièce de resistance, Schicchi, acting as Buoso, and to the accompaniment of a string tremolando, wills the mule and his house in Florence to his "great friend" Gianni Schicchi! Now the Donati family is furious, their familial tempest intensified astride an impatient chordal flurry drawn from the busy opening material of the opera, as well as Schicchi's "success" motive. As their mounting protests intensify to the cacophony of strings and brass, Schicchi sings his "stump" song, thus shutting them up most effectively. The notary, too, scolds the family for its inappropriate behavior. Finally Schicchi, his near-falsetto nasal squeal concealing his otherwise abundant baritone, awards himself the most valuable asset: the mills at Signa. With a generous wave of his arm and his double-cross a fait accompli, he orders Zita, to the tune of the stump song, to tip the witnesses and pay the notary. His hands a-tremble, he wishes the notary and his aids courage, and they in turn express their sorrow at the impending loss of such a great man. As they leave, Rinuccio makes a dash for the terrace, where he joins Lauretta.

The relatives attack Schicchi, calling him "Ladro, furfante, traditore!" (Thief, scoundrel, traitor!). Schicchi beats them back with Buoso's stick, gesticulating wildly and asserting his new rights as the homeowner. The family's call to arms is to steal whatever is in sight, be it linen or silver. Their battle continues, though by now the lot of them have gathered at the foot of the stairs, their spoils in hand.

But just then the glass doors swing open and Florence, awash in sunlit pastels and aquatints, emerges mirage-like in the distance. In the midst of all this natural beauty, Rinuccio and Lauretta stand in a passionate embrace. Rinuccio's "May Day" love theme for Lauretta now becomes a duet, as the lovers sing of the beauty that is Florence, a kind of paradise on earth, and evoke the memory of their first kiss. As they embrace again, Schicchi returns to his perch upstairs, his arms burdened with recovered loot. But it hardly impresses him; he throws it blithely onto the floor. The sight of his daughter with the man she loves touches him, and with that, he addresses the audience with this spoken (not sung!) sendoff:

"Tell me ladies and gentlemen, if Buoso's money could have had a better end than this. For this prank, they sent me to hell, and so be it; but with the permission of the great old man Dante, if you've been entertained this evening, allow me extenuating circumstances" (Ditemi voi, signori...). To the tune of his success motive, along with the bold blare of the brass and timpani, Schicchi claps his hands, takes a bow, and brings down the curtain.

Turandot

Characters	Voice Type
Princess Turandot	Soprano
The Emperor Altoum, her father	Tenor
Timur, the deposed king of Tartary	Bass
The unknown prince (Calaf), his son	Tenor
Liù, a slave girl	Soprano
Ping, lord chancellor	Baritone
Pang, majordomo	Tenor
Pong, chief of the imperial kitchen	Tenor
A Mandarin	Baritone
The prince of Persia	Tenor
The executioner (Pu-Tin-Pao)	Non-singing role

Imperial guards, the executioner's men, boys, priests, Mandarins, dignitaries, eight wise men (sages), Turandot's handmaids, soldiers, standard bearers, musicians, ghosts of suitors, crowd

In three acts. Libretto by Giuseppe Adami and Renato Simoni. Completed by Franco Alfano. Based on *Turandot* by Carlo Gozzi. Premiere at Teatro alla Scala, Milan, April 25, 1926.

Puccini's final opera, *Turandot*, may well have been for him what Beethoven's Ninth and Mahler's *Das Lied von der Erde* were to their composers: a mysterious, even mystical sign of mortality. In a letter to his friend and librettist Giuseppe Adami, he confessed his depression: "On my travels I have carried about with me a large bundle of melancholy. I have no reason for it, but that is the way I am made . . . I'm afraid *Turandot* will never be finished." Only a short time later, he wrote to his friend Sybil Seligman, "My work terrifies me, and I find nothing good anywhere. I feel as though from now on I'm finished."

If Puccini's sentiments proved more prescient than even he could have expected, it may not have been without reason. The year 1918 saw the death of his colleagues Leoncavallo and Debussy. His on-again, off-again relationship with the former, and the admiration he had for the latter (a mutual sentiment), stimulated his competitive instincts, but would no longer. A year later, he lost his brother-in-law, Massimo Del Carlo, as well as a childhood friend, Carlo Carignani. Elsewhere, Italy was left reeling in a sea of unemployment and hardship after World War I, the result of unfulfilled treaties, catastrophic losses, poor military planning, insignificant territorial gains, and an overwhelming war debt that wouldn't be repaid until the 1970s.

Though his enormous success and vast wealth insulated him from the woes of the common man, Puccini was hardly immune to quotidian concerns, political and otherwise. Mussolini's Fascist Party was making headway in Italy, auguring all manners of horror to come, while Puccini's advancing, though not advanced, age, impressed itself upon him without mercy. Puccini, in spirit a youthful and gentle man, was ill suited to the rigors of aging and said so on more than one occasion. An artist who continually looked for ways to reinvent himself, he needed as much energy as he could muster and then some. For him, composing was more than the stuff of professional endeavor; it was the life force itself that rekindled his desire as well as his ambition. It was, in effect, his fountain of youth.

Perhaps that is why in March 1921, over lunch with the playwright and theater critic Renato Simoni, he was relieved and delighted to hear about Carlo Gozzi's (1720–1806) *Turandot*, a play exceptionally well suited to his musical sensibilities. *Turandot* was one of a series of "fairy-tale" plays first performed in Venice in 1761; it had a peculiar effect on its audiences, who were enthralled by its exoticism and invention. Gozzi's influence on men of letters never ebbed, at least in Europe; Friedrich Schiller translated the play in 1802, and some years later, in 1809, Carl Maria von Weber wrote incidental music for a production of the play in Stuttgart. Puccini was not the only twentieth-century composer to have found inspiration in Gozzi; Sergei Prokofiev, too, based his 1919 opera *A Love for Three Oranges* on a Gozzi play of the same name.

The story is straightforward enough. Turandot, a beautiful but cruel princess with a wicked temper, has issued an edict: Anyone who dares to become her suitor must answer three riddles. Those who fail to do so will be decapitated; indeed, at the opera's opening, more than a dozen have been beheaded already. Calaf, a foreign prince unknown to her or the citizenry of Peking, is taken with her beauty and rises to the challenge, much to the consternation of his elderly father, Timur, the former king of the Tartars, and Timur's good-hearted slave girl Liù. Impervious to the entreaties of those, including Turandot's three ministers, who persuade him to abandon his quest, Calaf pursues it, only to beat Turandot at her own game. He successfully answers her riddles, compelling her to become his lover. She demurs, but her father, the emperor, won't let her back out of a commitment of her own making. Calaf offers her another chance. If she can find out, by dawn, what his name is, he will gladly go to the gallows. But the ruse doesn't work. Even Liù, who knows his name, refuses to disclose it, an offense for which she is tortured. Liù kills herself, thus becoming something of a martyr, and most certainly a catalyst in the battle of wills between Turandot and Calaf. Defeated, Turandot gives in, accepts Calaf's love, and melts in his embrace.

Puccini labored over *Turandot* for three years. His original outline proposed an opera in two acts, not three, as we know it today. Just as he had in *Madama Butterfly*, he harvested Oriental folk music to inform the mood, setting, and, ultimately, the verismo of his new opera. To this end he met with an Italian diplomat, the Baron Fassini Camossi, who had been stationed in Beijing. Camossi brought back to Italy a small memento, a music box, that likely meant nothing to him, but its contents proved enormously beneficial to Puccini when he discovered the box cranked out Chinese melodies. Among the indigenous tunes that inhabited it was the "Imperial Hymn," which Puccini would use frequently and to great effect throughout *Turandot*.

Camossi's music box was not Puccini's only source; he also availed himself of a J. A. van Aalst's 1884 *Chinese Music*, a chronicle of the country's musical (and dance) history and traditions. Van Aalst, who was a Belgian customs official in the employ of the Chinese government, remained the principal source of information about Chinese musical genres well into the mid-twentieth century, and his contributions are still greatly valued by musicologists everywhere.

A few points are worth mentioning, if only as a way to demystify some of the more puzzling details of this opera. That the etymological origins of *Turandot* point to central Asia, not Peking, as the center of action didn't bother Puccini or his librettists, Giuseppe Adami and Renato Simoni. But no matter, Turan was indeed a central Asian territory that was under the exclusive control of the Persian Empire. Turandot is in fact a Persian name, and in Farsi, the name of the original fairy tale is *Turandokht*—the daughter of Turan. As for the correct pronunciation of *Turandot*, well, that has always been a matter of some confusion. Most people prefer the French vogue, which does not pronounce the final "t," insofar as Puccini himself never pronounced it, according to at least one contemporary, the Polish soprano Rosa Raisa, the first Turandot.

The sad story of Turandot parallels the composer's own fate. In the winter of 1924 Puccini developed a persistent sore throat and a hacking cough. Visits to an exclusive spa the following May brought no relief. Even so, he didn't give the symptoms much thought, attributing them to a prolonged case of the flu. Consultations with doctors and specialists proved no help, either, as they either misdiagnosed his condition or failed to acknowledge their inability to diagnose it at all. Finally, he went to see a specialist in Florence, who recommended surgery. What this doctor did not have the heart to tell his patient was the truth: that he had an inoperable tumor that would prove fatal. Only Puccini's son, Tonio, knew the extent of his father's illness; the doctor thought it best to inform him.

Leaving behind his wife, Elvira, who didn't feel well, either, Puccini took off on November 6, 1924, for Brussels, where he was to be treated at a clinic that had had some success with cancers of his kind. He submitted himself to therapy and, for a while, appeared to be doing well. On November 24 he underwent surgery, the results of which at first looked promising; but only five days later, on November 29, he died from heart failure. He was sixty-five years old.

Puccini had completed the first two and a half acts of *Turandot*, up to the crowd's elegiac choral sendoff of Liù's body midway through act 3. He left behind only sketches for the rest, which were entrusted to his student Carlo Alfano for completion. There was testy disagreement over just who would be allowed to complete the opera. Puccini's publisher

Ricordi vigorously lobbied on behalf of its client Franco Vittadini. But Arturo Toscanini, for decades a champion of Puccini's music and his favorite conductor, favored Riccardo Zandonai (1883–1944), the composer of a popular opera, *Francesca da Rimini*. It was an odd choice, insofar as Puccini never hid his distaste for Zandonai or his music.

Tonio Puccini adamantly rejected Toscanini's recommendation. The weighty task eventually fell to Alfano, who was a skilled and successful composer in his own right and familiar with Puccini's musical idiom. Indeed, Alfano's own music, especially his opera *Sakantula*, incorporated a number of Oriental elements of which Puccini would have approved. For his part, however, Toscanini was not especially happy with the fruits of Alfano's skillful work. With his customary autocratic manner, he demanded that Alfano make substantial edits, even though that meant compromising the music's compositional logic. Nevertheless, Alfano complied, and *Turandot* was given its world premiere, to mixed critical reaction, on April 25, 1926, at La Scala in Milan.

On this occasion Toscanini omitted Alfano's ending altogether and, in an uncharacteristically modest moment, put down his baton and turned toward the audience where Liù's funeral cortege leaves the stage. Though accounts of what he actually said differ, there is at least consensus on the thrust of his remarks, which have gone down in musical history as having been, "Here the maestro put down his pen." However, one eyewitness, Enrico Minetti, tells a different story. He was the concertmaster at La Scala that evening and was thus in close proximity to Toscanini. According to Minetti, Toscanini's exact words were "Qui finisce l'opera, rimasta incompiuta per la morte del Maestro" (Here ends the opera, which remains incomplete because of the composer's death).

Act I

The walls of the great violet city

Though brief, the brass- and timpani-infested fanfare that opens *Turandot* cuts like a knife through the silence from which it emerges. The mood is grim. A burst of parallel octaves gives way to alternating oscillations that pulsate ruthlessly underneath in staccato proclamations. The ambience, so bleakly created by the strings, brass, and woodwinds, is made all the more prescient by the inclusion of an ambiguous tritone and the ominous beating of timpani.

As the curtain opens, the sun sets on the Imperial (Forbidden) City of Peking, as it was known then and in Puccini's day. (Most productions nowadays preserve the name as it appears in the libretto, rather than changing it to Beijing.) Awash in the amber light of the north, it materializes gradually out of the crepuscular shadows, like a silver emulsion coming into view. Expansive mahogany ramparts, seamlessly constructed and sloping upward in serpentine dovetails, surround the stage. On one side is an imposing loggia, where elaborate oak and rosewood dragons snarl beside winged phoenixes carved from jade. As if to protect the dead, a small army of emerald-embedded terra-cotta turtles lurks solemnly beside a row of wooden stakes ornamented with human skulls, whose hollowed eyes and clattering jaws peer out as if in mockery of anyone who would challenge their presence. In the midst of this reservoir of severed heads, the unnerving clack of a xylophone and a distant gong sing a skeleton's song before any human voice is even heard. Looming in the rear, three gates cut rough-hewn paths through a thick, fifty-foot oak wall adorned with gigantic brass rings,

A Mandarin, in this case a high-ranking Chinese official whose embroidered silk robe reflects his preeminent position, addresses a large gathering of his compatriots as he proclaims the law of Peking: The princess Turandot, he tells them, will marry whoever solves three riddles of her making. But woe unto those who fail to discern the enigma she sets forth, as they will be beheaded. Indeed, in light of her proclivities, the castration symbolism that informs decapitation, at least in the household of theater, assumes a whole new meaning in this opera; Turandot's aim, as we shall see, is nothing if not the emasculation of her victims. Surrounded by imposing guards, whose Tartar origins radiate proudly from every pore of their wide and handsome faces, the Mandarin sets a stentorian tone in brutal parlante spurts that hobble repetitively astride the back of two pitches. The prince of Persia, it seems, has failed Turandot's challenge and has been sent off to the gallows, where he will, out of the audience's range of vision, lose his head.

As the orchestra regurgitates the sparse and bareboned motivic material, the pace quickens and the bloodthirsty crowd calls for the head of the Turandot's latest victim, the prince of Persia. ("Muoia! Sì, muoia!"—He must die! Yes! Die!) As the guards push the impatient crowd aside with ruthless dispatch, an assertive contrasting theme in 3/4 time traces its *fortissimo*, stepwise descent atop uneasy syncopations and is capped off in cadence by a falling fifth.

An old man, bruised and distraught, has been shoved to the ground in the rush of the crowd. His slave girl, the gentle Liù, calls out for help amid a variant of the aforementioned crowd motive. A well-clad stranger, Calaf (the "unknown prince"), hears her and is astonished to recognize the old man to be his father, Timur, the exiled king of the Tartars. As the populace prepares to witness the gruesome execution of the prince of Persia, Timur entreats his son, to the rumble of timpani, to hear him out. It was Liù who remained loyal to him when, in the heat of battle, his authority collapsed and he fled for his life. Calaf is puzzled; why would Liù want to put herself at such terrible risk? She replies, "Perchè un dì . . . nella reggia, mi hai sorriso" (Because one day . . . in the palace, you smiled at me).

With these loyalties now firmly established, Puccini again turns his attention to the Peking masses, who cheer on a coterie of men in the executioner's employ, whose only duty it is to sharpen his scimitar. "Gira la cote!" (Grind the whetstone!) A vivacious patch of parallel chords in inversion, colored by the steely ring of a triangle and a dozen basses, flutters *pianissimo* in 2/4 time and spells out the crowd's excitement. ("Ungi, arrota, che la lama guizzi, sprizzi fuoco e sangue!"—Oil it, sharpen it, let the blade gleam, spatter fire and blood!) The otherwise sepulchral blare of trumpets and trombones, at first played offstage, serves to heighten the intensity of this fragile and nervous motivic confection as it accumulates energy. The crowd anxiously anticipates the appearance of Turandot's next suitor, taunting him for his audacity before they even set eyes on him. ("Chi quel gong percuoterà, apparire la vedrà!"—Whoever strikes that gong will see her appear!)

The opening motive in parallel octaves resurfaces to announce an ethereal chorus, a diaphanous engagement of strings, woodwinds, and voices that pays homage to the magic of the moon. The music, for all its quiescence, establishes a voluptuous new motive in D major that migrates upward in tepid, disjunct triplets, which then lightly flutter downward. This "moon" motive is implicitly bitonal, in that it outlines in lateral juxtaposition a dominant seventh chord alongside B-minor arpeggiations constructed on the sixth degree of the scale. As the moon rises, so do the dynamics and the tonality, which migrates gradually from D major to F major, and finally to E-flat. To the rhythm of an anapest on a single pitch astride another oscillating ostinato, the crowd invokes the name of the executioner, Pu-Tin-Pao, as their voices dissolve into the shallow moonlight and the ensuing boy chorus.

Discreetly supported by two saxophones and a wordless chorus of heavier voices, the boy singers, extolling Turandot's ravishing enchantments, alight in veiled diffusion upon a Chinese folk tune, the "Jasmine Flower" (Moh-li-hua). Its motivic significance cannot be overestimated, given that it will soon enough come to be associated exclusively with Turandot herself. As a funeral cortege leads the Persian prince to the scaffold, the crowd, in tandem with Calaf, launches a weary lament, their belligerence having turned into pity.

Here, Puccini introduces an exotic new motive in E-flat minor, its aura of resigned melancholy drawn out by its slow ascent and subsequent descent in quarter- and half-notes. With its second scale degree raised a half tone, from A-flat to A-natural, its exoticism is empowered, conveying something of the ancient mystery that informs the story. As if conjured by these sad tones, Turandot materializes on the balcony, her figure bathed in moonlight. For the first time in a Puccini opera, the entrance of the heroine's body precedes that of her voice. The disembodiment that enveloped Tosca and Butterfly in an aura of sanctity is here reversed; Turandot's corporeality grounds her, investing her, ironically, with human qualities. It is as if Puccini resolved to dispose of the usual prefabricated baggage—the image repertoire, if you will— that accompanied his previous operas' eponyms. Thus is Turandot introduced as flesh and blood, rather than concept; her body becomes a promise that remains unfulfilled until the next act precisely because she has nothing to say in this one.

The crowd kowtows, fearful of her next move, but Calaf, feeling himself her equal, remains standing, as do the executioner and the doomed Persian prince. All beg for Turandot's mercy, but she refuses. With a single, perilous gesture, and in the embrace of a dynamically expanded Moh-li-hua, she orders the execution to go ahead. Turandot doesn't say a word or sing a note, which is unusual enough for a Puccini heroine; but then again, some princesses are better seen than heard.

At that moment, Calaf, transfixed by Turandot's gaze and her beauty in spite of her cruelty, resolves to make her his lover. ("O divina bellezza, o meraviglia, o sogno!"—Oh, divine beauty, oh, marvel, oh, dream!) The crowd, powerless to alter the fate of the condemned man, accedes to the prayers uttered sotto voce by the wizened priests, their voices rising solemnly from the impending darkness.

Alone now with his father, Timur, and Liù, an enchanted Calaf discloses his infatuation. Timur makes every attempt to dissuade his son from the likely terror that awaits him, but to no avail. As the pace of their tense dialogue increases, Calaf gives voice to the name Turandot, and in so doing, his bright tenor, climbing to a high B-flat, surmounts the jagged blaze of trumpets that accompany her motive, the Moh-li-hua. Calaf repeats her name three times, only to be echoed by the Persian prince, whose life has already begun to ebb in the distance. So as to signal Turandot of his intention to take on the challenge and answer her riddles, Calaf moves toward the summoning gong with vigorous determination but is stopped by the emperor's ministers, Ping, Pang, and Pong (also known, from Gozzi's play, as "the masks").

The ministers, though amused, are determined to bring Calaf to his senses; to the rapid patter of another Chinese folk tune in alternating duple and triple meter, they take turns berating him with exaggerated threats and insults. ("Fermo! Che fai? T'arresta!"—Wait! What are you doing? Stop!) Their demeanor, though mocking, is also comical, as if they spent every waking moment needling anyone who would challenge them. But their behavior is hardly capricious; on the contrary, the ministers are fundamentally emblems, in opposition to the passions respectively brought to life and rejected by Calaf and Turandot. They are the opera's resident intellectuals, at once critical, probative, reasonable, analytical, and pessimistic. Calaf repeatedly interjects with a persistent response, "Lasciatemi passare!" (Let me by!), but to no avail. A playful thematic fragment, given to Pang and Pong only, angles upward in whole tones. ("O scappi, o il funeral per te s'appressa!"—Run along, or else your funeral will be prepared for you!)

A lonely oboe, set astride a barely audible blurs of cellos, ushers in Turandot's handmaidens, who demand quiet; the princess is sleeping. ("Silenzio, ola!—Hola, silence!) The music here, thinly scored with a celeste, harp, and flute, evolves into an ethereal, even magical sheen, its texture and minor-key tonality providing an antidote to Wagner's sensuous Rhine maidens at the opening of *Das Rheingold*. The ministers, once again in unison, shoo the maidens away, then return their attention to the stubborn Calaf. They resolve to have a word with him; even bronze, rock, and the gloom of night are easier to penetrate, they explain, than Turandot's riddles. ("Ferro, bronzo, muro, roccia . . . son men duri degli enigmi di Turandot!"—Iron, bronze, walls, rock . . . are less hard than Turandot's enigmas!) A deftly arranged pentatonic stream, ornamented by rapid-fire appoggiaturas and articulated by flutes and percussion, pokes at the ministers' staccato patter. The fragment paints itself as an orientalism of unknown origins.

Calaf remains unmoved but is growing weary of the ministers. Suddenly, a group of phantoms arises from the shadows, all of them lost souls who failed to satisfy Turandot's demands. Their voices, eight in number and divided equally between contraltos and tenors, merge in a vague and eerie hush. "Non indugiare!" (Don't hesitate!) is the motto of their brief participation, bolstered still by the colorful instrumentation, which in this instance is a wash of sound effects. A hypnotic strain of strings reiterates an irresolute pedal point in a high register, as flutes, a gong, and a piccolo chirp like birds alongside them. Dismissing the phantoms' entreaties to the princess that killed them ("Fa ch'ella parli! Fa che l'udiamo! Io l'amo!"—Make her speak! Let us hear her! I love her!), Calaf protests that he alone loves Turandot ("No, no, io solo l'amo"—No, only I love her!), a comment that the ministers greet with cold resistance. She is only a figment of Calaf's imagination, they insist;

she does not exist, any more than the phantoms do. Try as they may, the sarcastic ministers fail to persuade Calaf, though Pang and Pong's cheerful "O scappi" (Run along) motive lends their words the scantest bit of optimism.

Calaf tries again to beat the gong but is now interrupted by the executioner, Pu-Tin-Pao, who, emerging haughtily on the bastion, shows off the prince of Persia's severed head, a gruesome emblem of Turandot's castration fantasy. He is accompanied by a light reminiscence of the act's opening motivic material, here reinvented among a host of woodwinds and colored by the inclusion of a celeste and a glockenspiel. Timur's commanding bass wells up in concern as he rails at Calaf to avoid the danger that awaits him. To an accompaniment of dusky strings, his heart heavy, he implores Calaf to change his mind, but his plea again falls on deaf ears. ("Aiuto! Non c'è voce umana che muova il tuo cuore feroce?"—Help! Isn't there any human voice that can move your fierce heart?)

Liù has overheard everything. Here, she breaks into one of the most well-known arias in opera, "Signore, ascolta!" (My lord, listen!). Though she holds her love for Calaf in secret, her sinuous pentatonic plea is a model of musical and theatrical sincerity. A simple binary form to which Puccini adds a heartbreaking coda in a high tessitura, it is buttressed by the discreet doubling of the vocal line with woodwinds. The harp halo that enshrouds the concluding phrase "Liù non regge più! Ah, pietà!" (Liù can bear it no more! Ah, have pity!) sanctifies Liù as a kind of earth angel.

Moved but hardly disavowed of his determination to capture Turandot's steely heart, Calaf's sympathetic response is an impassioned lament, lushly scored. He returns the plea, begging her never to leave Timur's side. Now, in a richly polyphonic concertato, Calaf, the ministers, Liù, and Timur engage each other simultaneously while a chorus of bystanders issues a chilling warning that it is already digging Calaf's grave. But as is Puccini's wont in his concertatos, where emotions run high and the theatrical crosscurrents move swiftly, the characters debate at cross-purposes: the ministers, failing to give up, insist Calaf leave as they persist in their deception that Turandot is not real; Liù asks for pity, as does Timur, who also makes one last entreaty to Calaf, claiming that no one, not even he, can win her heart; while Calaf, now completely consumed by Turandot's image, at last throws himself on the gong, striking it three times and thus summoning the ice princess. The act draws to a conclusion in a feverish bluster of Turandot's "Moh-li-hua" theme, while the ministers, their derisive laughter having hemorrhaged into biting mockery, skitter offstage with the peevish diffidence of unpaid psychoanalysts. ("Quando rangola il gong, la morte gongola! Ah, ah, ah!"—When the gong clangs, death is happy! Ha, ha, ha!)

Act 2, scene 1

A pavilion adjacent to the great square of the royal palace, before sunrise

Absent from the opening of act 2 is an interlude or even a prelude. By jumping directly into the action, thus thrusting the characters into the forefront, Puccini allows the drama to prevail over the music, at least temporarily. In any case, what we intuit is a conduit that links the previous act to this one.

A cavernous tent looms large over the stage, its silken drapes embroidered in satin stitchery with indigo images of flowering peach, lotus blossoms, and peony flowers. Standing solemnly in the middle of the tent is Ping, who is soon enough joined by Pang and Pong. Three servants tiptoe in behind them, each carrying a colored lantern—one red, one green, and one yellow. Setting the lanterns on a table, the servants retreat to the rear, leaving the three ministers to ponder events to the accompanying strain of another puckish Chinese folk tune, its lilting pentatonic figurations delicately perfumed by string pizzicatos and a sprinkling of brass and percussion. Pong is charged with making preparations for a wedding, in the event that Calaf succeeds in his quest to win Turandot's love. Pang, accustomed to the string of failures that have befallen the ice princess's many other suitors, is more sanguine about his obligation, which is to plan for yet another execution and, in consequence, another funeral, as well.

Here the ministers bemoan the state of things in China since the birth of Turandot, who has served only to spread misery and barbaric cruelty. The lyrical "O scappi" fragment, with which Pong and Pang urged Calaf to leave while he still had a chance, resurfaces as they evoke him by innuendo, if not by name. Calaf will become Turandot's thirteenth victim, an unlucky number even in the Year of the Tiger. Just as a recall of the executioner's theme suggests, the ministers have become, under Turandot's ruthless regime, nothing more than pawns of the executioner, whose light but unnerving motivic thread accompanies them here.

With this, each waxes nostalgic about his native province. ("Ho una casa nell'Honan . . . Tornar laggiù!"—I have a house in Honan . . . To go back there!) This small but significant scene serves to humanize the ministers, who until now have been little more than pat, even comic, characters. Ping pines for his lake home in Honan, while Pong ponders the shaded forests of Tsaing. Pang regrets ever having left the garden he enjoyed near Kiu. Their daydreaming is supported by a docile but somewhat irresolute thematic fragment; given over to the flutes and a harp, it is a stream of alternating intervals, tethered to an expression of its dominant pitch, in perfect and augmented fourths. It broadens admirably into a lyrical, amiably harmonized profusion, as bucolic in character as the landscapes it describes. The addition of a raised fourth (G-sharp) to the texture is especially piquant, conveying as it does a certain bittersweet pungency to this otherwise sympathetic phrase.

But the time for dreaming is up; the ministers cynically disparage the folly of love such as they have observed it. ("O mondo, pieno di pazzi innamorati!"—Oh, world, filled with mad lovers!) Certain that the worst is yet to come, at least for Calaf, they recall Turandot's victims, and thus Turandot's ruthless agenda, one by one. Echoes of the executioner's motive are introduced in tandem with a people's chorus, which calls upon him to sharpen the blade. ("Ungi, arrota, che la lama guizzi e sprizzi fuoco e sangue!"—Oil and sharpen the blade till it shines and splatters fire and blood!)

The ensuing trio, which the ministers sing in unison with each other and the strings, is remarkable for combining its pessimistic message with such optimistic music. ("Addio, amore"—Farewell to love!) They bid farewell not only to love, but also to their heritage, to Chinese culture, and to China herself; their shared song is a not-too-subtle swipe at Turandot's grotesquely authoritarian politics. Again, Puccini yields to a Chinese melody, or the semblance of one, given its pentatonic construction.

As the orchestration lightens to an airy pastiche of xylophone, triangle, and woodwind coloring, the ministers consider the alternative, contemplating the possibility of a wedding rather than an execution. For this, Puccini introduces "Tao-Yin" (Guiding March), a cheerful Chinese melody that has its roots at the imperial court. ("Poi tutt'e tre in giardino"—Then the three of us in the garden.) Imagining the victory of a suitor, whoever that might be, they envision a China where love and humanity have been restored to the royal household.

But duty calls. The guards and servants are already preparing the riddle ceremony, where Calaf will meet his fate with Turandot. The music tenses as a flurry of trumpets repeatedly disclose themselves in a dotted rhythm atop a persistent pentatonic-colored ostinato. The ministers ready themselves once again for Turandot's treachery and what they believe will surely be her suitor's death sentence.

Act 2, scene 2

A vast square inside the palace walls, sunrise

As the scene shifts, the orchestration expands into a nervous array of woodwinds, triangle, snare drum, and strings, while the aforementioned ostinato continues to cling selfishly to its status. An ornate marble staircase winds steeply upward to a plateau that in turn opens onto a wide landing. The servants, their long braids aflutter beneath their silk hats, bustle impatiently as they adorn the ceremonial area with brightly colored lanterns. The crowd of citizens, perhaps every bit as bloodthirsty as in act 1, fills the plaza as the Mandarins, attired in blue and gold robes, make their way to their appointed place. Affixed to their silken garments are square badges representing earth and exquisitely embroidered with images of exotic birds; such was the customary emblem of rank that distinguished Chinese civil officials, at least in the Ming dynasty. On the Mandarins' heels are eight sages (wise men in any other play), their authority implied by their slow gait, enormous size, and advanced age. The sages seem to glide in, as if on rollers, glowing in a halo of portentous solemnity. They carry with them the official scrolls, which will not only allow them to inaugurate and document the proceedings, but also hold the answers to Turandot's riddles.

In deference to the sages, the music evolves into the Chinese "Imperial Hymn," a tune that came to Puccini's attention by means of a music box belonging to one Baron Fassini Comossi, a diplomat at the Italian Embassy in Beijing. This heroic march, here embodied in a blaze of clarinets and horns, breaks the autumnal hush of the crowd, which falls prostrate upon the appearance of Emperor Altoum. With his arrival, the citizens, their voices rising in unison atop a short but strident dotted-note motive, pay homage to their old and wizened leader, who takes his place on a carved ivory throne. ("Diecimila anni al nostro Imperatore!"—Ten thousand years' life for our emperor!)

Altoum is no stranger to compassion. Just as Timur, Liù, and the ministers did so eloquently, the emperor, introduced by a bright trumpet fanfare, pleads with Calaf, offering him one last chance to flee and thus avoid Turandot's savage vendetta. ("Un giuramento atroce mi costringe a tener fede al fosco patto. Basta sangue! Giovine, vá!"—A ghastly oath forces me to keep faith with this horrid pact. Enough of this blood! Young man, go!) Altoum's entreaty rings all the more austere, as he sings a cappella, with only momentary interruptions of a single chord blurted out *forte* by the brass and timpani, or brief pentatonic fragments played in unison by the strings and percussion. Calaf's by-now-predictable response, likewise unaccompanied, and which he proffers three times, is adamant: "Figlio del cielo, io chiedo d'affrontar la prova!" (Son of heaven, I ask to undergo the trial!). Altoum, seeing that he is getting nowhere, reluctantly leaves Calaf to his own fate and allows the ceremony to continue.

Here, the "Imperial Hymn," as if giving its consent, reappears, its mood no longer militaristic or noble, but attenuated; it has become an oddly melancholy but lyrical lament. The Mandarin returns to his musical roots, setting forth the official proclamation to the menacing motivic units that opened the opera. Turandot's theme ("Moh-li-hua") is heard once again in the throats of the boy's chorus.

At long last, Turandot speaks, or should I say, sings. That Puccini would wait this long to formally introduce his heroine—or antiheroine, as the case may be—is unique among operas. Cold and impenetrable, Turandot presides high above the crowd, intoning her extended aria, "In questa reggia" (In this palace) (CD Track 17), a model of vocal declamation. Though it challenges the singer with its unforgiving high tessitura and exceptionally long lines that spin out with merciless intensity, the overall mood onstage, as well as in the orchestral accompaniment, is both arid and mysterious. As Turandot pays tribute to the fallen princess of years past, horns and flutes, and then muted strings, quietly enshroud her song. Though the entire aria remains affixed to a single key, F-sharp minor, its harmonies migrate and then regroup, creating the impression that the key center is moving north. In fact, it is not; but Turandot's declamation, as it becomes more intense and moves into the vocal stratosphere, would make anyone believe otherwise.

En route to her mission of murder, she reveals the agenda that drives her: vendetta. Centuries earlier, her ancestress, the Princess Lo-u-ling, suffered torture, and then murder, at the hands of a foreign invader. It is to avenge Lo-u-ling's abduction, rape, and death that she has resolved to challenge all potential suitors, or so she says.

Of course, that's nonsense. Behind Turandot's icy demeanor is a woman hurt and terrified. While neither Puccini nor his librettists disclose the reasons that may have led to her peculiar psychopathology, and didn't have to—it's just an opera, after all—her claim to avenge a distant relation she never knew is patently ludicrous. Indeed, while she claims to have inherited the spirit of her ancestress, her words suggest something entirely different. "Mai nessun m'avrà . . . Ah, rinasce in me l'orgoglio di tanta purità!" (No one will ever possess me . . . Ah, in me is reborn the pride of such purity!), the ardent lyrical cadence that wraps up "In questa reggia," says it all. Her cruel game of chance is nothing more than a ruse that allows her to objectify her inadequacy, to wit, her inability to love. When you're a powerful princess, the next-best thing to castration is decapitation; take it or leave it. Indeed, Turandot is precisely what Butterfly might have become, had her fury turned outward rather than inward. What makes her all the more interesting among the protagonists of Puccini's operatic canon is her fundamental behavior, which is that of a sociopath. That much she shares in common with Pinkerton, Scarpia, and even Manon Lescaut, but to a degree far greater and, in the world of dramatic characterization, more dangerous.

So sure is Turandot of victory, she offers Calaf one final chance to withdraw honorably, perhaps her only demonstration of kindness. In the face of yet another stubborn refusal, the ceremony begins as she reveals the first of her three enigmas: "What is born each night and dies each dawn?" she asks in a belligerent outburst confined to only three notes, E, F, and C-sharp. In their libretto, Adami and Simoni cast her words as a statement, not a question ("Ed ogni notte nasce ed ogni giorno muore!"—And every night it's born and every day it dies!), lending to Turandot's declamation an arrogance that betrays her as both deluded and vulnerable. Calaf, imperturbable and confident, responds as if he had known the question, as well as the answer, all along: It is *hope*! ("La speranza"). The sages, scrutinizing the scrolls, confirm it. It is hope, indeed.

With the pronouncement of each riddle, Turandot's fateful enigmas gain support in the orchestra, which accompanies her ravenous query, duplicating her vocal line in the throes of three diminished chords, accentuated and *fortissimo*, played by strings and trumpets. Capping off this uneasy fragment in the bass is our ambiguous old friend, the *diabolus in musica*—the augmented fourth, two more of which are embedded in the middle instrumental voices of the preceding chords.

Calaf's response, an echo of Turandot's motivic material, rings victorious. It is extended by a wild orchestral flourish, a tumble of trumpets and cellos that then dissolve into the sages' growling bass. This additional motivic material might be viewed as symbolic in its own right, as it is not given to the ice princess; on the contrary, it adumbrates her frustration, disorients her, and throws her off her game. In any case, Turandot remains cynical: "Sì! La speranza che delude sempre!" (Yes! Hope, which always deludes!). The emperor and the citizenry are likewise unconvinced, as if Calaf were merely lucky; they again urge him to quit, repeating what has by now become a dramatic mantra.

Not yet defeated, Turandot declaims the second riddle: "Guizza al pari di fiamma, e non è fiamma!" (It flickers like a flame, but it is not flame!). Here, Puccini characterizes a flame, or rather its flicker, with a brief motivic dart that ascends and vanishes as quickly as it appeared. The crowd interrupts, as does Altoum, reminding Calaf that he will likely lose his life if he doesn't abandon his folly. Liù pipes in, admonishing him that love is at stake, too. Though the three words "È per l'amore!" (It is for love!) are Liù's only contribution to this act, her utterance is as ambiguous as it is selfish; she refers to what she expects to be her own loss, not Calaf's. Even so, this interruption, which delays Calaf's response, serves to heighten dramatic tension, much in the way of a pregnant pause. But Calaf has not been fooled. With a confident cry of "Il sangue!" (Blood!), he has won round two, and again the sages, surveying their scrolls, verify it.

Calaf has begun to sway the crowd, at least, to his side. They wish him courage as Turandot embarks on the last of her riddles. In an effort to intimidate him, Turandot leaves her royal perch and descends, her long silk train slithering down the white marble staircase as if it had a life of its own. She is not pleased with the mood of the crowd, which has become antagonistic to her interests. Livid, she orders the guards to beat them: "Percuotete quei vili!" (Lash those wretches!). She approaches Calaf, unmoved as she looms over him as if he were already dead. He falls to his knees, evidently in an effort to signal defeat, but he is merely mocking her. Now the stakes really are higher, at least for the soprano: Puccini raises the pitch by a half-tone, confronting Turandot with an even riskier tessitura, an apt musical metaphor indeed for both her tension and rage. She shouts, "Su, straniero, il gelo che dà foco, che cos'è?" (Stranger, what is like ice but burns like fire?). Here, Calaf gets up and, assuming a stiff and noble posture, relishes what is about to become his ultimate triumph: "La mia vittoria ormai t'ha data a me! Il mio fuoco ti sgela: Turandot!" (My victory now has given you to me! My fire will thaw you: Turandot!).

With the sages' final confirmation, the swelling crowd congratulates Calaf, extolling his victory, ironically, to the "Mo-li-hua"—Turandot's motive—now emboldened by the full orchestra. ("Gloria, o vincitore!") The chorus, its dream come true, drifts *pianissimo* into a pious, even ethereal, cadence.

Turandot's defeat turns to shame as she begs her father to spare her from being surrendered to Calaf. ("Non gettar tua figlia nelle braccia dello straniero!"—Don't cast your daughter into the stranger's arms!) But a promise is a promise, and the oath, the emperor reminds her, is sacred. The music becomes labyrinthine, slithering this way and that between major and minor tonalities, with the orchestration entrusted largely to the strings. The crowd, echoing their emperor's unwavering edict, overwhelms Turandot, who resists the legally binding entreaty that would impale her convictions. That the crowd persists in its demands with Turandot's own thematic fragment, the "Moh-li-hua," paints her as being all the more humiliated by events of her own twisted making. Indeed, assuming her motivic fragment now heightened to stratospheric vocal proportions, she bellows *fortissimo* her familiar but defiant refrain, "Mai nessun m'avrà!" (No one will ever possess me!). Of course, that said, who would want to? But again, it's opera, not politics.

Bitter and confused, Turandot poses another riddle, but this one off the books. "Mi vuoi nelle tue braccia a forza, riluttante, fremente?" (Would you have me in your arms by force, reluctant and enraged?) she asks Calaf. Calaf, in a machismo bid to win another game, recoils with a resounding, "No, no," but his ambitions are hardly magnanimous. He reopens negotiations by offering an enigma of his own, one that will give Turandot, now defeated, an opportunity to escape her commitment. Alongside the riveting three-chord motive that articulated Turandot's riddles, Calaf challenges her to find out his name by dawn, and if she does, he will go willingly and happily to the gallows. ("Dimmi il mio nome prima dell'alba"—Tell me my name before dawn.) Here, a shadow of Calaf's searing act 3 aria, the famous "Nessun dorma," tiptoes in, leased, as it were, to the violins, which are entrusted to its forecast. The emperor, duly impressed and accompanied by a thinly orchestrated restatement of the "Tao-Yin" (Guiding March), wishes him luck, saying only that, when dawn breaks, it is a son he hopes to gain. The curtain comes down as the chorus proudly declaims the "Imperial

Hymn," which is no longer merely a matter of ceremonial procedure, but an earnest expression of its collective conviction.

Act 3, scene I

The garden of the palace

As night falls and the curtain rises, a splendid, lavishly appointed pavilion that segues into the palace comes into view. Just behind the door that links the palace and pavilion is the suite of rooms where Turandot is known to lurk. An offstage chorus of heralds and anonymous voices issues Turandot's royal edict, a warning to all citizens that no one is to sleep until the name of the unknown prince, familiar to the rest of us as Calaf, is revealed.

Calaf, neither weary nor discouraged, listens to the heralds' chilling proclamation: "Questa notte nessun dorma in Pekino!" (Tonight no one must sleep in Peking!). Clarinets, violins, and a harp spread out in a restless sequence of slurred couplets, marked "misterioso," atop a dark rumble of string tremolandos. No one should confuse the ministers' words for Calaf's celebrated aria (CD Track 18), which ensues only moments later and where he vows now one will discover his name. Perhaps he expects Turandot will hear his defiant boast, as he exclaims it in "Nessun dorma," that even she should not sleep.

A crowd follows the ministers through the surrounding shrubbery. Turandot, true to form, has everyone in a panic, as no one's safety is guaranteed so long as Calaf's name remains a secret. Now their lives are in his hands. At wit's end, the ministers, their desperation showing, attempt to bribe him with a coterie of seductive young girls, and then with gold and precious gems, but again in vain. The sultry, Eastern flavor of the local accompaniment bleeds into a florid new Oriental motive in 2/4 time.

Just then, the guards run in, their grubby hands firmly wrapped around the arms of their two detainees, Timur and Liù. They and the ministers, having seen them in Calaf's company, demand they reveal his name. Calaf comes to their defense, protesting they know nothing, but to no avail. The ministers and the crowd intone the name of Turandot, and no sooner than they mouth, "Principessa," does she appear. A grand, brass-rich restatement of her "Moh-li-hua" theme anticipates her response to the obsequious Ping, who fills her in on the status of the two prisoners and what they may know about Calaf. ("Principessa divina! Il nome dell'ignoto sta chiuso in queste bocche silenti"—Divine princess! The stranger's name is enclosed within these silent mouths.)

Now her claws are out. The rhapsodic thematic fragment from act 1's opening minutes—where the guards restrain the crowd and push Timur to the ground—urgently resurfaces in the midst of a testy exchange between Turandot and Calaf. Liù, in an act of genuine selflessness, turns the tables and comes to Calaf's defense. Claiming only she knows his name, Liù promises never to reveal it, no matter the consequences. ("Io so il suo nome ... M'è suprema delizia tenerlo segreto e possederlo io sola!"—I know his name ... My supreme pleasure is to keep it secret and to have it for myself alone!) The guards try to extract it, as a dark variant of the once-placid "moon" theme from act 1 rears its head underneath, its disjunct rhythms now ominous and sinister. The crowd, once more bloodthirsty, self-absorbed, and looking for a way out, demands her torture and death. Calaf throws himself in front of Liù, so as to protect her, but that only serves to infuriate Turandot all the more. She orders the guards to seize and shackle him. He is helpless now to stop Liù's torture at the hands of her captors. The music, having already drifted into the barest wisp of vague motivic recalls, is merely atmospheric as Liù pursues her thoughts to the accompaniment of a melancholy new motive, a descending scale pattern echoed by the oboe and clarinets. ("Signor, non parlerò"—Lord, I won't speak!)

Turandot again demands that Liù reveal the name. But Liù means business: "Piuttosto morrò!" (I'd rather die). Turandot is resolute but quizzical; where does a slave girl find such courage, she wonders. ("Chi pose tanta forza nel tuo cuore?"—Who gave your heart such strength?). Predictably, Liù's answer is "Principessa, l'amore!" (Love, Princess!). In her penultimate aria, "Tanto amore, segreto e inconfessato" (Such love, secret and unconfessed), Liù, her voice adrift in a tender sequence of descending slurred duplets, reveals to everyone the love she harbors for Calaf but will never consummate; here she offers him a symbolic gift of that love.

Unmoved and spurred on by the wicked crowd and the crafty Ping, Turandot orders her guards to continue torturing Liù. Already, Liù's life force is ebbing. She implores Turandot to accept Calaf's love, something she, Liù, will never be able to do. In support of her plea, Puccini introduces a variant of Turandot's "Moh-li-hua" motive, its thematic and rhythmic design nearly identical but its pitch patterns slightly altered, and its harmonization darkly cast G-flat minor. If Liù is a would-be Butterfly, she certainly succeeds here: she grabs a guard's knife and, with Calaf in full view, stabs herself. She dies, but not before the crowd, fearing for its own safety, demands she give up her secret: "Parla! Il nome!" (Speak! His name!). The crowd shows itself here to be nothing more than a reflection of Turandot's cruelty, an extension of her psychosis. Even as Calaf mourns her, Turandot's sadism lingers unsatisfied; wrestling a whip away from one of the executioner's men, she whips the guard who allowed Liù to do herself in.

Turandot orders Calaf freed, while Timur, horrified, kneels over Liù's limp body and begs her to awake, his words transformed by the woodwind-rich music into a dark, funereal lament. ("Liù . . . Liù sorgi!"—Liù . . . get up!) Ping chides him for wasting time over a dead body, while Timur inspires fear in the superstitious crowd, which now believes Liù, a victim of gross injustice, may become an evil spirit bent on revenge. An impromptu cortege forms as the crowd, their voices now a reverent whisper, observe two handmaidens as they enshroud Liù in a white veil. As her body is removed to the discreet resonance of the timpani, Timur fumbles for her petite hand, which he takes ever so delicately in his. Here, Timur, accompanied by Liù's elegiac variant of the Moh-li-hua motive, bids her an aggrieved farewell with a solemn promise to follow her into the unknown. ("Liù . . . bontà! Liù . . . dolcezza!"— Liù . . . goodness! Liù . . . sweetness!) Even the ministers are not left untouched, joining Timur and the crowd in their mournful expression of regret. The chorus, bearing Liù aloft, mourns its way offstage and into the distance, their voices fading as suddenly as Liù's young life.

At this point, as Toscanini sadly explained at the opera's premiere at La Scala, Puccini died. Here, his student Franco Alfano stepped in and completed the score from twenty-two pages of sketches that Puccini left behind. Though Alfano appropriated the opera's thematic material to paint the characters and situations of the closing scenes, it remains an interpretation of what Puccini might have done, but by no means can it be construed to equal precisely his intentions. What's more, Toscanini's rather arbitrary edits probably didn't help; Alfano was a sufficiently gifted composer in his own right to understand just what his obligation entailed and how to make the best of a difficult challenge. It would have been impossible then, just as it would be now, to imitate Puccini, nor would it have been a good idea. Alfano's authoritative command of compositional technique and procedures, as well as operatic convention, had an inner logic all of its own that Toscanini, had he been more objective, would have left untouched.

But back to the story. The show, as they say, must go on. Though not Puccini's, the music remains powerful and moving. With the funeral cortege a memory, Calaf is left alone onstage with Turandot. He is still in love with her despite her psychotic disposition, though even that doesn't stop him from launching into a virulent tirade against her. ("Principessa di morte!"—Princess of death!) Perhaps in dramatic counterpoint to the placement of a veil over the dead Liù, an act of posthumous consolation, Calaf rips Turandot's veil off her now-ashen face. A parade of hollow open fifths, blared *forte* by trumpets and strings, invests Calaf's fury here with chilling intensity. Turandot, now fancying herself a goddess ("Cosa umana non sono"—I am not human), feigns repulsion at Calaf's heated advances; evidently her sadistic cruelty is, for him, an aphrodisiac. Her earlier motivic protest—the expressive cadential material of "In questa reggia"—raises its melodic head again here but pales in the glow of Calaf's passionate entreaties ("No! Mai nessun m'avrà!"—No! No one will ever possess me!). With this, Calaf, ignoring her useless edicts, grabs and kisses her wildly. As they kiss, and the singing stops, the bass viols and timpani strike with a booming thud below. Whether Puccini would have resolved in such an abrupt manner the transition to an impassioned kiss from Calaf's contempt for her, and Turandot's vilification of him, remains unknown.

Turandot, reduced to jelly, gives in with a sheepish "Che è mai di me? Perduta!" (What has become of me? I'm lost!). Calaf smothers her in perfumed prose, extolling her more, let's say, salient qualities in a brief arioso. ("Mio fiore! Oh! mio fiore mattutino!"—My flower! Oh, my morning flower!) Here, a nearly imperceptible strain of a deftly layered woman's chorus contributes to the lavish harmonization, as does a brief reappearance of the boys' choir, which echoes the fragrant "Moh-li-hua."

Among the thematic fragments that Puccini left behind in his sketches was a particularly endearing *sostenuto*, a fluid melodic pendulum that swings back and forth over a dominant pedal point. ("Miracolo! La tua gloria risplende nell'incanto del primo bacio, del primo pianto"—Miracle! Your glory is radiant in the magic of a first kiss, of your first tears.) Alfano wisely appropriated it in support of Calaf's ecstatic testimony to Turandot's thaw, though again, it remains unknown if his assignment of it to woodwinds and strings conformed to Puccini's epigrammatic instructions. What is known is that Puccini had something else in mind, in that he did not intend to use the melody specifically at this juncture.

Turandot, now humanized as mysteriously as she was possessed of her long-dead ancestress, confesses her feelings, until now concealed, in a rambling aria set astride alternating seventh chords and a discreet ostinato. It is infused with the sostenuto "pendulum" theme, which, only moments earlier, dripped off Calaf's lips. She has been transformed into a proto-Isolde, inebriated by amorous longing, but, unlike Wagner's lass forlorn, she has taken out her pathetic aggressions on everyone *but* her new lover. Of all the suitors who vied for her favor, only Calaf inspired love, fear, and hatred in her, all at the same time. ("Del primo pianto"—My first tears.) She asks him to relish his victory and leave her, but he cannot; lest she has already forgotten, he reminds her that she is now his, and reveals he his name. ("Il mio mistero? Non ne ho più!"—My mystery? I no longer have one!) Behind him, the music swells in a crescendo of rising sequences that dissolve into a round of trumpets and trombones. These announce the ceremonial offices of the official proclamation.

Even now, Calaf has taken a risk, giving Turandot the upper hand in their game. Dawn has broken, and Turandot has learned the name of the prince, who is still willing to die for her. The riddle motive, here every bit as unnerving as it was in act 2 and besieged by augmented fourths, reinvents itself in Calaf's offer to submit his will. After all, he has at long last experienced her passion, which is quite enough to satisfy his compulsive longing. What's more, and not insignificantly, Turandot's body has evolved from its monolithic, Stone-Guest-like presence in act 1 to something pliant and vulnerable. But if there is any question that her intent is to hack off his head, it has become a moot point.

Act 3, scene 2

Outside the imperial palace (CD Track 19)

The transition to the last few minutes of the opera finds the stage bathed in a pallid light. Emperor Altoum, alongside his entourage of soldiers, wise men, and Mandarins, stands dead center atop a grand staircase not unlike that presided over by Gloria Swanson's Norma Desmond in *Sunset Boulevard*, though Salome is hardly his dramatic model. The citizenry, looking up toward Altoum with joy and admiration, to speak nothing of relief, has spread out en masse in the pavilion below.

The full orchestra and chorus, set alight by trumpets and horns and the "Imperial Hymn," accompany Turandot's ascent to her father's throne atop the staircase. Entirely transformed from an evil princess to a submissive, albeit aristocratic, housewife, Turandot issues her final proclamation in a tessitura so high as to shatter glass: that Calaf's real name is love. With that, Calaf, victorious, makes an athletic sprint up the staircase to join her. Now shorn of her independence and pretty much her character, too, the now emasculated Turandot welcomes his warm embrace as the full ensemble comes to rest in exultation of the "Nessun dorma" theme. What becomes of the pair afterward is anybody's guess, but there can be no question, if we are to speculate, that these two have some very serious issues indeed.

Turandot, essentially having proved herself to be Scarpia in drag, is hardly a creature of whimsy or idle pathology, but a symbol of bureaucracy gone mad. What Scarpia could not achieve—total dominion over those who dared challenge him—is left to Turandot to fulfill. Is it any wonder, then, that Calaf's infatuation takes on a patina of pure lust devoid of any real human compassion, concern, or intelligence? It may be that Puccini didn't see it that way, and it is unlikely that it was the outcome he sought. Yet, in drawing such unsympathetic characters as Turandot and Calaf, he would have been especially hard-pressed, like any composer, to reconcile their differences in any other way. The victory that they attribute to love rings hollow; it's *chacun à son gout* on steroids. Certainly, there is no logical reason that the otherwise noble Calaf, whatever his sexual proclivities, would have remained in love with a woman whose crimes are not only unspeakable, but which have also gone unpunished. And it is for this reason that the story fails to work on theatrical terms, as there is no dramatic payoff to speak of. Turandot is a sociopath who got away with murder, while Calaf, whose only motivation is lust, could not care less. But then again, in the embrace of such opulent music and stagecraft, does it really matter? That, in a word, is opera.

Glossary

allegro	Generally understood to be a fast or moderately fast tempo, but in music of the baroque and classical eras, especially, it refers to character and disposition; it can be construed to mean "cheerful" or "happy."
andante	A gracious, walking tempo, not too slow nor too quick. Subject to any number of gradations.
aria	A self-contained, lyrical, and extended vocal solo with instrumental accompaniment.
arioso	A vocal piece that combines the lyrical elements of an aria with the declamatory elements of a recitative. The term can also refer to a short vocal solo in the style of an aria.
articulation	The manner in which a performer distinguishes (by means of attack, prolongation, and release) certain tones, motives, phrases, and groups of pitches individually and in relation to each other. Composers either spell out or provide symbols to indicate types of articulation, such as staccato, legato, wedges, tenuto, and other accent marks.
barcarolle	A Venetian gondolier's song, or an instrumental or vocal work based on it, that is often set in 12/8 or 6/8 time against a lilting, pendulum-like repetitive accompaniment.
baritone	A male voice type whose range lies above bass and below tenor.

baroque music	Music composed roughly between 1590 and 1750 and that embraces certain styles and techniques attributable to the aesthetic ideas, formulations, and philosophy of the era. Because of its long run, it is usually divided into three distinct subperiods, each governed by specific innovations. Opera, the fugue, and the harmonization of a ground bass were products of baroque invention.
bass	The lowest male voice type, below baritone.
bel canto	Italian for "beautiful singing." The term refers largely to a lyrical style of singing, originally cultivated in seventeenth- and eighteenth-century Italy, that focuses on the beauty of vocal sound, authoritative and flexible phrasing, exemplary breath control (especially in *pianissimo*), and exceptional agility in florid passagework. It also refers to a singer's ability to attain high notes with ease and lightness.
brindisi	A drinking song, but literally a "toast."
buffo, buffa	An adjective to indicate "comic." An *opera buffa*, for example, is a comic opera.
cadence	A harmonic progression that demarcates the end of a phrase or larger section of a work and provides a sense of resolution, with varying degrees of finality. In its harmonic tendency to move back toward the key of the work, cadence is also an expression of a composition's tonality.
canonic	Defined by a thematic subject that is presented then successively imitated by one or more voices commencing on different pitches.
chest voice	Singers use this term, as opposed to "head voice," to distinguish pitches that vibrate in the chest rather than the head.

classical era	The period of musical composition that extended from the early eighteenth through the early nineteenth centuries. Its exact division into years is difficult to measure, as classicism evolved slowly and its attendant techniques and aesthetics eventually bled into romanticism. Characteristics of music of the classical era include periodic phrasing; longer harmonic rhythms; a prevalence of simpler, more natural melodic designs; homophonic textures; and greater use of specifically marked dynamic contrasts.
coda	The concluding section of a composition (or a part of one, such as an opera aria), which may encapsulate the work's principal themes. A coda can be as brief as a few measures, or elaborate and extensive.
contralto	The lowest female voice type, below mezzo-soprano.
counterpoint	The simultaneous unfolding of two or more melodies, and the various compositional principles that govern their existence and formulation—that is, their movement apart or away from each other, their rhythmic differences, and the resultant harmonies they create in relation to each other.
crescendo, decrescendo	A gradual, cumulative increase or decrease in volume indicated by hairpin signs or written out as a word by the composer. This intensification of sound in either direction informs the affective character of the passage it modifies.
diminution	The presentation of a melody in note values shorter than those in which it was originally cast.
ditty	A short song, often half sung and half spoken.
dominant	Every major and minor scale consists of seven pitches; the fifth scale degree is called the *dominant*. A chord constructed around this pitch includes the

seventh degree of the scale. The tendency of the seventh degree to move toward its neighboring tonic pitch is strong and creates in listeners a feeling of strong expectation and desire for resolution.

dotted notes A dot placed just alongside a pitch increases the temporal value of that note by one half of its original value. Two dots set in this way increase the value by yet another quarter of that value.

dramatic A term for a powerful voice capable of tremendous declamation, wide projection, and extraordinary power. Most of the great Wagnerian roles require such a voice, as do several roles of Puccini, including Calaf and Turandot.

fugato A usually brief contrapuntal section that occurs within a larger work and that does not develop into a full-blown fugue, although it is at once contrapuntal and imitative (the essential characteristics of a fugue).

fugue A musical composition or section in which a theme (also known as a *subject*) is stated and then repeated consecutively in two or more voices in imitative counterpoint. This confluence of voices is then elaborated, extended, varied, modulated, or developed in any number of ways.

Gesamtkunstwerk A term used by Richard Wagner to represent his ideal of the "total art work"—a fusion of music, poetry, drama, and the visual arts supporting a single artistic goal. Wagner felt that many operas, especially the bel canto operas of early-to-mid-nineteenth-century Italy, emphasized superficial elements over substance.

heldentenor A German term (meaning "heroic tenor") for an especially powerful and resonant tenor voice, capable of great projection and ringing tones. It is usually associated with Wagnerian leading roles.

hemiola A kind of rhythmic substitute, wherein two measures in triple meter are both notated and played as if they were three bars in duple meter.

intermezzo Originally a brief comic interlude set between acts of an opera. But in the nineteenth century, it also became a short and lyrical character piece that stood on its own in instrumental music.

libretto The words or text of an opera.

lirico spinto A lyric voice that is capable of "pushing," with somewhat greater heft than a conventional lyric, especially in dramatic climaxes. Cavaradossi from *Tosca* and Madama Butterfly are examples of lirico spinto roles in Puccini.

lyric A term for a voice that is less heavy and powerful than a dramatic voice. Lyric voices run the gamut from small to strong, from light lyric to full lyric to lirico spinto. They are capable of soaring fluidly, with great flexibility with a bright sound, into a high tessitura. Rodolfo and Mimì in Puccini's *La bohème* are considered lyric tenor and soprano roles.

march A militaristic processional piece meant to engender uniformity of the troops. It gives emphasis to the strong beats in regularly recurring patterns in 4/4 time.

minuet An elegant dance in 3/4 time that had its origins in seventeenth-century France. It is usually in two-part (binary) form, and its second beats are often accented. When danced, the minuet was a little slower than when performed strictly as instrumental music.

mezzo-soprano A female voice type whose range lies below soprano and above contralto.

motive, motif	A brief rhythmic unit of a specific duration and design that acquires its own identity and becomes the basis of more elaborate structures, movements, and whole works.
ostinato	A repetitive rhythmic and melodic pattern reiterated over the course of a composition, usually carried in the bass.
pedal point	A single tone, reiterated and sustained under changing harmonic patterns and over an extended period. While pedal points frequently occur in the bass, they can also be dispatched in any voice to enhance harmonic and rhythmic tension.
piano; pianissimo	Soft; very soft.
pizzicato	For stringed instruments, an articulation wherein the string is plucked with the fingers rather than bowed.
polyphony	Wherein several musical voices, or lines, are heard in combination, and where each line has an independent character.
soprano	The highest female voice type, above mezzo-soprano.
staccato	The distinct separation of a pitch from its neighboring notes. From the baroque era onward, staccato was an articulation marking, indicated by a dot above the note that instructed the player to cancel the prevailing legato.
subdominant	Refers to a pitch, chord, or tonality based on the fourth degree of a major or minor scale.
syncope (short for syncopation)	A temporary shift of accent that contradicts the metrical organization within a bar line or phrase, though the metrical identity of he passage stays intact. For example, an accent on a weak beat of a bar on the heels of unaccented strong beat will modify the function of those beats, turning a weak

beat into a strong beat, and can thus affect harmonic orientation, articulation, and rhythmic trajectory.

tempo   The rate of speed at which a piece of music is played; a specific tempo is indicated by the composer, who relies on a performer to respect his instructions according to the universally understood precepts, and in accordance with contemporary performance practice.

tenor   The highest male voice type, lying above the baritone range.

terzetto   A piece for three voices, with or without accompaniment; a vocal trio.

tessitura   Where most notes lie within a given aria, role, or voice type, not typically including the highest or lowest notes sung. It corresponds roughly to the "comfort zone" of a singer. Not to be confused with *range*, which includes all notes sung, regardless of how often they occur. A particular soprano's aria might have exactly the same range as a particular mezzo-soprano's aria—say, middle C to high A-flat—but the soprano's tessitura will lie higher within that range than the mezzo's.

tonality   The organization of tones around a single central pitch, or tonic. Tonality comprises all twelve major and minor keys, as well as the scales, triads, and harmonic functions that define them.

tremolo   The rapid repetition of a single pitch or chord. Used for purposes of affective and dramatic intensification.

triplet   Three notes of equal value played in place of two notes of equal value.

verismo   A naturalistic style of opera akin to realism, distinguished by its emphasis on the passions—including violence and sensuality—made popular at the turn of the twentieth century in Italy.

CD Track Listing

1. *Crisantemi* (elegy for string quartet) (6:23)
   Hungarian Operetta Orchestra
   ℗ 2008 Naxos. Courtesy of Naxos.
   From Naxos 8.555304

2. *Manon Lescaut*: "Sola, perduta, abbandonata" (4:48)
   Miriam Gauci (Manon); Alexander Rahbari, conductor, Belgian Radio and Television Philharmonic Orchestra
   ℗ 2008 Naxos. Courtesy of Naxos.
   From Naxos 8.660019-20

3. *La bohème*: "Sì, mi chiamano Mimì" (4:33)
   Luba Orgonasova (Mimì), Jonathon Welch (Rodolfo); Will Humburg, conductor, Czecho-Slovak Radio Symphony Orchestra
   ℗ 2008 Naxos. Courtesy of Naxos.
   From Naxos 8.660003-04

4. *La bohème*: "Ehi! Rodolfo! . . . O soave fanciulla" (4:22)
   Jonathon Welch (Rodolfo), Luba Orgonasova (Mimì), Boaz Senator (Schaunard), Ivan Urbas (Colline), Fabio Previati (Marcello); Will Humburg, conductor, Czecho-Slovak Radio Symphony Orchestra
   ℗ 2008 Naxos. Courtesy of Naxos.
   From Naxos 8.660003-04

5. *Tosca*: "Vissi d'arte" (3:56)
   Nelly Miricioiu (Tosca); Alexander Rahbari, conductor, Czecho-Slovak Radio Symphony Orchestra
   ℗ 2008 Naxos. Courtesy of Naxos.
   From Naxos 8.660001-02

6. *Tosca*: "Tosca, finalmente mia!" (5:19)

   Nelly Miricioiu (Tosca), Silvano Carroli (Scarpia); Alexander Rahbari, conductor, Czecho-Slovak Radio Symphony Orchestra

   ℗ 2008 Naxos. Courtesy of Naxos.

   From Naxos 8.660001-02

7. *Tosca*: "E lucevan le stelle" (3:00)

   Giorgio Lamberti (Cavaradossi); Alexander Rahbari, conductor, Czecho-Slovak Radio Symphony Orchestra

   ℗ 2008 Naxos. Courtesy of Naxos.

   From Naxos 8.660001-02

8. *Madama Butterfly*: Orchestral introduction (1:01)

   Alexander Rahbari, conductor, Czecho-Slovak Radio Symphony Orchestra

   ℗ 2008 Naxos. Courtesy of Naxos.

   From Naxos 8.660015-16

9. *Madama Butterfly*: "Dovunque al mondo" (3:06)

   Yordi Ramiro (Pinkerton), Georg Tichy (Sharpless), Joseph Abel (Goro); Alexander Rahbari, conductor, Czecho-Slovak Radio Symphony Orchestra

   ℗ 2008 Naxos. Courtesy of Naxos.

   From Naxos 8.660015-16

10. *Madama Butterfly*: "Un bel dì vedremo" (4:36)

    Miriam Gauci (Butterfly); Alexander Rahbari, conductor, Czecho-Slovak Radio Symphony Orchestra

    ℗ 2008 Naxos. Courtesy of Naxos.

    From Naxos 8.660015-16

11. *Madama Butterfly*: "Humming Chorus" (2:55)

    Alexander Rahbari, conductor, Slovak Philharmonic Chorus and Czecho-Slovak Radio Symphony Orchestra

    ℗ 2008 Naxos. Courtesy of Naxos.

    From Naxos 8.660015-16

12. *La rondine*: "Ch'il bel sogno di Doretta" (2:53)

Luba Orgonasova (Magda); Will Humburg, conductor, Czecho-Slovak Radio Symphony Orchestra

Ⓟ 2008 Naxos. Courtesy of Naxos.

From Naxos 8.552119-20

13. *La rondine*: "Bevo al tuo fresco sorriso" (3:03)

Roberto Alagna (Ruggero), Angela Gheorghiu (Magda), Inva Mula (Lisette), William Matteuzzi (Prunier); Antonio Pappano, conductor, London Symphony Orchestra and Chorus

Ⓟ 2008 EMI Classics. Courtesy of EMI Classics.

From EMI Classics 7243-5-56338-2-8

14. *Il tabarro*: "Sgualdrina! . . . Bocca di rosa fresca" (1:54)

Carlo Guelfi (Michele), Roberto Alagna and Angela Gheorghiu (Two Lovers); Antonio Pappano, conductor, London Symphony Orchestra and Chorus

Ⓟ 2008 EMI Classics. Courtesy of EMI Classics.

From EMI Classics 7243-5-56587-2-2

15. *Suor Angelica*: "La grazia è discesa dal cielo! . . . Suor Angelica ha sempre una ricetta buona" (4:58)

Cristina Gallardo-Domâs (Angelica), with Christopher van Kampe, cello; Antonio Pappano, conductor, Philharmonia Orchestra

Ⓟ 2008 EMI Classics. Courtesy of EMI Classics.

From EMI Classics 7243-5-56587-2-2

16. *Gianni Schicchi*: "O mio babbino caro" (2:09)

Tatiana Lisnic (Lauretta); Alexander Rahbari, conductor, Malaga Philharmonic Orchestra

Ⓟ 2008 Naxos. Courtesy of Naxos.

From Naxos 8.660111

17. *Turandot*: "In questa reggia" (5:26)

Giovanna Casolla (Turandot), Lando Bartolini (Calaf); Alexander
Rahbari, conductor, Malaga Philharmonic Orchestra and Choral Society
of Bilbao

Ⓟ 2008 Naxos. Courtesy of Naxos.

From Naxos 8.660089-90

18. *Turandot*: "Nessun dorma" (2:32)

Lando Bartolini (Calaf); Alexander Rahbari, conductor, Malaga
Philharmonic Orchestra and Choral Society of Bilbao

Ⓟ 2008 Naxos. Courtesy of Naxos.

From Naxos 8.660089-90

19. *Turandot*: "Diecimila anni al nostro Imperatore" (2:35)

Giovanna Casolla (Turandot); Alexander Rahbari, conductor, Malaga
Philharmonic Orchestra and Choral Society of Bilbao

Ⓟ 2008 Naxos. Courtesy of Naxos.

From Naxos 8.660089-90